The Local Church, Agent of Transformation

An Ecclesiology for Integral Mission

Tetsunao Yamamori
and C. René Padilla, editors

Buenos Aires - Año 2004

Translated by Brian Cordingly
from the Spanish
La iglesia local como agente de transformación
Ediciones Kairós, 2003

José Mármol 1734 - B1602EAF Florida
Buenos Aires, Argentina

Queda hecha el depósito que marca la ley 11.723

Impreso en Argentina
Printed in Argentina

www.kairos.org.ar

Yamamori, Tetsunao
The Local Church, Agent of Transformation : An Ecclesiology for Integral Mission / Tetsunao Yamamori y Carlos René Padilla. – 1ª. ed. – Buenos Aires : Kairós, 2004.
322 p. ; 20x14 cm.

ISBN 987-9403-67-3

1. Iglesia Local. I. Padilla, Carlos René
CDD 250

Contents

II. EXAMPLES OF CHURCHES THAT PRACTICE INTEGRAL MISSION

Editors and Contributors

Tetsunao Yamamori: Japanese by birth and living in the United States, he obtained his doctorate in social sciences at Duke University. He was President of Food for the Hungry for many years. He is presently associate lecturer in sociology at the State University of Arizona and assistant lecturer in mission studies at the Christian University of Tokyo.

C. René Padilla: Ecuadorian, PhD in New Testament from the University of Manchester, he was General Secretary for Latin America of the International Fellowship of Evangelical Students and later of the Latin American Theological Fraternity (FTL). He is currently President emeritus of the Kairos Foundation of Buenos Aires, Argentina, Publications Secretary of the FTL, International President of Tearfund-U.K. and Ireland, and President of the Micah Network for Integral Mission.

Esteban Voth: Born in the United States and reared in Argentina, he graduated from Bethel College and Bethel Seminary, and then did a PhD in Hebrew Bible and Ancient Near Eastern History at the Hebrew Union College in Cincinnati. For many years he taught at the Christian and Missionary Alliance Bible Institute in Buenos Aires and then at Bethel Theological Seminary in San Diego, California. He works now as a translation consultant with the United Bible Societies.

Nancy E. Bedford: Argentine, she studied communication sciences, romance languages and theology in the United States. She gained a doctorate in theology at the University of Tübingen, Germany. Between 1995 and 2000 she was teaching in the field of systematic theology at the University Institute ISEDET and in the

Baptist International Theological Seminary, both in Buenos Aires. Currently she is a lecturer at the McCormick Theological Seminary of Chicago, and is author of both academic and popular articles on theological questions.

Samuel Escobar: Peruvian, he did a PhD in Philosophy in the *Universidad Complutense* in Madrid, and for several years developed his mission work in the university world in Argentina, Brazil, Spain, Canada and Peru. He held the Chair of Mission Studies at the Eastern Baptist Theological Seminary in Philadelphia. He has been a visiting lecturer in several theological institutions in Latin America, and currently lives in Spain where he works with several centres of theological education. He is author of several books and writes regularly for journals in mission studies.

Alberto Fernando Roldán: Argentine, Doctor of Theology from the University Institute ISEDET, in Buenos Aires. He is a member of the presbytery of the Independent Presbyterian Church, Londrina, Brazil, has a pastoral and teaching ministry in Argentina, and is the academic secretary of the Latin American Doctoral Program. He is author of thirteen books and many articles.

Pedro Arana-Quiroz: Peruvian, he studied theology in Scotland and is a Presbyterian minister. He worked for many years with the International Fellowship of Evangelical Students and served as General Secretary for Latin America. He is currently Executive Secretary of the Peruvian Bible Society and Chair of Urban-Rural Mission of Lima, Perú. He is the author of several books.

Hugo Santos: Argentine, a graduate in psychology at the *Universidad del Salvador* in Buenos Aires, Argentina. He is a Professor at the University Institute ISEDET and a minister in the Evangelical Methodist Church of Argentina. He is currently Executive Secretary of the Association of Theological Seminaries and Institutions (ASIT).

Alberto Guerrero: Argentine, he obtained his master's degree in theology at the International Baptist Theological Seminary of Buenos Aires. A Baptist minister for many years, he was then appointed Executive Director of the Kairos Foundation of Buenos Aires, Argentina. He is now involved as a lecturer in theological education.

Josué Fonseca: Chilean, received his master's degree in theology from Regent College of Vancouver, Canada. He is Dean of the Baptist Theological Seminary of Santiago, Chile, where he lectures in spirituality. He has written articles for many journals.

Mauricio Solís-Paz: Honduran, a graduate in psychology, he is coordinator of the Interchange Ministry of the Willow Creek Church in Costa Rica. He is a member of the International Assembly of Habitat for Humanity, and also a member of the Coordinating Committee of *El Camino* Network for Integral Mission in Latin America.

Dafne Sabanes Plou: Argentine, she is a journalist specializing in issues of church and society. For several years she was President of the World Association of Christian Communicators and managed *El Estandarte Cristiano*, the official journal of the Methodist Church of Argentina. She is author of several books, including *Caminos de unidad: itinerario del diálogo ecuménico en América Latina 1916-1991* (Paths of unity: the itinerary of ecumenical dialogue in Latin America 1916 -1991).

Translator's Preface

The choice of one or two words and phrases merits some explanation. The expression ***"integral mission"*** is gaining in currency in liberal and evangelical church circles. Sometimes called "holistic mission," it translates the Spanish *"misión integral"* and it means the mission of the whole church to the whole of humanity in all its forms, personal, communal, social, economic, ecological, and political. Following its understanding of God's purpose as revealed in Jesus Christ, it has a particular concern for the poor, the outcast and the marginalized people of the world.

The word "integral" used in this context does us a linguistic favor too, by restoring its original sense of "whole" and "complete," a sense that it has almost lost in English except in the field of mathematics.

In the Spanish of the Latin American churches, the word "*evangélica*" is used in a very broad way, from signifying churches which are to be distinguished by the "clamorous joy of their worship" and a theology preoccupied with individual salvation, and some literalism in the interpretation of Scripture, to meaning something as general as "protestant." I have chosen to translate the word as ***"evangelical"*** even though a strict European English might demand some differentiation. The thinking behind that is that it is important to recognize that in the culture of the people writing a single word does describe that wide range of Christian allegiance, a kind of linguistic ecumenism. And I was also conscious of my Nordic Christian friends who are happy to call their Lutheran churches "evangelical."

Something of the same thinking underlies my transliteration of the word ***"pastor."*** It refers in the book to the usually professional, usually paid leader of a local church, regardless of denomination, and to search for the alternatives of minister, vicar, even priest, depending on the denomination in question, as would be the case in Britain and Ireland, would lose that unity of awareness in the Latin American use. However, in the ideology of the book the word "minister" would better convey the idea of a "servant-leader."

Just a word about quotations. Biblical qoutations are from the New Revised Standard Version, with the exception of Chapter 2, which qoutes the New International Version. It has occasionally been possible, where the original work was in English, or where there is a standard translation into English, to find and use the original quotation. Where that has not been the case the quotation has been directly translated or re-translated from the Spanish text.

Editors' Preface

An important deficiency in Latin American evangelical theology has been in the area of ecclesiology. For Roman Catholics the church constitutes one of the fundamental theological issues, whereas for evangelicals it is a secondary question. By way of illustration, it is sufficient to glance at the last Spanish edition (the eighth) of *Christian Books in Existence*, published by the Association of Hispanic Evangelical Publishers in 2002: among 7100 titles registered, it includes only 41 which bear any relation to the theme of "the Church." Of those 41 titles, only two or three can be included in the category of theology of the Church—ecclesiology—while the rest deal with ecclesiastical issues such as church administration, Christian education, women's ministry and church growth.[1]

It is hard to calculate the consequences of this lamentable deficiency. The least one can say is that, when the church lacks an ecclesiology rooted in biblical revelation, what takes priority is the church as institution, regulated by human traditions and preoccupied with the achievement of secondary objectives, such as numerical growth, to the detriment of qualitative growth.

---

[1] It should be noted, however, that the bibliography mentioned does not include publications on ecclesiology written by Protestants but published by Catholic publishers in Spain, as is the case with *La Iglesia, fuerza del Espíritu* by Jurgen Moltmann (Salamanca: Sígueme, 3ra ed., 1978) and *Ética y eclesiología* by Wolfhart Pannenberg (Salamanca: Sígueme, 1985).

In the light of the foregoing, this book seeks to fill a gap in evangelical literature. The impulse for its publication emerged from the editors' concern with the need for a work which would set out clearly the qualities that a local church must have to be prepared to undertake the task of being "salt of the earth" and "light of the world" in its own sphere of action. The result is this book which the reader now has at hand. It was made possible by the collaboration of writers associated with the Latin American Theological Fraternity.

The work is in two parts. The first, which comprises chapters 1 to 9, is concerned with a theoretical framework for an ecclesiology of integral mission. The second, chapters 10 to 13, offers four models of churches engaged in integral mission —"models" not in the sense of perfect exemplars to be followed in other contexts, but rather as concrete illustrations of how the principles of integral mission have been embodied in local churches in specific situations.

In the Introduction ("An Ecclesiology for Integral Mission") C. René Padilla establishes the biblical-theological basis of the church as agent of transformation of human life in all its dimensions—the personal and communal transformation, for which it has been called and equipped by God. This chapter offers a view of the basic themes running through the whole work.

In chapter 2 ("The Biblical Basis for Integral Mission in the Context of Poverty"), Esteban Voth takes as his starting point Jesus' words in Mark 14:7 ("The poor you will always have with you, and you can help them any time you want") to show Jesus' deep commitment to the poor. Such a commitment, says Voth, had its roots in the Old Testament and provides a solid basis for integral mission. Jesus saw himself as the one who came to fulfil God´s purpose to establish his kingdom of justice and peace. In order to gain a better understanding of the dimensions of integral mission the author suggests looking at Jesus' view in light of A. P. Fiske's socio-theology of poverty. In this way, according to Voth, it becomes clear that in both the Hebrew Bible and Jesus's life and work the purpose of God is the restoration of each aspect of human dignity.

Nancy Bedford, in chapter 3 ("The Theology of Integral Mission and Community Discernment"), argues from the outset that the theology of integral mission must be a trinitarian theology. The reason is clear: "Mission means sending, and refers in the first place to the sending of the Son by the Father in the power of the Spirit, and consequently to those who have come to be sons and daughters in the Son." This sending can take many forms, and that then requires the exercise of community discernment. For this the author proposes four *marks* of mission, or *notae missionis* ("pentecostality," ecumenicity, inclusiveness, and ubiquity) as indispensable marks of the wholeness of mission, in a trinitarian dynamic. They are also the cardinal points which keep us orientated in our search for ways into integral mission.

In chapter 4 ("The Church as Community") Samuel Escobar looks at the "main thrusts of the apostolic teaching on the growth of the people of God to fullness of life in Christ"—personal growth for the members of the church, but also growth in the church as a body, "growth in the quality of relationships within the church, the community of faith and life that has been called to carry out the mission." According to the author, this growth-to-fullness of the community relates directly to the variety in the kinds of service which society requires from the Christian mission.

In chapter 5 ("The Priesthood of All Believers and Integral Mission") Alberto Roldán addresses a fundamental question for the life of the church: How does the practice of universal priesthood relate to our undertaking of what has come to be called "integral mission"? The conclusion of his reflections is that integral mission needs an integral church, that is to say "a church that lives out freedom in love and uses all the gifts of the Spirit in the appropriate spheres of ministry," proclaiming the Kingdom of God and his justice "in every area of life—spiritual, personal, family, social and political."

Pedro Arana-Quiroz in chapter 6 ("Integral Mission in the Framework of Grace, World and Church") expounds his conviction that "integral mission springs from the very *grace* of God, it challenges us to get involved in our own *world* understood as a particular 'theological situation,' and it requires an integral *ecclesiology*, with a trinitarian base, in which the community of faith experiences the tension of being called out as it is also being sent out, consequently recognizing the need to embody creatively those images and tasks of the church that are to be found in Scripture." He maintains that the globalized world, as it exists at present, calls for a vision of the church which recognizes the dimensions of the mission—ecumenical, liturgical, soteriological, diaconal, prophetic, both in stewardship and *koinonia*.

Hugo Santos in chapter 7 ("Church Structures: The Perspective of Institutional Psychology") maintains that "Integral mission assumes an integral vision, giving access to different viewpoints and strategies that will extend the range of our perception and action." On this premise he turns to institutional psychology to describe a number of the characteristics of healthy institutions—characteristics which can be recognised in the context of the local church, but also in the church more generally. He affirms that "the human sciences are useful instruments for the analysis and operation of the community of faith."

In Chapter 8 ("Servant-leaders, Facilitators of Integral Mission") Alberto Guerrero poses the question, "What are the characteristics of the leaders of a local church that, in the power of the Spirit, is fulfilling its responsibility to be 'salt of the earth' and 'light of the world?'" He recognises that, in the present circumstances of the church, unless the leaders of the church are willing to get back to an integral gospel, it is hard to expect change on the part of the congregation. He affirms that the primary task of servant-leaders is that of facilitating the full development of the local church, in a way that enables it to fulfil its redemptive purpose in society.

Josué Fonseca puts the finishing touches to the first section of the book with Chapter 9 ("Integral Mission in Worship"). From a critique of the kind of theology which is reflected in the worship services of the majority of churches in our circles, dominated these days by religious *marketing*, he proposes five characteristics for a kind of worship in keeping with integral mission: genuine spirituality, enrichment by contributions from many traditions, an awareness of personal and social needs, use of folk idiom, and Christian ecumenicity.

The second section draws together four experiences from churches committed to integral mission in different Latin American countries. It would have been advantageous to have produced a whole book of such experiences, as the authors originally intended. However that proved impossible for a number of reasons, not least of which is the fact that an oral culture such as ours militates against the documenting of ecclesiastical and other experiences. We hope that the examples included here will at least serve to illustrate what is meant by the church acting as an agent of transformation in its concrete situation. We hope too that these "models," which are only *examples of what is possible* will inspire in other communities the same commitment to the mission of God in the world, to the glory of Jesus Christ, Light of light and King of kings.

I

A Theological Framework for an Ecclesiology of Integral Mission

1

Introduction: An Ecclesiology for Integral Mission

C. René Padilla

There is a solid basis for stating that the concept of *integral mission* has found its place in the evangelical community in Latin America. Of course, there is a risk that the frequent use of the phrase could make it a mere cliché, an expression bearing no relation to the actual life of Christians or churches. However, there is abundant evidence to show that for a growing number of Christians and churches, the phrase *integral mission* encapsulates a distinctive way of perceiving their role in the world as disciples of Christ.

Intellectual assent to the concept of integral mission, however, is not enough to make it take concrete form in the real life situation of the local church. For this to take place, the church itself must fulfill *certain conditions or requisites that qualify it to practice integral mission.* This does not mean that there are formulae or strategies which will convert a church overnight into an agent of spiritual and social transformation in its community. What it does mean is that churches that are making an impact that is truly *evangelical*—rooted in the gospel and consequently bringing about transformation in society—are churches that share certain characteristics that contribute to that impact.

What are these characteristics? What are the marks of a church which, through the power of the Spirit, is prepared to fulfill its role in its own surroundings as "salt of the earth" and "light of the world," a task to which all followers of Jesus Christ have been called? Obviously, one prerequisite for practicing integral mission is to be *an integral church*. Of course, that does not mean that it must be a perfect church, for then integral mission would be impossible. It means that it has to be a church in which God's Spirit is free to act so that in it the Word of God becomes flesh—a church which is making progress in its own transformation and the transformation of the community which it serves. More concretely, an integral church is a community of faith which gives priority to 1) commitment to Jesus Christ as Lord of everything and everyone; 2) Christian discipleship as a missionary lifestyle to which the entire church and every member have been called; 3) the vision of the church as the community that confesses Jesus Christ as Lord and lives in the light of that confession in such a way that in it can be seen the inauguration of a new humanity; and 4) the use of gifts and ministries as instruments that the Spirit of God uses to prepare the church and all its members to fulfill their vocation as God's co-workers in the world.

1. Commitment to Jesus Christ as Lord of Everything and Everyone

Integral mission is the concrete expression of commitment to Jesus Christ as Lord of the totality of life and of all creation.

The Lordship of Jesus Christ

New Testament scholars generally agree that the confession "Jesus Christ is Lord" was the basic confession of the early church, the criterion which defined a person's relationship with God and with the community of faith. It is with respect to this confession that the following observations are offered.

In the first place, a cursory reading of the New Testament will reveal the frequency with which the word *Kyrios* ("Lord") appears referring to Jesus Christ. In evangelical circles, the title "Savior" takes preference, reflecting the characteristic emphasis on the "salvation of the soul."[1] In the New Testament, however, the title "Savior" is applied to Jesus on only a few occasions,[2] whereas "Lord" is used hundreds of times. Although it is certain that in many of these references, especially in the Gospels,[3]

---

[1] This is by no means to deny the importance of the spiritual dimension of salvation. However, it is one thing to affirm this dimension; it is something quite different to reduce the gospel to an otherworldly message, which loses sight of the fact that eternal life is not simply life after death—not just an eschatological idea—but a whole different lifestyle, characterized here and now by the love of God and the love of one's neighbor.

[2] E.g., in Ac 5:31, 13:23; Eph 5:23; Php 3:20; 2Ti 1:10; Tit 1:4, 2:13, 3:6; 2Pe 1:11, 2:20, 3:2, 18; 1Jn 4:14. It must be remembered, however, that the name Jesus means "savior."

[3] See, e.g., Lk 7:6, 9:59, passages in which *kyrios* is no more than a polite address, like "Mr. Jones." There are also passages where *kyrios* carries the idea of "master" or "boss" (cf. Mt 18:25, 27). These meanings, however, stand in contrast to many other passages, especially in Paul's letters and the last two chapters of John's Gospel, in which the term is used with christological connotations, probably associated with a Christian reading of Psalm 110:1, where the Messiah is referred to as "Lord." Most probably the designation of Jesus as "Lord" acquired the idea of deity only

kyrios does not carry the idea of deity—a "high christology" in the language of theological definition—, there are many examples which leave no room for doubt that the term is used to present Jesus as one deserving the same honor as that which is offered to God.

In the second place, to understand fully the significance of the confession of Jesus as *Kyrios*, we need to interpret it with reference to certain facts about the historical context in which this confession took shape during the first century until it became a sort of synthesis of the faith and message of the primitive church. One of these facts is that *Kyrios* is the Greek translation of YHWH (Yahweh), the name of God in the Septuagint. Therefore, to speak of the Lord is to speak of God, no more and no less. It is not surprising then that there are Old Testament texts that use the word *kyrios*, originally referring to God, which in the New Testament are quoted as referring to Jesus Christ. Another fact is that in the emperor worship of the first century, the emperor was referred to as *Kyrios* to emphasize the absolute nature of his authority, characteristic of a god. Furthermore, in the same period in Asia Minor, Syria and Egypt there were religions in which the gods and goddesses (for example Isis and

---

after his resurrection and exaltation. David J. Bosch, however, notes that in Matthew the only ones who use the word "Lord" in reference to Jesus are the disciples or those who came to him looking for help, whereas his adversaries always call him "Rabbi" ("Teacher"), never "Lord." The designation of Jesus as "Lord" by his disciples in this gospel is so consistent that, where his sources use "Teacher," Matthew changes it to "Lord." On this basis Bosch concludes that "it can hardly be doubted that Matthew understood it (i.e. the title 'Lord') primarily as a divine title." [*Transforming Mission: Paradigm Shifts in Theology of Mission* (Maryknoll, N.Y.: Orbis, 1991), pp. 75-76].

Osiris) also acquired the titles *Kyrios* and *Kyria*. The confession of Jesus as *Kyrios*, therefore, stands over against other confessions and allegiances present in the religious world, and led Paul to affirm:

> we know that "no idol in the world really exists," and that "there is no God but one." Indeed, even though there might be many so-called gods in heaven or on earth—as in fact there are many gods and many lords—yet for us there is one God, the Father, from whom are all things and for whom we exist, and one Lord, Jesus Christ, through whom are all things and through whom we exist (1Co 8:4-6).

When these facts are taken into consideration, it becomes clear that *the confession of Jesus Christ—the risen Christ—as Lord is essentially a recognition of his sovereignty over the whole of human life and over the whole creation.* According to the apostle Paul, such a recognition is possible only through the action of the Spirit of God (1Co 12:3). Christians are, by definition, "those who call upon the name of our Lord Jesus Christ" (1Co 1:2; cf. Ac 9:14, 21; 22:16; 2Ti 2:22), those who have received "the word of faith" which the apostle to the gentiles summarizes: "If you confess with your lips that Jesus is Lord and believe in your heart that God raised Him from the dead, you will be saved. For one believes with the heart and so is justified, and one confesses with the mouth and so is saved" (Ro 10:9-10).

In the third place, the confession of Jesus Christ as Lord, which could well be considered the core of the apostolic message,[4] amounts to saying that *the Kingdom of God has*

---

[4] Cf. Oscar Cullmann, *The Christology of the New Testament* (London: SCM, 2nd ed., 1963), Ch. 7.

become a present reality in history, in the person and work of Jesus Christ, an affirmation which is corroborated by the Gospels, without putting in doubt the future dimension of the Kingdom.

Among New Testament scholars there is a consensus that the Kingdom of God was Jesus' principal message, and there are few who would not recognize that for him that Kingdom was as much present as future. This double dimension of the Kingdom derives from the fact that *basilea* ("reign" or "kingdom" in Greek) in the New Testament, as in many cases with *malkut* ("reign" in Hebrew) in the Old Testament, means something dynamic: "sovereignty," "dominion," or "government." It does not, therefore, refer to a territorial realm in the present, nor to an eschatological realm which will come into being in the future. Rather, it refers to the power of God in action—the royal power of God which, anticipating the end, manifests itself in the present through Jesus Christ and will manifest itself in the future in all its fullness.

A question remains, however: If in the preaching of Jesus the Kingdom of God holds such a prominent position, why does it scarcely appear in the preaching of Paul and the other apostles?[5] The best answer appears to be that in the Greco-Roman world it made much more sense to proclaim the universal sovereignty of Jesus Christ in terms of his *lordship* rather than his *kingly power* as David's heir. The use of *Kyrios* in the proclamation of the gospel by the apostle to the gentiles is a clear New Testament illustration of the contextualization of the message in the first

---

[5] See, however, Ro 14:17; 1Co 6:9,10; 15:24, 50; Gal 5:21; Col 1:13; 4:11; 2Th 1:5; 2Ti 4:1.

century. The use of the same title in preaching in a Jewish context, however, shows that, as Cullmann says, "it is clear that whenever Paul mentions the confession of Christ as Lord, he draws upon an old tradition and presupposes acquaintance with it as the foundation of all proclamation of Christ."[6] It is evident that, from the very beginning of the church, Christians understood the exaltation of Jesus Christ, after his resurrection, to be his enthronement as Lord and King of the universe. Thus Acts 2:36—when Peter in his Pentecost sermon says about Jesus that "God has made him Lord and Messiah"—provides evidence, along with other passages, that this conviction was already part of the message of the church in Palestine.

The relation between the resurrection and exaltation of Christ and his enthronement as *Kyrios* is shown clearly in a passage in which Paul writes that the power of God in the lives of believers is the same as that which

> God. . . put to work in Christ when he raised him from the dead and seated him at his right hand in the heavenly places, far above all rule and authority and power and dominion, and above every name that is named, not only in this age, but in the age to come. And he has put all things under his feet and has made him head over all things for the church (Eph 1:20-22).

This is another way of claiming that the risen Christ has been made "Lord of everything and everyone;" that he has been enthroned to exercise, by the power of God, sovereignty over all creation ("all things"): "Jesus Christ is Lord." Along the same line, the christological hymn in Philippians 2:6-11 traces the

---

[6] Cullmann, *ibid*., p. 215.

trajectory of Jesus Christ from his position of equality with God, through his descent to the condition of a slave, to his humiliation in death—the death of the cross—, to his exaltation to the highest place as Lord, at whose name every knee shall bow and every tongue confess that he is *Kyrios Jesus Christos.* It is as such, says Paul to the Ephesians (1:22), that God has given him to the church for it to confess him and proclaim him to all nations.

From Christology to Ecclesiology

The lordship of Jesus Christ is the foundation of both the life and the mission of the church. In the so-called "Great Commission" according to Matthew 28:16-20, the charge to "make disciples"[7] is preceded by the affirmation of universal sovereignty by the risen Christ: "All authority in heaven and on earth has been given to me," he says. "Go *therefore* and make disciples of all nations" (vv. 18-19a, italics mine). Because Jesus Christ is the Lord of the whole universe, he must be proclaimed as such among all nations, and in all nations disciples must be made who will confess his name and live in the light of that

---

[7] The verb "make disciples" (*mathetuein*) occurs only four times in the New Testament, three times in Matthew (13:52, 27:57, and 28:19) and once in Acts (14:21). Only in the "Great Commission" in Matthew does the verb appear in the imperative and in this passage it defines the main action, the content of the mission. The participles "baptizing" and "teaching," on the other hand, outline *how* the action of making disciples is to be carried out.

The noun "disciple" (*mathetes)* is common in the Gospels and Acts, but it does not appear in the rest of the New Testament. It appears 73 times in Matthew, 46 in Mark and 37 in Luke. In the synoptic Gospels, it is the word used to refer to the followers of Jesus, although in Mark and Luke it is restricted to the twelve, while in Matthew it is used more widely: it includes the Twelve, of course, but not exclusively.

confession. The compass of this confession of his lordship must match the degree of authority conferred on him by the Father. The christology summarized in the confession "Jesus Christ is Lord" constitutes the basis of an ecclesiology that sees the church as the community that confesses and proclaims Jesus as Lord of the whole of human life and of the whole of creation.

Without the proclamation of Jesus as Lord, there is no integral Gospel, and without an integral gospel there can be no integral mission. It is here that the problem arises with those versions of the Christian message which restrict the action of Jesus Christ to the realm of private religion—"the spiritual"—and leave out all references to his authority over other aspects of human life. If Jesus Christ is Lord of the whole universe and has been granted sovereignty in heaven and on earth, his dominion extends over the economic and the political spheres, over the social and the cultural, over the aesthetic and the ecological, over the personal and the communal. Nothing and no one is excluded from his authority.

When the church loses sight of the centrality of the Lord Jesus Christ, it ceases to be the church and is reduced to being a religious sect, incapable of relating its message to daily life and to public life. *The integral church is one which recognizes that all spheres of life are "mission fields" and looks for ways of asserting the sovereignty of Jesus Christ in all of them.* The lordship of Christ is the foundation of an integral ecclesiology and of integral mission. Questions about *what the church is and why the church exists* can only be answered after we have answered the prior question of *who is Jesus Christ.* If Jesus Christ is Lord of everything and every one, the church is the *church of Christ* in the measure that it sees itself as "the community of the King"—Jesus the Christ—and defines the purpose of its existence in terms of witnessing to him, not only by what it says, but also by what it is and by what it does. If Jesus Christ is Lord of everything and everyone, the church is not an agent of "individual salvation" which brings into people's grasp the benefits of Christ's work, but rather the community of faith called to incarnate the testimony to his lordship over the whole of life.[8]

2. Christian Discipleship

Christian discipleship understood as a missionary lifestyle—the active participation in the realization of God's plan for human existence and the creation, revealed in Jesus Christ—to which the whole church and each of its members have been called, expresses, in a word, the essence of the church's mission.

If, as we have stated above, the church is the community that confesses Jesus Christ as Lord and lives in the light of that confession, it follows that the proclamation of Jesus Christ as Lord and the all-inclusive invitation to submit to his authority are inescapable elements of the church's mission. As Paul argues,

> For there is no distinction between Jew and Greek; the same Lord is Lord of all and is generous to all who call on him. For, "Everyone who calls on the name of the Lord shall be

---

[8] For an excellent exposition of this way of understanding the Church in relation to the lordship of Christ see Darrell K. Guder, *Be My Witnesses: The Church's Mission, Message, and Messengers* (Grand Rapids: Wm. B. Eerdmans Publishing Company, 1985). According to this author, "It is a tragic heresy to reduce the lordship of Christ to the religious and spiritual side of life, when he clearly said that he had been given all authority in heaven and on earth" (p. 177).

> saved." But how are they to call on one in whom they have not believed? And how are they to believe in one of whom they have never heard? And how are they to hear without someone to proclaim him? And how are they to proclaim him unless they are sent? (Ro 10:12-15a).

The person who hears the gospel and responds positively sets out to *follow Jesus, a process of transformation lasting a whole lifetime and extending to every aspect of life*. Several comments are in order here.

First, in evangelical circles there has been a marked tendency to emphasize conversion as an event that takes place at a particular moment, in which a person passes from death to life, through a personal decision and (it is assumed) the action of the Holy Spirit. It is not uncommon, therefore, for the believer to give the date of his or her conversion. Of course, without repentance and without faith there is no discipleship. However, beyond the experience with which the Christian life begins, and which one cannot always date, it must be affirmed that God's aim is to recreate in the believer the image of his Son Jesus Christ, the New Man, and that this involves a process of transformation which lasts throughout life. Jesus' words in Matthew's "Great Commission" about *how* to "make disciples" call attention to this process: 1) "baptizing them in the name of the Father and of the Son and of the Holy Spirit," the rite of initiation into following Jesus and, therefore, into the Christian life; and 2) "teaching them to obey everything that I have commanded you," the process of formation *in* the practice and *for* the practice of Jesus' teaching—the will of God—without which there can be no genuine discipleship.

From a Biblical perspective, *orthopraxis,* obedience to all that Jesus taught his disciples, is at least as important as orthodoxy, if not more so, since the disciples' goal is to live out the practice of love and thus to be "children of your Father in heaven," "perfect as your heavenly Father is perfect" (Mt 5:45, 48). Jesus' disciples are not distinguished by mere adherence to a religion, a Jesus cult, but rather by a lifestyle which reflects the love and the justice of the Kingdom of God. The church's mission, therefore, cannot be reduced to proclaiming the "salvation of souls." Its mission is to "make disciples" who will learn obedience to their Lord in all the circumstances of daily existence, private and public, personal and social, spiritual and material. *The call of the gospel is a call to a total transformation that reflects God's purpose to redeem human life in all its dimensions.* Integral mission is possible only when there are disciples who have the vision to ensure that the leaven of Kingdom values permeate every sphere of society.

Secondly, Jesus assumes that there is a whole body of teaching which he has entrusted to the keeping of his disciples and which they, in turn, need to communicate to new disciples. The assumption is that there is a tradition which is passed on from one generation to the next, a tradition essential for putting into practice the commission to make disciples of the Lord Jesus Christ. This is actually a reference to the *apostolic tradition* (or *teaching*) to which several later New Testament passages will refer (see, e.g., Ac 2:42; Ro 6:17; 1Co 11:23; Gal 1:8-9; Col 2:6-8).

It must be kept in mind, however, that Jesus' teaching was not merely, or even primarily, doctrinal or theoretical, but rather practical and paradigmatic. That is to say, his pedagogy consisted, above all, of his example and his actions, through which he communicated the values of the Kingdom of God incarnated in himself. So, for example, in order to teach the importance of humble service in the community of his followers, on his last journey to Jerusalem he referred to himself as "the Son of Man [who] came not to be served but to serve and to give his life a ransom for many" (Mk 10:43-45). In the upper room, shortly before his crucifixion, he washed his disciples' feet and then said to them, "I have set you an example, that you also should do as I have done to you" (Jn 13:15). There can be no doubt that this sort of teaching is an essential part of the apostolic tradition, the "commandment" which he entrusted to his followers so that they could fulfil their mission to make disciples. Consequently, the disciples' mission would not be limited to making converts in order to increase the numbers of church members. It would be directed, rather, to making disciples in whose lifestyle the example of Jesus Christ would be reproduced: an example of unconditional love for God and neighbor, of humble service and solidarity with the poor, of commitment to the truth and unshakeable opposition to all forms of hypocrisy. In other words, the mission of the church would consist of an invitation and a challenge to set out as followers of Jesus as a means to "recover" Jesus, "the most radical way of recovering the concrete reality of Jesus and making of it the origin and basis of the whole of life."[9]

Understood in these terms, discipleship is costly, and it is a cost that cannot be evaded. One aspect of this cost is the renunciation of everything that interferes with absolute fidelity to Jesus Christ as Lord. In a time of popularity when "great multitudes" were following him, Jesus turned to them and said, "Whoever comes to me and does not hate father and mother, wife and children, brothers and sisters, yes, and even life itself,

---

[9] José María Castillo, *El seguimiento de Jesús* (The Following of Jesus) (Salamanca: Sígueme, 1986), p. 13.

cannot be my disciple. Whoever does not carry the cross and follow me cannot be my disciple." He spoke about counting the cost, as when one plans to build a tower, or when a king is about to go to war with another king. Then he added, "So therefore none of you can become my disciple if you do not give up all your possessions" (Lk 14:25-33). Jesus is the one who defines the conditions of discipleship. He defines them in a way that leaves no doubt that his call is to an integral discipleship, one that requires radical obedience to the will of God in all areas of life, from family relationships to material possessions.

Thirdly, the formation of disciples after the pattern of Christ takes place in the context of the community of faith, not separate from it. Jesus said: "By this everyone will know that you are my disciples, if you have love for one another" (Jn 13:35). Clearly, for Jesus the mark of discipleship is love. However, nobody can learn to love in isolation from others. In effect, the knowledge—the experience—of the love of Christ, which, in Paul's words "surpasses knowledge," is possible only "with all the saints" (Eph 3:18-19). It is in the church, "the family of God," that disciples learn to love, and not only to love, but to serve, to pray, to renounce evil, and to do good. It is in the church, "the body of Christ," that disciples discover and use their gifts and grow into "the unity of faith and of the knowledge of the Son of God, to maturity, to the measure of the full stature of Christ" (Eph 4:13). It is true that starting out on the road of discipleship clearly requires a personal decision, a decision involving an irrevocable renunciation of a life independent of God and a readiness to identify oneself with Jesus in his sufferings. It is also true, however, that those who embark on the way as followers of Jesus can only make progress in this pilgrimage to the extent that they are able to experience the grace of God *in* the church and *through* the church.

The practice of integral mission assumes that the church and each of its members will give absolute priority to following Jesus in terms of a missionary lifestyle: a way of life modeled on Jesus for the purpose of bearing witness, by word and action, to Jesus Christ the Lord; a way of life centered on Jesus Christ as the Event through whom God has definitively wrought the re-establishment of his purpose for the whole of his creation. Such a lifestyle is truly "evangelical," not in a sectarian sense, in which to be evangelical means to be identified with a ghetto-church that thinks it has a monopoly on truth, but in the broad meaning of the word: to be evangelical means to be entirely dependent on the grace of God shown in Jesus Christ, to be committed to him as Lord of the whole of life and the whole of creation, and to join in the spreading of the good news of Jesus as "the way, the truth and the life" (Jn 14: 6). As John H. Yoder says,

> The message cannot remain in the ghetto because the good news by its very nature is for and about the world. The good news is not information which will remain true even if people in a ghetto celebrate it only for themselves; it is about a community-building story for which the world beyond the ghetto is half of the reconciling event.[10]

3. A Biblical Vision of the Church

The church is the community that confesses Jesus Christ as Lord of everything and everyone and lives in the light of this

---

[10] John H. Yoder, *The Priestly Kingdom: Social Ethics as Gospel* (Notre Dame, Indiana: University of Notre Dame, 1984), p. 55.

confession in such a way that in it may be seen the inauguration of a new humanity.

The church is not just the sum total of the individuals who come together on the basis of shared religious interests. From the point of view of the New Testament, the church holds a central place in salvation history because it is the testimony to God's great purpose in Jesus Christ. Its witness, however, is not limited to words only. Its witness is essentially *incarnational*. What does this mean?

Obviously, this adjective refers to the central act of God in history, the incarnation. At the outset, it is fitting to warn that the idea of the church as "extension of the incarnation," common in Roman Catholic dogmatics, does not do justice to the enormous difference which, from a biblical standpoint, exists between Jesus Christ and the church. That, however, is not to deny that there is a close relationship between the life and mission of the church, on the one hand, and the life and mission of Jesus Christ, on the other. Without denying the unique character of Jesus' work through the "salvific events," we can still affirm, without fear of contradiction, that this work is extended and made effective in history, through the power of the Spirit, by means of the life and mission of the church.

As was stated above, the basis of the mission of the church is the lordship of Jesus Christ. Because he has received all authority in heaven and on the earth, the church is called to make disciples in all nations. Jesus Christ in this way provides the *why* of the mission. At the same time, he provides us with the content, the *what,* of the message. Thus Paul says, "we do not proclaim ourselves; we proclaim Jesus Christ as Lord" (2Co 4:5). What is the gospel if it is not precisely *good news about Jesus Christ?* The mission of the church is incarnational when it is centered on the Word of God who was made man.

The incarnation of God in Jesus Christ, however, provides not only the *why* and the *what* of the mission; it also provides the *how*. The risen Christ said to his disciples, "As the Father has sent me, so I send you" (Jn 20:21). The implications are clear. The form of Jesus' sending by the Father provides the model or paradigm for the commissioning of his followers—the commissioning whereby disciples are made.

To understand in what sense Jesus' mission serves as a paradigm for the mission of the church, it is necessary to take into account the totality of the "saving events" by which Jesus fulfilled his mission: his life and ministry, his death on the cross, his resurrection and his exaltation. Each of these events points towards integral mission as the means whereby the church continues Jesus' mission throughout history, and whereby the redemptive work of Jesus takes effect under present circumstances.

The Church and the Life and Ministry of Jesus

The traditional tendency to separate the death of Jesus from his earthly life and ministry—a marked tendency in evangelical circles— in order to give prominence to the cross, has resulted in a sad lack of attention to the significance of his life and ministry for the mission of the church. It is true that the four Gospels emphasize the passion and death of Jesus Christ to the point where there is a lot of truth in what has been said, namely, that they are essentially narratives about the happenings immediately prior to the crucifixion, with more or less extensive introductions. And then Paul, too, emphasizes the centrality of the cross when he says that he preaches "Christ crucified" (1Co 1:23; cf. 2:2). However, what gives validity to the death of Jesus Christ as "the atoning sacrifice for our sins" (1Jn 4:10) is that it was the sacrifice of the perfect man, whose way of life established the foundations for the definition of what it means to love God above all things and to love one's neighbor as oneself. His earthly life and ministry in this way came to be the model for the life and mission of the church.

One of the more praiseworthy elements of the Latin American theology of liberation was its emphasis on the historical Jesus as a paradigm for the mission of the church. The gospel as the proclamation of good news to the poor, the preaching of freedom for captives, of the recovery of sight for the blind, and the liberation of the oppressed became the criterion by which to assess how far the mission of today's church was really the continuation of the mission of Jesus of Nazareth.[11] The option of some liberation theologians for Marxist communism as the preferred socio-economic and political system for all nations should not prevent our recognizing the solid Biblical grounding

---

[11] Many years before the emergence of liberation theology in Latin America, E. Stanley Jones, a Methodist missionary in India, interpreted Jesus' "keynote discourse" in the Nazareth synagogue (Lk 4:18-19) as the program, in general terms, of the Kingdom of God on earth. Cf. *Cristo y el communismo* (abridged edition) (El Paso: Mundo Hispano, 1974). The original work in English, *Christ's Alternative to Communism,* was published in 1935. According to Jones, Christ "has given us a kingdom, which is no less than the New Order, the ultimate Order that opens the way to transcend the existing order and change it; and we have turned it into a sheepfold that we rush into, looking for refuge and hoping that Jesus will carry us up to heaven" (p. 83). Only the Spanish translation available to the author.

and the missionary value of this emphasis on Jesus' solidarity with the poor and oppressed as a model for the mission of the church. As John Perkins says, the church is called to "be the replacement of Jesus in a given community, doing what he would do, going where he would go and teaching what he would teach."[12]

The Church and Jesus' Cross

The cross represents the culmination of Jesus' surrender in submission to the will of God for the redemption of humankind. "He made him to be sin who knew no sin, so that in him we might become the righteousness of God" (2Co 5:21). This is at the very heart of the gospel. However, *the cross also represents the cost of discipleship and of faithfulness to God's call to take part in bringing to fruition his redemptive purpose*. The mission of the church provides the link between the death of Jesus Christ on the cross, on one hand, and the appropriation of the justice of God by faith—justification—on the other. As Paul states, the work of reconciliation contains two closely related aspects: God "reconciled us to himself through Christ, and has given us the ministry of reconciliation; that is, in Christ God was reconciling the world to himself, not counting their trespasses against them, and entrusting the message of reconciliation to us" (2Co 5:18-19). The practice of the "ministry of reconciliation" has its cost, however, both in terms of sacrificial surrender for the sake of others—a self-giving which reproduces that of Jesus Christ—and also in terms of suffering for the sake of the gospel. The church is not truly the church unless it is, according to Bonhoeffer's

---

[12] John Perkins, *Beyond Charity: The Call to Christian Community Development* (Grand Rapids: Baker Books, 1993), p. 39.

description, "the church for others," in which the image of "the man for others" —the man who "came not to be served but to serve, and give his life a ransom for many" (Mk 10:45)—is reproduced. Then too, when Jesus sent his disciples out on their mission during his earthly ministry, he warned them:

> You will be hated by all because of my name. But the one who endures to the end will be saved. . . . A disciple is not above the teacher, nor a slave above the master; it is enough for the disciple to be like the teacher, and the slave like the master. If they have called the master of the house Beelzebul, how much more will they malign those of his household! (Mt 10:22, 24-25)

Suffering would be a constituent part of the disciples' mission, as it was for their Lord. It would not be fortuitous or accidental, but the logical consequence of membership in the community of followers of the way of the Suffering Servant. So Paul would write to the faithful in Philippi:

> Only live your life in a manner worthy of the gospel of Christ . . . striving side by side with one mind for the faith of the gospel, and in no way intimidated by your opponents. For them this is evidence of their destruction, but of your salvation. And this is God's doing. For he has graciously granted you the privilege, not only of believing in Christ, but of suffering for him as well (Php 1:27-29).

The cross was also the means whereby, according to Paul, Christ broke down the wall of separation between Jew and gentile, thus producing a new humanity, one body (Eph 2:14-16). The church therefore is called to demonstrate, both in its life and in its message, this reconciliation with God and between individuals and groups. Among those who gather beneath the shadow of the cross of Christ, ethnic, social and gender divisions disappear so that "there is no longer Jew or Greek, slave or free, male or female," but "all of you are one in Christ Jesus" (Gal. 3:28). The church provides a glimpse of a new humanity that in anticipation incarnates God's plan, that plan which will be brought to fruition in "the fullness of time," "to gather up all things, things in heaven and things on earth" in Christ (Eph 1:10).

The Church and the Resurrection of Jesus

The fulfilment of God's plan for the life and mission of the church relies on one incomparable resource, the power with which God raised Jesus from the dead, the power of the resurrection. No wonder, then, that Paul in his prayer for the faithful asks God that they might experience the "immeasurable greatness" of that power (Eph 1:19-20).

The resurrection of Christ is the dawn of a new day in the history of salvation. It was the confirmation that his sacrifice had succeeded in overcoming the fatal consequence of sin, which is death. For those who put their trust in him, therefore, death does not have the last word. "The sting of death is sin, and the power of sin is the law. But thanks be to God, who gives us the victory through our Lord Jesus Christ!" (1Co 15:56- 57).

Because death has been vanquished, Christian hope in the final victory of God's plan is based on a solid foundation. The risen Christ is the first fruits of the great harvest, a new humanity. By his resurrection he has introduced into history a principle of life which guarantees not only the survival of the soul for all eternity, but also the permanent validation of all that the church does through the power of the Spirit for the cause of Jesus Christ, that is, the cause of love and justice. That leads to Paul's exhortation, "Therefore, my beloved, be steadfast, immovable, always excelling in the work of the Lord, because you know that in the Lord your labor is not in vain" (1Co 15:58). *The cause of Jesus Christ is the only cause that has a future.* So it makes sense to pray, "Thy kingdom come, thy will be done on earth as it is in heaven," and to strive that the power of the resurrection may become manifest in the here and now, and in every sphere of human life and in the whole of creation.

The Church and the Exaltation of Jesus

The close relationship that exists between the present dimension of the Kingdom of God and the presence of the Holy Spirit who works in history to make the mission of the church possible is clearly seen in Jesus' reply to a question posed by his close followers just before his ascension: "Lord, is this the time when you will restore the kingdom to Israel?" (Ac 1:6). Even after the crucifixion and the resurrection, two events which should have completely transformed the apostles' idea about the real nature of Jesus' mission, they are still clinging to those Jewish nationalist aspirations which had prompted them to follow Jesus from their first encounter and right up to the crucifixion of their Master. Jesus' reply does not seem to have much to do with the question. Rather, it sets in relief the combination of factors which are going to come into play in salvation history after the ascension of Jesus Christ. "It is not for you to know the times or periods that the Father has set by his own authority. But you will receive power when the Holy Spirit has come upon you; and you will be my witnesses in Jerusalem, in all Judea and Samaria, and to the ends of the earth" (vv. 7-8). The following comments are germane.

First, according to Luke these are Jesus' final words before his ascension. They include the fifth account of the "Great Commission,"[13] in which the missiology of the whole book of Acts is summarized in narrative form. Beginning in Jerusalem, the gospel spreads first to the adjacent areas, Judea and Samaria, and then progresses until it arrives in Rome. In the whole process, the church occupies a vital place, but not the church alone: *the church in the power of the Spirit.* The mission is no mere human project. It is the result of Jesus' mission being extended in history, an extension made possible by the action of the Holy Spirit. As such it is brought to fruition, not only by what the witnesses to Jesus *say*, but also by what they *are* and *do.*

Second, Pentecost follows immediately upon the ascension and is inseparable from it. Jesus Christ is enthroned as "Lord and Messiah" (Ac 2:36), King of the universe, and from this position sends his Holy Spirit to equip the church for the purpose of making disciples of all nations. The universal horizons of the mission are foreshadowed by the presence in Jerusalem of "devout Jews from every nation under heaven" (v. 5) on the day of Pentecost. The risen Christ, to whom the church bears witness, has been glorified to reign and put his enemies under his feet. Peter explained it to the believers in his Pentecost sermon: "Being therefore exalted at the right hand of God, and having received from the Father the promise of the Holy Spirit, he has poured out this that you both see and hear. For David did not

---

[13] The other four accounts are in the four Gospels: Mt 28:18-20, Mk 16:15-18 (although the most ancient manuscripts do not include Mk 16:9-20), Lk 24:46-49 and Jn 20:22-23. For an excellent exegetical and contextual study of these passages see Mortimer Arias, *La Gran Comisión* (Quito: CLAI, 2001).

ascend into the heavens, but he himself says, 'The Lord said to my Lord: Sit at my right hand, until I make your enemies your footstool'" (vv. 33-35). Years later, in agreement with Peter, the apostle Paul will affirm "for he must reign until he has put all his enemies under his feet" (1Co 15:25). With the exaltation of Jesus Christ and the coming of the Holy Spirit at Pentecost, a new era has been inaugurated in salvation history: the era of the Spirit, which is at the same time the era of Jesus Christ exalted as Lord and Messiah, and the era of the church and her mission to make disciples in the power of the Spirit.

Thirdly, Jesus' promise to his apostles that he would be with them "always, to the end of the age" (Mt 28:20), a promise which accompanied his commission to make disciples of all nations, is fulfilled through the presence of the Spirit and the Word, the combination that made possible the existence of the church and the success of her mission. As Emil Brunner says, "The *Ecclesia* is what it is through the presence of Christ dwelling within it. He is present in it through His Word and His Spirit."[14]

Finally, Acts 2:41-47 clearly shows that the result of the Pentecost experience is no ghetto-church, devoted to cultivating individualistic religion and an exclusive, separatist church. On the contrary, it is a community of the Spirit, a community that becomes a center of attraction, "having the goodwill of all the people" (v. 47), because it incarnates the values of the Kingdom of God and affirms by its way of life the lordship of Jesus Christ over all of life, including economics. It is a missionary community which preaches reconciliation with God and the restoration of all

---

[14] Emil Brunner, *The Misunderstanding of the* Church (London: Lutterworth Press, 1952), p. 12.

creation by the power of the Spirit. It is a community which provides a glimpse of the birth of a new humanity, and in which can be seen, albeit "in a mirror, dimly" (1Co 13:12), the fulfilment of God's plan for all humankind. "Although immersed in this world, the church by her way of being represents the promise of another world, which is not somewhere else but which is to come here."[15]

4. Gifts and Ministries

Gifts and ministries are the means used by the Spirit of God to equip the church as an agent of change in society—change that reflects God's plan for human life and the whole creation—and to equip all the faithful for the fulfilment of their vocation as God's co-workers in the world.

The is essentially the eschatological community, the community of the end time, empowered by the Spirit to bear witness to the Lord Jesus Christ as Lord of everyone and everything. This empowerment is offered in the form of various gifts and ministries, which all members receive for the edification of the Body of Christ. As Paul says from his trinitarian perspective, "Now there are varieties of gifts, but the same Spirit; and there are varieties of services, but the same Lord; and there are varieties of activities, but it is the same God who activates all of them in everyone" (1Co 12:4-6).

The importance of this statement for the articulation of an ecclesiology for integral mission cannot be exaggerated. And yet, all too frequently evangelical churches display a considerable

---

[15] Yoder, *op. cit.*, p. 94.

deficiency in this area. The reasons for the deficiency are many and varied, but perhaps the most important is a tendency to reduce Christianity to a religion given over to the satisfaction of those needs most closely linked with the human sense of the sacred and with worship services divorced from life. Seen in those terms, Christianity depends on "priests," who undertake the function of mediators between God and the faithful. From this standpoint the church is a religious institution, managed by specialists in religious matters, dedicated primarily to worship services and the care of the "spiritual needs" of the people. There is a sharp distinction between "clergy" and "laity," between "religious life" and "daily living," and between "the sacred" and "the secular."

A vision of the whole church with every member as an agent of integral mission, engaged in all areas of human life and creation, cannot possibly take root and flourish in a narrowly religious Christianity. Proof of that is to be found in the sad history of what were called "base Christian communities" that sprang up and grew in several Latin American countries from the middle of the last century. What might have been a genuine rebirth in the church, "an authentic ecclesiogenesis" as Leonardo Boff called it,[16] deeply rooted in Scripture, in the heart of the Roman Catholic Church, developed into a threatening flame which had to be extinguished with every means at the Vatican's disposal. And it was practically extinguished.

---

[16] Leonardo Boff, *Eclesiogénesis: Las comunidades de base reinventan la iglesia* (Ecclesiogenesis: Base Communities Reinvent the Church) (Santander: Sal Terrae, 1984), p. 10. The English translation was published by Orbis Press.

It must be admitted that the New Testament does not provide answers for all the questions which can be asked about the church, especially those concerned with institutional matters. That is the case with certain matters of church governance, which is an occasion of dissent among different Protestant denominations. But what is certain is that a New Testament perspective provides no basis for making the church a hierarchical institution in which a small elite holds a monopoly of gifts and ministries, leaving the majority to limit themselves to "submitting" to their leaders.

Integral mission demands the "declericalization" of ministries and a "laicization" of the clergy. In other words, it requires a recognition of the apostolic nature of the whole church. This implies, on one hand, that all members, by the simple fact of being disciples of Christ, share in the commission to go into the world in the name of Jesus Christ, as his witnesses. It also implies, on the other hand, that the leaders are a part of the *laos*, the people of God, just as are all the rest of Christ's followers, no more and no less.

All this is in accordance with the biblical doctrine which formed one of the pillars of the Reformation of the sixteenth century, *the priesthood of all believers*. The classical reformers like Luther and Calvin, however, emphasized the *soteriological consequences* of that doctrine, namely that a person could have a direct relationship with God without the need for intermediaries. But they did not pay much attention to the *ecclesiological consequences*: that all believers are called to Christian ministry, whatever their vocation. In consequence, it was a common idea in the Protestant world that the benefits of salvation could be separated from the responsibility for mission. Integral mission demands the recovery of the priesthood of all believers to the extent that the church becomes a community in which all members, equally, encourage each other to discover and develop their gifts and ministries in those countless areas of human existence which need transformation by the power of the gospel. As Boff says, the basic essential, without which the church does not exist, is "faith in the active presence of the Risen One and of his Spirit at the heart of the whole human community, causing it to live out those fundamental values without which there is no humanity," and this leads to "accepting the co-responsibility of all in the building up of the Church, and not only some members of the clergy."[17]

What then is the place for the leaders of the church? Is there no room for "specialized" ministries such as those exercised by the apostles, prophets, evangelists, pastors and teachers referred to in Ephesians 4:11? There is nothing in what has been said so far which would preclude a positive answer to these questions: the risen and exalted Christ has distributed gifts and has established these ministries for the fulfilment of his plan. But this list of gifts (in this case person-gifts rather than special skills) needs to be seen alongside another three lists, two in 1 Corinthians 12 (vv. 7-11 and 28-30) and one in Romanos 12 (vv. 6-8). Putting the four lists[18] together leads to the conclusion that there is no hierarchy of gifts or ministries, that all are valued equally, and that all have been conferred by "one and the same Spirit, who allots to each [member of the body of Christ]

---

[17] *Ibid.*, p. 39.

[18] 1Pe 4:11 could be added to the passages noted, but this passage does not actually offer a list of gifts. It refers only to two general categories in which the others could be classified; those concerned with speaking and those concerned with serving.

individually just as the Spirit chooses" (1Co 12.11). What is essential in the church in carrying out her task as witness to Jesus Christ is not a hierarchy, but a community of gifts which complement each other and contribute equally to the common good. Peter's exhortation to the elders or "presbyters" (pastors) shows the extent to which there was a real longing to avoid that church leaders become dependent on formal rights of office in exercising leadership in the community: "Tend the flock of God that is in your charge. . . Not under compulsion but willingly. . . not for sordid gain, but *eagerly. Do not lord it over those in your charge, but be examples to the flock*" (1Pe 5:2-3, italics mine). In the community of the Spirit two principles apply: the principle of service and the principle of teaching by example. These principles were incarnated in Jesus Christ as basic norms for the exercise of power. The church needs leaders, certainly, but servant-leaders; it needs teachers, but apprentice-teachers. As Guder puts it: "The organizational leadership of the church. . . is functional; that is, it is there to serve and equip the whole people for their ministry."[19] Actually, Ephesians 4:11-12 indicates this, stating that person-gifts have been given to the church "to equip the saints for the work of ministry, for building up the body of Christ."

Of course this is not to deny that the church has to have an organizational or institutional structure. Brunner argues in *The Misunderstanding of the Church* that the church-institution, characterized by institutional organization and the result of centuries of ecclesiastical history, must not be confused with the *Ecclesia* of the New Testament, characterized by an order

---

[19] Guder, *op. cit.*, p. 193.

established by the Spirit.[20] For him an acknowledgment of this by all the churches would be the first step toward creating a greater sense of unity among them, for none of them would claim direct descent from the original *Ecclesia*, and all would see their need for continual reformation. On the other hand, such an acknowledgment would remove one of the prime obstacles to the preservation of the true church, because "the main enemy of the Christian message and the communion which is rooted in Christ is not the hostility of the unbelieving world, but clerical, parsonic ecclesiasticism."[21] Even so, toward the end of his stimulating book he suggests that it might well be God's will that new church structures "of a very different order" could emerge in response to contemporary situations, structures which could favor the development of "the essence of the New Testament *Ecclesia* , the oneness of communion with Christ by faith and brotherhood in love."[22] Without rejecting Brunner's thesis, we need to add here that structures which favor "the unity of communion with Christ through faith and brotherhood in love" are just as necessary for the internal life of the church as for its external life. The historical nature of the church requires organization, but it is one thing for the church to be organized to maintain itself institutionally and to ensure its own survival, and something different to organize itself

---

[20] Cf. *op. cit.* For Brunner "the *Ecclesia* as *koinonia Christou* and *koinonia pneumatos*, like the 'body of Christ,' is a pure communion of persons entirely without institutional character" (pp. 16, 17), while the historical church "is rather something which has arisen in the course of a long and complicated history, through a process of development, transformation and retrogression, out of the New Testament *Ecclesia*" (pp. 14, 15).

[21] *Ibid.*, p. 117.

[22] *Ibid.*, p. 118.

for integral mission, for collaboration with God in the fulfilment of his plan for human life and all creation. It is vital that the church be structured for the task of integral mission. Without the working of God through the Spirit, organization will never ensure that the church attain its goals as witness to Jesus Christ as Lord of everything and everyone. But what is also sure is that the lack of an adequate organization will militate against the development of mission.

All churches are called to cooperate with God in the transformation of the world based on the gospel centered in Jesus Christ as Lord of the universe whose lordship provides the basis for an integral ecclesiology and integral mission. The mission of the church is the formation of disciples from all nations, disciples who are identified with Christ in his death and resurrection through baptism, and who are learning obedience to him in every aspect of life. The church depends for its incarnate witness on the "saving events" through which Jesus brought about redemption, namely, his life and ministry, his death on the cross, his resurrection and exaltation. Through the power of the Spirit, the church constitutes the beginning of a new humanity, and in what it is, does and says bears witness to Jesus Christ and cooperates with God in the fulfilment of his plan. It is a community of gifts and ministries; a community of hope, faith and love; a community structured for the task of integral mission for the glory of God.

2

The Biblical Basis for Integral Mission in the Context of Poverty

Esteban Voth

In a time of much tension and uncertainty Jesus said these words: "The poor you will always have with you, and you can help them any time you want. But you will not always have me" (Mk 14:7).

The subject at hand is the Biblical basis for integral mission in the context of poverty. Although there is an abundance of literature on this topic, there is no excess of praxis of integral mission; we find ourselves immersed in a context which demands a constant revision of our ideas and suggestions. The evangelical church today invests much of its time and effort in the development of personal spirituality, in the search for a more genuine approach to worship, in music groups that will attract youth, and in endless methods for Bible study and evangelization. The question that therefore arises is whether "religious" people are at all concerned with their responsibility towards the poor.[1]

---

[1] See the study made by R. Wuthnow, "What Religious People Think About the Poor," *Christian Century*, Sept. 7-14 (1994): 812-816.

Let's return to Jesus' words. They were spoken when some indignant people angrily questioned the woman who had anointed Jesus in Bethany with a very expensive perfume.[2] These words have been interpreted in many ways, though in my opinion none has been adequate. For this reason we will examine some of these interpretations as a way of beginning to approach the problem of discovering the biblical bases for integral mission.

One of the most common interpretations of Christ's statement suggests that we have to resign ourselves to the fact that the poor will always exist and there is nothing that can be done about it. Jesus' assertion is taken out of context to legitimize a passive and irresponsible attitude towards the reality of poverty. One has the right to ignore the situation of the poor because Christ insinuated that nothing could be done about it.

Another common interpretation similar to the one above suggests that, in some way or other, Jesus' statement implies that poverty has been predetermined by God. It follows, therefore, that if poverty has been "predestined," a lack of commitment to the crude reality of poverty can be justified once again. This interpretation allows the Christian to close his eyes to the suffering of millions and continue his spiritual pilgrimage along other paths.

Hendriksen provides us with a rather different interpretation. He states that it was not a case of the Teacher being indifferent to the situation of the poor, but that the possibility of showing love

---

[2] According to Garland the perfume cost the equivalent of a workman's salary for one year. See David Garland, *Mark, The NIV Application Commentary* (Grand Rapids: Zondervan Publishing Co., 1996), p. 515.

and honor towards him was about to disappear, for he was going through humiliating circumstances. The events at Gethsemane, Gabatha and Golgotha were getting nearer. What the woman had done was very good; it had been a beautiful deed.[3]

Lane proposes a different approach when he mentions that the woman's gift was a beautiful expression of love, with a deeper meaning of which the woman was most likely unaware. The gift was appropriate precisely because Jesus' death was imminent.[4] Lane accepts Danker's suggestion that this event and Jesus' words should be understood in the context of Psalm 41, where the poor and innocent suffer but in the end emerge victorious over their enemies.[5] Like the psalmist, Jesus is poor and innocent and suffers as a result of his righteousness. The woman in this instance, unlike the other guests, acknowledges that Jesus was the poor *par excellence.*

In his commentary on the parallel text in Matthew, Lenski states that the most important point in this passage revolves around the chiasm "always-not always." This is not to establish a difference in value between Jesus and the poor. The marked contrast is not between Jesus and the poor, but between "always" and "not always." They would "always" have the poor and "always" be able to work for their well-being. Jesus, on the

---

[3] W. Hendriksen, *Exposition of the Gospel According to Mark, New Testament Commentary* (Grand Rapids: Baker Book House, 1975), pp. 559-560.

[4] W. L. Lane, *The Gospel according to Mark, The New International Commentary on the New Testament* (Grand Rapids: William B. Eerdmans Publishing Co., 1974), pp. 493-494.

[5] F. W. Danker, "The Literary Unity of Mark 14,1-25," *JBL* 85 (1966): 467-472.

other hand, would only be among them for a few more days, and this would be the woman's only opportunity to honor him.[6]

I would like to suggest that each of these interpretations has overlooked the context in which Jesus spoke these words. It is crucial to understand the position from which Jesus made this statement and what his world view was when he made it.

A review of the circumstances in which Jesus is found shows us that this encounter between Jesus and the woman who anoints him with the expensive perfume is situated between two key events in Jesus' life. In Mark 14:1 we find that the chief priests and the teachers of the Law were attempting, through sly maneuvers, to find a way to arrest Jesus. Later, at the end of this section, in vs. 10 and 11, we learn of Judas' betrayal. This encounter takes place between these two events, creating a tremendous contrast. In the midst of such malice and disloyal treachery, which ironically includes a financial transaction, we find the woman's expression of love and devotion. This love, devotion and honor are expressed through an act of incredible generosity. The woman doesn't hold anything back. She offers everything to him who truly identified with the poor and, as it were, was the poor par excellence. In this sense it is imperative to note that Jesus' words are, in my opinion, a direct quotation of Deuteronomy 15:11: "There will always be poor people in the land" (NIV). But that is only the first part of the verse, which continues: "Therefore I command you to be open-handed toward your brothers and toward the poor and needy in your land."

---

[6] R. C. H. Lenski, *The Interpretation of St. Matthew's Gospel* (Minneapolis: Augsburg Publishing House, 1961), p. 1009.

There are several points here that should be highlighted. To begin with, I'd like to call attention to the assertion "therefore." The idea of cause and effect is very prominent in the Hebrew text. The fact that the poor exist elicits an order from Yahweh to his followers, that they take care of the underprivileged and the "needy." In other words, there is no place here for an attitude of resignation or justification. Neither is there room for excuses for a lack of commitment to the reality of the poor. This is a clear mandate, highlighted in Hebrew by the emphatic use of the subject "I." There can be no doubt about the command or from whom it comes.

It is interesting to note that in Deuteronomy 15:4 an ideal had been expressed:

> However, there should be no poor among you, for in the land the Lord your God is giving you to possess as your inheritance, he will richly bless you.

Nevertheless, accepting that in the end Israel would break the covenant and that this ideal would not be possible, we find this passionate call to take care of the poor.

It is also worth noting the parallelism that exists between the generosity of the woman who anoints Jesus and the call to be generous with the poor. When Jesus replies to the indignation of the guests, he is doing so from this perspective. The woman had served with utter generosity, holding nothing back. By quoting Deuteronomy, Jesus is declaring that the woman is complying with the deuteronomic mandate. The order in Deuteronomy is expressed by the repetition of a verb. It appears first in the infinitive, followed later by the imperfect form *patoaj tiftaj*. This is one of the ways in which emphasis and intensity are expressed in Hebrew.[7] Literally, the text is saying "open (truly) your hand." This command clearly demands generosity that exceeds any kind of legislation to help the poor. This is Yahweh's demand, which gives a practical dimension to the teaching in Leviticus 19:18: "Love your neighbor as yourself. I am the Lord." I submit, therefore, that this is the background needed to understand Jesus' words. When Jesus answers on this occasion, he is quoting Deuteronomy, with the background of the Old Testament as a part of his understanding. Therefore, those who interpret that Jesus' words imply an attitude of resignation towards the reality of poverty, or that poverty was somehow divinely predetermined, are mistaken because they have ignored the context from which Jesus was speaking.

Lastly, the text we are exploring speaks of a total devotion to Jesus. In light of the biblical context, and keeping in mind especially the words of Jesus found in Matthew 25:31-46, those who truly honor Jesus are those who are concerned for the poor. This means that Jesus' words are a form of judgment directed towards all those that claim to honor him. The very existence of the poor is a sign that Christ's disciples are not obeying the mandate of Deuteronomy. In this regard, I would agree with the ideas presented by Garland.[8] When Jesus says: "The poor you will always have with you, and you can help them any time you want," he is saying that our help must not be sporadic or limited to certain times; it should be continuous. Furthermore, Jesus' words: "She did what she could" imply that helping the poor does not depend on abundance. The woman gave everything

---

[7] See R. Williams, *Hebrew Syntax: An Outline*, 2nd. ed. (Toronto: University of Toronto Press, 1976), pp. 37-38.

[8] D. E. Garland, *Mark*, p. 520.

she could. We will return to this point later since, on the basis of the widow's offering (Mk 12:41-44), the issue is evidently not "how much one gives" nor whether "one gives all he or she can" but rather "how much one keeps."

Finally, it is striking how Jesus associates this action with the preaching of the gospel:

> I tell you the truth, wherever the gospel is preached throughout the world, what she has done will also be told, in memory of her.

As Garland has pointed out, "What is the Gospel if not good news for the poor?" (cf. Mt 5:3; 11:5; Lk 4:17-19).[9] Jesus understands that biblical mission is necessarily integral mission through which every human being is cared for as a whole person. In this sense I propose that the words of Jesus found in Mark 14:7 in reference to the poor are paradigmatic and programmatic. They represent a model of integral mission and offer a practical example of what the *praxis* of integral mission meant in everyday life in Israel during the first century. Far from being a text which justifies indifference and resignation towards the anguish of poverty, this text is a guide, a challenge and a call to a profound and proactive commitment to the "neighbor" who lives under humiliating conditions.

This example from Jesus' life was chosen as an introduction to this study for the purpose of establishing the theoretical framework within which we will work. We consider that it is crucial to discern Jesus' world view, as he was the missionary par

---

[9] *Ibid.* See also the view offered by G. Cook y R. Foulkes, *Marcos, Comentario Bíblico Hispanoamericano* (Miami: Caribe, 1990), pp. 324-326.

excellence. Jesus became flesh in a specific historical period, in a specific place, in a specific culture, and he spoke a specific language. As such, Jesus expressed himself in cultural terms which were understandable in the Ancient Near East of the first century. Furthermore, we know that Jesus was shaped by the Hebrew Bible, which provided a context, an authority and a basis for his mission. For all these reasons, we will trace some of the key passages of the Old Testament that we believe were fundamental for establishing the theoretical framework on the basis of which Jesus articulated his mission and put it into practice.

1. Integral Mission in the Old Testament

In the first few chapters of Genesis we find two opposing realities. On the one hand, we have the liturgy of creation, characterized by extraordinary abundance and generosity. The whole of creation is considered very, very good. The creation, with human beings as a part of it, has everything it needs to be fruitful and live with dignity. But the entry of sin affects the entire creation. Sin not only causes harm in the spiritual realm, it also alters the harmony in the realm of human relationships, in ecology, in the body, and in the access to a dignified life for all human beings. Though it is true that the terms *poverty* and *oppression* do not appear in these first chapters of Genesis, the account narrates events that illustrate these conditions. Starting with the fratricide committed by the stronger brother, followed by the violence of Lamech and culminating with the construction of the tower of Babel which was most likely built by slave labor, we encounter a reality which demands a mission that will deal with everything that has been affected by sin. We can see from looking at the very beginning of all things that a simplistic or "reductionist" vision of what the creation needs is unacceptable. Jesus knew this text from Genesis quite well, and I propose that that is why the reality which is described there was a part of his world view. This world view influenced the way in which Jesus approached people and the situations which they were experiencing.

Jesus also knew the instructions written in the book of Leviticus. One of them is relevant to our discussion. In Leviticus 19:9-10 we read the following:

> When you reap the harvest of your land, do not reap to the very edges of your field or gather the gleanings of your harvest. Do not go over your vineyard a second time or pick up the grapes that have fallen. Leave them for the poor and the alien. I am the Lord your God.

Hebrew legislation was very clear about providing for the poor. In other words, it paid attention to the dignity of human beings in several aspects. In the first place, it was concerned with their need to eat properly. It is necessary to point out, however, that the possibility of working was implicit in this law. "Gleaning" the fields and "picking up" the fallen grapes is work, not charity. Work is essential for the dignity of the person. Once again the text confronts us with an integral proposal. It is not simply about feeding someone, but about creating a context in which human beings can also regain their dignity.

Obviously, this legislation is directed towards an agrarian society. In a society of this kind, land is the determining factor for subsistence. The Hebrew text states categorically that the earth belongs to God. Humans are called to be faithful stewards of the earth, which belongs to God. This does not mean that private property should not exist, but it does mean that even private property must be submitted to God's sovereignty. This basic principle is expressed in different practical ways. The Year of Jubilee confronts us with a principle through which there is the restitution of land lost by the poor. The Mosaic law also declares that a brother must "redeem" property that his poor brother was forced to sell. Similarly, the institution of "levirate" marriage shows a concern for the integrity and the welfare of the widowed sister-in-law. Through all these laws God expresses his will that all his people have the right to a decent life.

Following the canonical order of the sacred text in Hebrew, in Deuteronomy 10:18-19 we find God's profound concern for those who lack a family structure to protect them:

> He defends the cause of the fatherless and the widow, and loves the alien, giving him food and clothing. And you are to love those who are aliens, for you yourselves were aliens in Egypt.

In the same way that God had extended his justice to the slaves in Egypt, now the recipients of that justice should pass it on to the widows, the orphans and the aliens. Why are these groups specified and not others? Because they all share a common condition: the lack of a family support network. In traditional societies, family networks were crucial as a form of "social security." God is extremely concerned about those who have lost their social security, and as a result, their place in society. This concern is transformed into a mandate for the community that calls itself "the people of God." In the rest of Deuteronomy this mandate has two main concerns: food and justice. A reading of Deuteronomy teaches that God's law is an integral law that cares for the whole person. Jesus is well aware of all this legislation and, simply but profoundly, comes to fulfill it and embody it. By doing so he shows us that it is possible to make it a reality.

The story of Ruth inserted in the deuteronomic history exemplifies an extreme situation. The narrative speaks of two women. The simple fact of being a woman at that time in Israel already meant being at a disadvantage. These two women had become widows. Both of them, at different places and times, are foreigners. Lastly, both of them are in a situation of extreme poverty, to the extent that Naomi expresses a lament on her return to her land:

> I went away full,
> but the Lord has
> brought me back empty.
> Why call me Naomi?
> The Lord has afflicted me;
> the Almighty has brought
> misfortune upon me.
> (Ruth 1:21)

In this situation of complete vulnerability in which Naomi had lost everything—husband, children, and one of her two daughters-in-law—two institutions established in the law take on active meaning and make possible the rehumanization of these two widows. We have already mentioned one of them, which refers to the permission for the poor to collect a part of the harvest. The other institution that we find here is the "kinsman redeemer" or "family protector" (*go'el*).[10] The role of this

---

[10] Cf. E. Jenni y C. Westermann, *Diccionario Teológico Manual del Antiguo Testamento*, vol. I (Madrid: Cristiandad, 1978), pp. 549-564.

mandate is decisive and provides a permanent solution to the desperate situation of the widow. In the first place, the "kinsman redeemer" rescues (*redeems*) the property of the relative who is in need and, in the second place, marries the widow of the deceased relative. In this case it may be that the guidelines for the "levirate" and the "kinsman redeemer" merge. This example is important because it shows how divine legislation affects structures. Through these two institutions a structure of poverty, helplessness and discrimination is transformed into a structurally good situation. Israel's society has a framework within its reach to provide a permanent solution for the well-being of the powerless. We can suggest therefore that in this framework of wholeness, the strong intervene in favor of the helpless.

During the period of the monarchy in Israel, deuteronomic literature provided clear instructions for the kings regarding their conduct and their actions. In Deuteronomy 17:14-20 we find legislation which does not legitimize the institution of the monarchy but which sets clearly defined limits for it. First of all, the king must be chosen by Yahweh and must belong to the people of God (v. 15). Secondly, the king "must not acquire great numbers of horses for himself;" in other words, a limit is placed on his military power. Thirdly, the king "must not take many wives" (v. 17). This means that a limit is established on his political power, since marriage with foreign women was aimed at making alliances to extend political power. Fourthly, "he must not accumulate large amounts of silver or gold" (v. 17), which indicates that his economic power is also restricted. Why? Because in this way the king will learn to fear Yahweh, to follow his words and his precepts, and therefore "not consider himself better than his brothers" (v. 20). These limits are established so that the king, who has power, will not take advantage of his people or oppress them because he considers himself "above them."[11] Without a doubt, the text is proclaiming an ideal of "equity and equality." Jesus, King of Kings, embodied this teaching by serving his neighbors, curing the sick, liberating the oppressed and giving dignity to women.

This same perspective and concern are found in the poetic literature in the anthology known as The Psalms. Psalms 9-10 (which are in fact only one Psalm), in particular, present Yahweh as Savior of the poor and oppressed.[12] In these Psalms, terms which describe people in need are repeated several times: the oppressed (*dak*); the suffering (*'anavim*); the needy (*'evyon*); the helpless, defenseless (*'ani*); the victim (*helekah*); and the orphan (*yatom*).

In each of these situations, Yahweh is presented as the one who brings justice. All of these disadvantaged members of society have the right to cry out to Yahweh about their individual or social situation and Yahweh will answer and will respond to their plight with justice. Salvation is not merely something that has to do with the future, nor is it something strictly "spiritual." The salvation of Yahweh that brings justice is palpable, immediate and integral. The text says:

> The Lord reigns forever;
> he has established his throne for judgment.
> He will judge the world in righteousness;
> he will govern the peoples with justice.

---

[11] Compare with the ideals for a king set forth in Psalm 72.

[12] There are numerous arguments in favor of considering these two Psalms as one. See H.-J. Kraus, *Psalms 1-59* (Minneapolis: Augsburg Publishing House, 1988), p. 191.

The Lord is a refuge for the oppressed,
a stronghold in times of trouble.
(Ps 9:7-9)

Once again, it is evident that a poem such as this one from the Hebrew Bible could have been the basis for the way in which Jesus carried out his mission here on earth.

In the Hebrew text, wisdom literature has characteristics of its own and a theoretical framework which is significantly different from that of the other literary genre we have been looking at up to this point. Nevertheless, generally speaking this literature suggests that wisdom is directed towards conduct which seeks to do justice. Now, the wisdom literature that we find in the book of Proverbs states that one of the causes which has contributed to the existence of poverty is laziness:

Laziness brings on deep sleep,
and the shiftless man goes hungry.
(Prov 19:15)

Do not love sleep or you will grow poor;
stay awake and you will have food to spare.
(Prov 20:13; cf. 20:4; 21:17; 21:25)

In this context of reflection upon different experiences in life, the text states that sometimes poverty is the result of an incorrect attitude.

This same literature, however, proposes that many times poverty is caused by injustice. Therefore one cannot generalize and attribute the existence of poverty to laziness alone. The author of Proverbs states:

A poor man's field may produce abundant food,
but injustice sweeps it away.
(Prov 13:23)

A ruler who oppresses the poor
is like a driving rain that leaves no crops.
(Prov 28:3; cf. 14:31; 22:16, 22-23)

Wisdom literature accepts that one of the most important causes of poverty is injustice. That is why it also declares that God will defend the cause of the poor, in particular when their situation has been caused by injustice:

Do not exploit the poor because they are poor
and do not crush the needy in court,
for the Lord will take up their case
and will plunder those who plunder them.
(Prov 22:22-23)

The God of justice warns that he will intervene to defend the poor when they are not treated with justice and dignity. God's mission is not limited to establishing a spiritual relationship with people, though this is extremely important. God's mission also concerns itself with concrete aspects of human existence. Wisdom literature, throughout Proverbs and Job (29:14; 31:13-23; 24:1-12), reaffirms this concept and proclaims that justice is fundamental to the practice of mission. If justice is of such great importance for God's mission, it should be more so for the mission of his Church.

Perhaps the literary genre which most challenges us on this subject is the prophetic literature. When the prophets of the Hebrew Bible proclaimed God's word, they took into account people's entire existence. These men cared for the religious experience of their people: their spirituality, their loyalty to God and their physical condition. The prophets challenged in equal measure, therefore, both the religious leaders and those that had political power. One of the issues that most concerned the prophets was justice. In contrast to the wisdom literature, for the prophets the true cause of poverty was found in the presence of injustice. This injustice had become institutionalized in royalty as well as in the clergy. These were, precisely, the two institutions that had received God's mandate, through the Mosaic law, to look after the welfare of the people and to make sure that all were treated with justice. As well as concerning themselves with the problem of injustice, the prophets also condemned idolatry and the disobedience to the law.

One of these prophets was named Amos. He was sent from the small kingdom of the south to denounce the powerful Northern Kingdom. He went to the capital, Samaria, and spoke against idolatry, sin and the terrible oppression of the poor. Amos made an integral denunciation in order lo proclaim an integral hope. He attacked the religiosity empty of all ethical content and at the same time spoke against the prevalent injustice. His words are already a classic:

> For three sins of Israel,
> even for four, I will not turn back my wrath.
> They sell the righteous for silver,
> and the needy for a pair of sandals.
> They trample on the heads of the poor
> as upon the dust of the ground
> and deny justice to the oppressed.
> (Am 2:6-7a)

Amos, however, did not only speak out against the oppression of the poor in general. He also uncovered the oppression of women: "Father and son use the same girl and so profane my holy name" (Am 2:7b). Though there are a number of different interpretations of this text, I submit that Amos is here pointing out two problems. One of them is immorality, which is an offense against Yahweh's holy name, and the other is the terrible oppression of women by men. Amos' mission was directed not only to the whole human being as such, but also to all the circumstances surrounding him. Though Amos was aware that injustice in his time was practically legal and legitimized by the powerful interests of the royalty and the clergy, his mission was not limited to speaking out against idolatry and the theological aberrations of his time. He confronted the powerful, who had the possibility of doing something about the appalling situation of the poor, and in that way his mission was much broader. Jesus, in our view, was deeply familiar with Amos' mission and embodied it in his own mission. We would suggest that the life and praxis of Amos may have been a source of inspiration for Jesus and may also have served as a way of legitimizing his ministry by tradition. In other words, when Jesus presents the demands of the Kingdom he does not do so in a vacuum. On the contrary, he is supported by an authoritative tradition.

Micah was another prophet of the eighth century B.C.E. whose mission was to engage the various evils that afflicted his society. Micah also confronted the false prophets that were in league with the royalty and proclaimed only what was favorable for the king. But this prophet also denounced other social ills such as oppression and corruption. His mission included announcing the punishment that would befall the rich oppressors, those who

> . . . plan iniquity,
> to those who plot evil on their beds!
> At morning's light they carry it out
> because it is in their power to do it.
> They covet fields and seize them,
> and houses, and take them.
> They defraud a man of his home,
> a fellowman of his inheritance.
> (Mic 2:1-2)

And, without any reservations, the prophet speaks to the corrupt governors:

> Listen, you leaders of Jacob,
> you rulers of the house of Israel.
> Should you not know justice,
> you who hate good and love evil;
> who tear the skin from my people
> and the flesh from their bones;
> who eat my people's flesh,
> strip off their skin
> and break their bones in pieces;
> who chop them up like meat for the pan,
> like flesh for the pot? (Mic 3:1-3)

The circumstances were so desperate for people that Micah described them in detail. His mission not only included a call to repentance and renovation of their loyalty to God but also a call to take responsibility for the socioeconomic situation of the people. Micah's description of the actions of the corrupt leaders of his time is quite fitting for those who today impose a neo-liberal economic plan, and also for those throughout Latin America who accept it with open arms. In Micah's mission there is a place for courageously exposing all the spheres of leadership that define and determine the situation of the masses:

Her leaders judge for a bribe,
her priests teach for a price,
and her prophets tell fortunes for money.
(Mic 3:1 l)

Only an integral mission can redefine and reorient the realities that people are living. A partial, reductionist, dualistic mission cannot offer an alternative, one which transforms people's situations. The example of the prophet is a warning to the church of Jesus Christ, which only utters words that seduce and entertain but which are inadequate to perform the complete surgery that our Latin American society needs.

The prophet Isaiah was one of the few prophets that had direct access to the king's court. This suggests that his family belonged to the nobility. Nevertheless, this man who was called by God did not try to protect the interests of the royalty, but carried out a countercultural mission that put his life in constant danger. One of his main concerns was to speak out against the monopolization of property by the royalty and the rich. lsaiah cried out with all his might:

Woe to you who add house to house
and join field to field
till no space is left
and you live alone in the land.
(Isa 5:8)

There are two modern parallels to the situation Isaiah describes: large landowners and the "private suburbs" where only people of the same kind live. This process of taking away the opportunities for people to live with dignity was not acceptable according to the deuteronomic law, and the prophet made sure he pointed it out. To seek justice for everyone was part of the integral mission of the prophet.

Isaiah was also concerned about the relationship that his people had with God; in other words, the spiritual condition of the community was not a secondary issue. The prophet says:

> . . . wash and make yourselves clean.
> Take your evil deeds
>   out of my sight!
> Stop doing wrong,
>   learn to do right!
> Seek justice,
>   encourage the oppressed.
> Defend the cause of the fatherless,
>   plead the case of the widow.
>   (Isa 1:16-17)

It is imperative to notice that the concern for purity of heart and for justice went hand in hand. The prophet did not separate one from the other. His call to live according to God's will, to be pure of heart, was interwoven with the call to seek justice, care for the orphan and protect the widow. The prophet lived out an integral mission, not one that was dualistic and divisive. Isaiah understood that the message he had received from God was one which encompassed all aspects of life and of the person. Greek dualism and missiological reductionism do not fit into the biblical vision.

Another aspect of the prophet's mission was not only to confront unjust laws but also to confront those who established them. The rich and the powerful of Israel made it a point to pass laws that legitimized oppression. They created the legal framework within which oppression was legitimized. That is why the prophet, upon seeing this situation, does not spiritualize it nor avoid it, but rather confronts it directly:

> Woe to those who make unjust laws,
> to those who issue oppressive decrees,
> to deprive the poor of their rights
> and withhold justice from the oppressed of my people,
> making widows their prey
> and robbing the fatherless.
> (Isa 10:1-2)

It is interesting to remember Jesus' answer to the teachers of the law when one of them asked which was the most important commandment. Jesus answered categorically: to love God with all your heart, soul, mind and strength, and love your neighbor as yourself. Later he added: "There is no commandment greater than these" (Mk 12:28-33). This shows us that neither Jesus nor the Mosaic law reduced or limited the commandments to only a correct relationship with God. The challenge was to live the Gospel in a holistic way. That is why the prophet's mission also included dealing with the legal system, with what happened in the courts, and with the creation of unjust laws. The corruption of magistrates, in ancient Israel as much as in our Latin American nations today, is not an issue which can be left out of an integral biblical mission. The proposal that arises from God's revelation demands that those who are missionaries should make his message of life penetrate into all aspects of existence and thereby influence people's whole lives.

Jeremiah is the last prophet and author we will consider from the Hebrew Bible. This prophet had the misfortune of seeing how his prophecies of judgment and destruction were fulfilled. No one suffered as he did, in his own flesh, the experience of seeing how his people were taken into bondage like cattle. But before this happened, Jeremiah had repeatedly warned the leaders of the nation. He had addressed the king, the priests and the prophets repeatedly, holding them responsible for the critical situation of the people. The people were far from God, far from a life of dignity and very close to political disintegration, due mostly to their leadership. The false prophets cried out "Peace, peace, peace," when there was no peace. The priests had emptied the sacrificial system of all meaning and ethical content. The kings oppressed the people openly. This situation required the appearance of someone who could embody an integral mission and offer a viable alternative, an alternative of hope.

When Jeremiah denounced the oppression caused by Jehoiakim, he used the following words which came from Yahweh:

> "Does it make you a king
> to have more and more cedar?
> Did not your father have food and drink?
> He did what was right and just,
> so all went well with him.
> He defended the cause of the poor and needy,
> and so all went well.
> Is that not what it means to know me?"
> (Jer 22:15,16)

Knowing God, a condition *sine qua non* for developing a healthy spirituality, was intimately related to doing justice. Once again it is evident that the Biblical text keeps both these dimensions together. For Jeremiah, mission demanded proclaiming a message that included a willingness to "know God," but this knowledge should be demonstrated through actions that sought to practice justice. These dimensions are inseparable.

One of the most important concerns for God's people was to be able to continue living in the land that God had given them after the miracle of the Exodus. The priests had convinced the people that if they went to the Temple and faithfully complied with their sacrifices, they would surely be able to inhabit the land forever. Jeremiah passionately refutes this theology:

> Do not trust in deceptive words and say, "This is the temple of the Lord, the temple of the Lord, the temple of the Lord!" If you really change your ways and your actions and deal with each other justly, if you do not oppress the alien, the fatherless or the widow and do not shed innocent blood in this place, and if you do not follow other gods to your own harm, then I will let you live in this place, in the land I gave your forefathers for ever and ever (Jer 7:4-7).

Jeremiah's mission, later incarnated by Jesus as the God-man, was a mission that spoke out against both idolatry and injustice. The alternative of hope that he proclaims, therefore, is one that seeks justice within a context of absolute loyalty to God.

2. Integral Mission in the Gospels of the New Testament

Although the above study of the text of the Hebrew Bible does not represent an exhaustive analysis, it will serve as a theoretical framework to understand Jesus' words and proposals. We would like to stress again that it is fundamental to acknowledge that Jesus "speaks" and "acts" on the basis of his complete identification with a world view which stems from the message of the Hebrew Bible. It is impossible to understand Jesus apart from the background of God's actions in history, which are narrated in the sacred literature of the people of Israel.

The Great Omission

According to the Gospel of Luke, the first public words spoken by Jesus were those he read from the book of the prophet Isaiah in the synagogue in Nazareth:

> "The Spirit of the Lord is on me,
> because he has anointed me
> to preach good news to the poor.
> He has sent me to proclaim freedom for the prisoners
> and recovery of sight for the blind,
> to release the oppressed,
> to proclaim the year of the Lord's favor."
> (Lk 4:18-19)

Jesus appears on the scene and introduces himself by means of a reading from the prophet Isaiah. In that precise moment he makes the words of the prophet his own. By doing so, he is declaring that he has been authorized by someone, that is, by the Lord himself. In the Hebrew text the divine title is intensified: it is the Sovereign Lord, the Lord of Lords, the one who is unequalled. Jesus does not appear on the scene alone, without support. He is not a "lone ranger" on the "mission field" to do and undo at will. His credentials are established through two images. First of all, the text states that the Spirit of the Lord is upon him. This is not an esoteric or mystical spirit, "new age" style. This Spirit is one who has power to transform reality. It is the same Spirit that eradicated the powers of chaos in creation and opened the waters during the Exodus, when the Israelite slaves were liberated from the oppressive clutches of the Egyptian pharaoh. Secondly, the text states that Jesus has been anointed by Yahweh. The act of anointing is a liturgical act through which a community gives someone authority.[13] Jesus, therefore, comes to be a "missionary" with this double dose of authority.

Jesus' mission is essentially to put into action the complete scope of the gospel. Interestingly enough, this is expressed through a series of verbs that speak of action, commitment and sacrifice. In Luke's narrative we find the following verbs: preach (announce), proclaim, give sight, release (liberate) and proclaim (make known). But in the Hebrew text of Isaiah we find three additional verbs: heal, console and comfort. All of these verbs are important because they indicate and define ministries towards the poor, the marginalized, the handicapped and the powerless, with the purpose of restoring them as human beings so that they can operate as such in the community.

This is the essence of *mission* for Jesus. This is what he carne to do. The problem is that the Church has decided to "spiritualize" these verbs to such an extent that they have lost their power. The evangelical church in general has domesticated these verbs and has taken away their ability to do major surgery. For this reason we have called this section of the New Testament "The Great Omission," in contrast with the well-known text popularly called "The Great Commission." Nonetheless, it is important to remember that these verbs were spoken with the authorization of the Spirit of the Lord. And this Spirit has the power to change reality, to convert chaos into order, slavery into freedom and condemnation into salvation. This means that "the great omission" (Lk 4:18-19) should become "the great mission,"

---

[13] See W. Brueggemann, *Isaiah 40-66*, *Westminster Biblical Companion* (Louisville, KY: Westminster John Knox Press, 1998), pp. 212-215.

so that the church can truly carry out "the great commission" (Mt 28:16-20).

In the Gospel of Luke we find a continuous interest in Jesus' commitment to the poor and in his mission which was so clearly expressed in his presentation in the synagogue. As Bosch[14] has pointed out, Luke had already made reference to the poor in the Magnificat:

> He has brought down rulers from their thrones
> but has lifted up the humble.
> He has filled the hungry with good things
> but has sent the rich away empty.
> (Lk 1:52-53)

This interest continues with the blessing of the poor: "Blessed are you who are poor, for yours is the kingdom of God" (6:20), together with the warning for the rich (6:24); the parable of the rich fool (12:16-21); the story of the rich man and Lazarus, the poor man (16:19-31); the case study of Zacchaeus, the tax collector of Jericho (19:1-10). All these examples, with the exception of the blessing, belong to Luke. They do not appear in the other Gospels. Luke uses the word *ptojos* (poor) ten times, twice as often as Matthew or Mark. In light of these facts, Schottroff and Stegemann have said the following:

> If we didn't have Luke we would probably have lost an important, if not the most important, part of the oldest

---

[14] David Bosch, *Transforming Mission: Paradigm Shifts in Theology of Mission* (Maryknoll: Orbis Books, 1991), pp. 98-104.

> Christian tradition, together with his intense regard for the person and the message of Jesus as the hope of the poor.[15]

Luke's concern for the poor, according to Bosch, can be seen in the use of the word *ptojos* as a collective term. Bosch shows that this can be clearly seen when Luke gives a list of people who suffer. In these lists he places the poor either at the beginning (cf. 4:18; 6:20; 14:13; 14:21) or else at the end as a sort of climax (see 7:22). All those who in some way experience some type of misery are, in a very real sense, poor. In Luke, then, "the poor" represents a social category.[16]

Following this train of thought, it is interesting to remember the phrase from Isaiah 52:7 that the Apostle Paul quotes in Romans 10:15: "How beautiful are the feet of those who bring good news!" Those that bring the gospel that Jesus described in the synagogue of Nazareth are considered beautiful by the poor of this world. They are feet that are "fitted with the readiness that comes from the gospel of peace" (Eph 6:15). The word "readiness" is a translation of the Greek word *hetoimasia*. This is the only time that this Greek term appears in the New Testament, and can be translated in various ways: ready, available, prepared. In reference to this verse and the use of this word, Vincent informs us that the Roman soldiers wore the *caligae* or sandals tied around their ankles.[17] These sandals were not used by superior officers, but only by soldiers. Common soldiers were

---

[15] L. Schottroff y W. Stegemann, *Jesus and the Hope of the Poor* (Maryknoll: Orbis Books, 1986), p. 67.

[16] D. Bosch, *op.cit.*, p. 131.

[17] M. Vincent, *Word Studies in the New Testament*, vol. III (Grand Rapids: William B. Eerdmans Publishing Co., 1946), p. 409.

therefore called *caligati*. They were the ones that had to be "ready," "prepared" to fulfill their task.

It is possible to argue that for those who have been anointed to preach the good news of the Gospel to the poor there is a movement from up to down, from the center to the periphery, from the elite to the poor, from the powerful to the oppressed. The emphasis changes towards those that are burdened by the effects of what we call modernization, capitalism and globalization. Those who carry the Good News have walked the roads of the poor and have been identified with those who experience poverty: they have learned their language, have entered their cultural environment, have learned to empathize with their values, share their world view and know how to represent their needs before the oppressors. They have walked many miles wearing the sandals of the poor, and, as a consequence, have "beautiful" feet. Such are the feet of those who proclaim the gospel of peace, those that practice integral mission. We would venture to suggest that those who share the gospel of peace are the "foot-washers" of the world (Jn 13).

The second New Testament passage which we will analyze tells us the story of the widow who gave an offering at the Temple (Mk 12:41-44). In this passage we can see at least two different categories of people: those that have a lot (the rich) and those that have little (the poor widow and Jesus' disciples). In the latter we will no doubt find two subgroups: those that live in absolute poverty (*ptojos*) and, as a consequence, cannot meet their basic necessities (shelter, clothing, food); and those that barely have what is essential for survival. They have no money to spend, but they do survive. This means that all the others have "a lot." All those that have more than the basic necessities have "a lot."

In this narration we are told that Jesus sat opposite the place where the offerings were put. Some suggest that this act of "sitting opposite to" is an act of judgment (cf. Mk 2:6 where the scribes are sitting to judge).[18] According to the *Mishnah* (*Shekalim* VI, 5), in the treasury of the Temple there were thirteen trumpet-shaped chests against the wall, in the women's courtyard. Each of these chests represented a particular cause (i.e. an item of the budget). Long lines would form behind these chests. Religious people would come with their offerings and stand in the line that formed behind the chest of their choice. Upon arriving at the chest, they would report to the priest the amount of the offering and for what cause it was to be employed, and later the offering was placed in the chest. The rich would often exchange the amount of their offering for smaller coins (with the money-changers outside the Temple; Jn 2:14) so that their money would make more noise in the chest and attract more attention.

Jesus took his disciples there to observe, study and evaluate what was happening, as a sort of ethnological experience. The disciples would have concluded that the rich were doing what was correct, that they had been obedient and faithful and therefore God had blessed them with material abundance. Jesus was observing both what was happening in the Temple treasury and what the disciples were saying and thinking. At that moment, "a poor widow came and put in two very small copper coins, worth only a fraction of a penny." We can imagine the situation. The widow had been standing in line. She had seen the rich, and perhaps the disciples who were watching everything. She was very poor. She represented the harsh reality of poverty. She only

---

[18] G. Cook y R. Foulkes, *op.cit.*, p. 304.

had "two very small coins." She held them tightly in her hand. She walked towards one of the chests (we don't know which one), announced her offering and threw in the two coins. She could have kept one, but gave both and, according to Jesus, this was all she had.

Jesus gathered his disciples right there, where they had observed what had happened, and spoke to them. He used the principle of "opposites," or of "paradox." He took the world view of the disciples, who most likely were thinking: "The truly pious are these religious leaders whose large donations to the Temple show us what it really means to give an offering," and he turned it upside down: "I tell you the truth, this poor widow has put more into the treasury than all the others." According to the logic of the disciples, this was ridiculous. They must have thought that Jesus had not seen clearly the donations the rich had made. But Jesus' teaching corrects the disciples' preconception: "They all gave out of their wealth; but she, out of her poverty, put in everything—all she had to live on." This means that faithfulness to God has little to do with what one gives, but it has a lot to do with what one keeps or holds back for oneself.

On the basis of a world view shaped by the Hebrew Bible, Jesus created a reality which was different from the one which was accepted by the dominant ideology and adopted by the disciples. But, at the same time, one could suggest another level of interpretation. In effect, Jesus rejected the conduct and the attitude of the rich and of the executives of the Temple. Implicitly, he criticized the fact that the Temple, which was full of wealth, in the end robbed the needy widow of all that she had. Just like the oppressors, the Temple took advantage of a misunderstood religiosity, and instead of protecting the widow ended up exploiting her.[19] This opportunity for reflection allowed Jesus to teach his disciples that mission cannot be ignorant of the reality of the poor, the widow and the homeless. All the pompous religiosity present in the Temple did not do justice to the reality of God nor to that of humanity.

Jesus' interest in integral mission did not spring exclusively from the world view derived from the texts of the Hebrew Bible. Although this was the basis from which Jesus received authority, it is also necessary to understand the political, economic and social situation of that moment in history. We have already stated that Jesus was immersed in a specific situation, he understood the life situation of his people and he spoke their language: in this way the God-Man became incarnate. The situation in first-century Palestine showed characteristics that make it comparable to the situation of contemporary Latin America. Irene Foulkes has described this reality in the following way:

> The all-encompassing framework is that of a uni-polar world: the Roman Empire exercised total hegemony, with absolute political control. Economic globalization was made easier by a universally recognized currency. There was "global" commerce with a flow of raw materials and finished products, as well as a captive work force—slaves and prisoners of war destined for slavery, a result of Rome's conquests in practically the whole known world. All this commerce was developed for the benefit of the hub, the center: Rome. There was only one military power, which imposed a peace that served it's own interests. Its military bases were strategically

---

[19] *Ibid*. See also a much more acute critique offered by A. G. Wright, "The Widow's Mites: Praise or Lament? – A Matter of Context," *Catholic Biblical Quarterly* 44(1982): 256-265.

located to make sure that the conquered peoples would not oppose the imperial will.[20]

In places like Palestine, the Roman Empire controlled everything, from the economy to political life. It did so through treaties cleverly made with the oligarchy of each conquered nation. That is how in Palestine the religious leaders and Jewish politicians collaborated with the Romans to protect their own interests. In this way, they facilitated the oppression of the common people. This oppression came in the form of high taxes which the people could not pay, and which produced an inevitable process of indebtedness and in the end the loss of their small plots of land. The result was the creation of large estates controlled by those who were friends of the Roman governors. Thus, in a context of subsistence based on agriculture, unemployment and poverty increased and the landless poor were forced into a very difficult position.

It was precisely this situation which demanded an integral mission that would take into account all of people's needs. Jesus, who was not unaware of that reality, lived out an integral mission which challenged the injustice of oppression and provided essential alternatives of hope.

---

[20] I. Foulkes, "Pedagogía desde la praxis de Jesús," *Educando como cristianos es el siglo XXI – Memoria del Primer Encuentro Latinoamericano de la Asociación Internacional para la Promoción de la Educación Superior Cristiana*, Gafos, Costa Rica, 1999, p. 13.

3. Towards a Theory of Integral Mission

Human beings are biological, social and spiritual beings. People everywhere need material "things" that they must seek with the help of others. This is usually achieved within the ideological framework of one's own world view, in order to satisfy physical and relational needs.

As humans we need a roof over our heads and clothes to sustain our corporal lives in different climates. We need vegetable and animal products to provide the necessary proteins and nutrition for a healthy life. We need the help and service of others, in various ways, during the course of our lives: as newborn babies we need basic nutrition to survive; as children, we need knowledge to face the real world; as young people, to achieve meaningful positions; and as adults, to build and maintain our families; as members of a community, we need others for security and defense. Furthermore, the need to worship presupposes a communion among believers that understand the physical and social reality from a shared ideological perspective.

Any given culture indicates or guides the ways in which people should act in their physical and social lives, and in every society cooperative social interaction requires the use of material goods and the exchange of services. The task of the various economic systems is to create a method for the provision of goods and services which will satisfy the needs of the body, the soul and the spirit. The production and distribution of these goods and services are the core of any economic system.

The prosperity or relative deprivation of any person or group is a function of its connection with that system. Those that attain a degree of control over the production and distribution of the material goods of any group of people possess a power that results in relative prosperity. Those that have little chance of exerting influence over the system, on the other hand, end up with little power and run the risk of living in relative poverty. It could be argued, therefore, that the economic system is a determining factor in the shaping of all the other cultural and social structures. The other spheres of social life—family and relatives, community, politics and religion—are shaped by the organization of power in the economic center.

In the last few years, words like "integral," "holistic" or "ecosystems" have been used frequently and are "in style." To speak of something "integral" is to refer to an emerging awareness of the complex interaction of many forces in our individual and social lives as well as in the world. The question we are trying to focus on in this essay, based on a Biblical perspective, is this: What happens when we apply an integral system or integral approach to our way of thinking about mission and, especially, to our Christian conscience in relation to the causes and the solutions for the poor and the culture of poverty?

The theory of systems is based on the supposition that in human events there is an ample and complete interconnection of the personal, social and cultural spheres. An approach based on "systems"—read "integral"—is centered on cycles and patterns and on the interaction between and within these spheres. Causality and purpose are rooted in the functional interactions of all the parts of the system. This is why any attempt at explaining human experience in holistic terms will invariably be different from the traditional and linear models, which seek "logical" explanations.

Christian theologians and missiologists are guilty of continuing to explain human suffering based on traditional paradigms, and of not making use of the contributions made by systemic thinking. We continue to depend on "scientific" models or on the logic of accepted theories to understand the problem of poverty. For too long, Western theologians have been speaking for others, as if they were superior. We have developed programs and policies for lives we have never lived. To account for the poverty in our midst we develop unilateral explanations that simply reflect our theories—capitalist, Marxist, or some other version of political-economic theories.

The search for an approach to the problem of poverty that is integral, systemic, meta-modeled, and based on the Bible will require the affirmation and integration of all the spheres of creation. We must affirm that everything created by God is good, not only in general terms but also in specific terms. It is imperative to resist the temptation of reductionism or the attempt to explain one level of creation by a reference to another level. We are seeking to develop a theory of integral mission that will take into account the contributions of social anthropology regarding systems of interaction which will, in turn, help us offer a proposal of integral mission that is biblical and at the same time interdisciplinary.

4. Dialogue with the work of A. P. Fiske

In a very real sense we lack an understanding of what we could call "a sociotheology of poverty" on the basis of ethnographic (*ideographic*) studies of specific societies, including "biblical" societies and their world views. It is necessary to develop, inductively, a universal understanding of poverty and its religious phenomena, based on genuine cases in diverse human contexts.

The recent work of A. P. Fiske is an example that challenges us to reflect on our task in the field of biblical theology. Fiske's ethnographic study among the Mossai in Burkina Faso describes "the implicit models that the Mossai. . . unconsciously use to generate and assess four types of social relationships."[21] Fiske identifies four types of social transactions that are "unmeasurable" within a society, but are "measurable" between human groups:

1. Communal sharing

People have an idea of group identity and unity which requires sharing with the members of the group. According to Fiske, this communal sharing is "a relationship based on duties and sentiments generating kindness and generosity among people conceived to be of the same kind, especially kin."[22]

2. Authority ranking

Human groups are organized according to hierarchical roles; in other words, in relational groups where power differences exist. Fiske says: "The relationship is not only of linear ranking,

---

[21] A. P. Fiske, "Relativity Within Mossai Culture: Four Incommensurable Models for Social Relationships," *Ethos* 18: 180.

[22] A. P. Fiske, *Structures of Social Life* (New York: The Free Press, 1991), p. 14.

but of hierarchical inclusion, insofar as people in higher ranks dominate successively greater numbers of subordinates."[23]

3. *Equality Matching / Egalitarian correspondence*

In societies, there are relationships between people that are considered equal or the same. "In a relationship of this type people do things *quid pro quo*, so that exchange is strictly reciprocal: what each person receives is equivalent to what he gives."[24]

4. *Market pricing*

Most societies have developed some form of "market economy," or have decided to be a part of some external market system. In this type of relationship, people establish some kind of parameter; in other words, a price by which two persons or products can be compared.

Although Fiske observed and reflected on the use of these structures within the Mossai economic system, he suggests that this model is applicable to all human relationships that are found within specific societies. The hypothesis has been presented; our proposal is to test Fiske's model and see in which ways it can be useful for the development of integral mission based on the biblical text.

---

[23] *Ibid.*

[24] *Ibid.*, p. 15. This type of relationship and its variations have already been described by M. Sahlins, "On the Sociology of Primitive Exchange," en M. Banton, ed., *The Relevance of Models for Social Anthropology*, Association of Social Anthropologists, Monograph 1 (London: Tavistock, 1965), p. 139ss.

5. Biblical Integral Mission and Fiske's Relational Model

The theoretical framework offered by Fiske proposes integrating the research on the circulation of things in all kinds of transactions (exchange, distribution, contribution, and *justice*), in the organization of work, in the many ways people relate socially with objects, land and time. According to Fiske—and this is precisely why we think it is relevant to our study—this theory includes and promises to integrate a wide range of social phenomena. The theory suggests, therefore, that there is a reasonable chance that a unifying theory (integral mission?) of social relationships may arise.

Fiske suggests that the four models and their significant roles in the creation of social relationships be analyzed using an imaginary example as a starting point. He suggests that we imagine the inhabitants of a small town arguing about how to extinguish a fire. Following this example, we propose working with the same model but reflecting on the problem of poverty. Let's imagine a society (community, people) meeting to consider the problem of how to combat a growing but unknown threat: poverty. What would they do?

1. One possibility would be to call a meeting to discuss the issue until a general consensus has been attained. Everyone can participate, all opinions can be expressed and the discussion continues until a unanimous agreement on a plan of action to combat poverty has been reached. If there is no consensus, there is no decision. If a consensus is reached, the plan of action is communal: the group works together. This is a decision based on

the *communal sharing* model, and can be illustrated in the following graph:

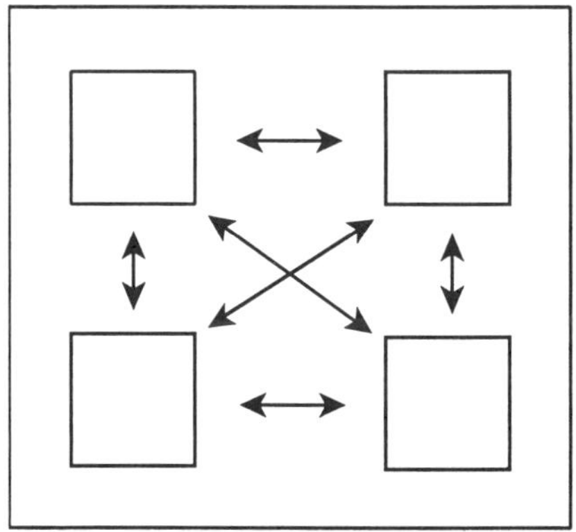

When the community has to confront the loss of economic self-sufficiency and the incapacity to maintain control of its personal and communal goods, the community unselfishly aids itself. Expressed in common terms: "All for one, and one for all." Maybe the best illustration for this is the existence of a healthy family; in other words, a cohesive group of equal members. In this sense, we can reflect on the concept of "family of God," or "the disciples of Jesus as friends," or even other examples.

Integral mission that considers poverty to be the result of injustice could benefit from this relational model submitted by Fiske, since in the Mosaic law and in the sayings of Jesus there is a lot on the concern for others and the consideration of the other's welfare.

2. Another possibility would be to submit the needs of the poor to a kind of social forum in which the distribution of resources and responsibilities would take place according to a

strictly equitable system. (Please note here that we have changed the order of the models submitted by Fiske). Each person would be assigned a task to fulfill, an amount to donate and a service to execute based on the role that has been assigned. There is an appeal mainly to friendship, companionship and group responsibility. Here the decision is based on the model of *equality matching*, which can be illustrated in this way:

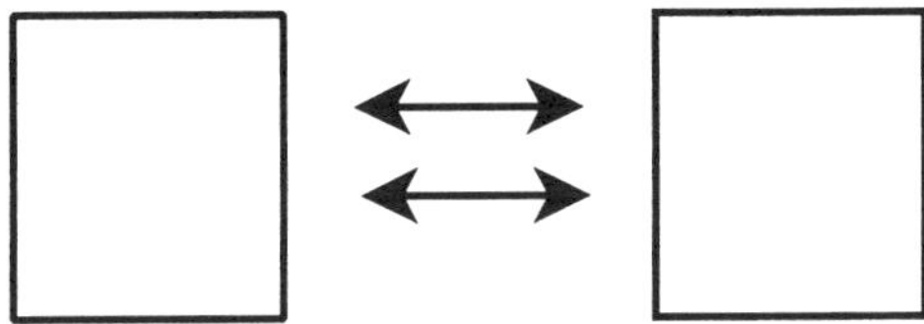

Perhaps here we can find a resemblance to Paul's image of the "body," that is, in other words, the equality of the members even though the "gifts" (social identities) are different. Relationships based on family, lineage, etc., become "one" through a shared faith. It is also possible that the example of the apostles, who accepted donations from the "haves," in order to distribute them among the "have nots" (widows, orphans, foreigners, etc.), may fit into this model of social relationships.

3. Another possible mechanism would be for a recognized leader, or an established authority, to seek a resolution for the problem of poverty unilaterally. A king, a president, a dictator, a "neighborhood kingpin" or a bishop with enough charisma orders his followers to solve the problem. The leader's will is put into practice within the realm of his authority.

The decision is based on the model of *authority ranking*:

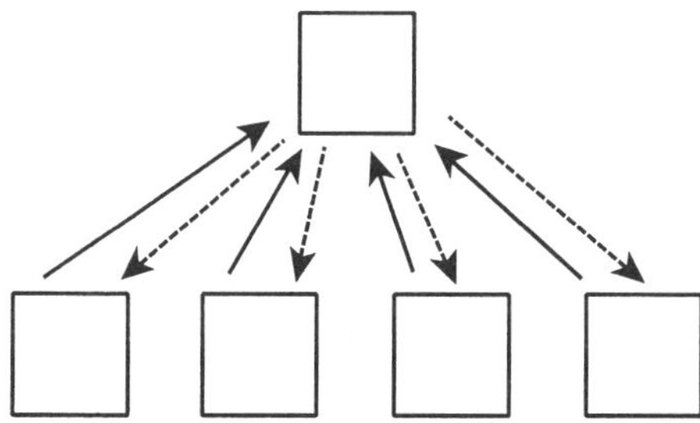

Two examples from the Bible seem to have some relationship to this model. In 2 Corinthians 8 and 9, and in other contexts, we find the Apostle Paul asking for contributions to mitigate the needs of the saints in Jerusalem and in other places. In 2 Corinthians 8:2 we can find the strange combination of difficult trials, overflowing joy, extreme poverty and rich generosity. What is incredible is that in the midst of what was seen as extreme need, the possibility of tremendous abundance arises. Paul says something that needs lo be urgently heard and understood by the Church:

> At the present time your plenty will supply what they need, so that in turn their plenty will supply what you need. Then there will be equality. . . (2Co 8:14)

The second example comes from the life of Jesus and his relationship with his disciples. On one occasion Jesus "ordered" his disciples to divide the crowd of people into groups and make them sit down. The reason for this order was to be able to distribute the "excess" of food produced by faith, even when the disciples could only see "scarcity."

4. Finally, another possibility would be to confront the problem of poverty by means of a social mechanism in charge of

redistributing goods and services on the basis of a "monetary system." A "price" for the help would be established, according to the parameters of the market, and in that way a decision is reached based on the model of *market pricing*.

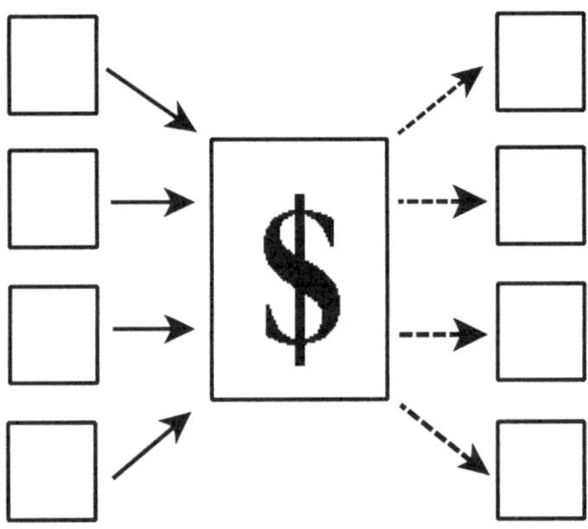

To continue with possible hypotheses, perhaps here we have a system similar to the elaborate one used in the Temple in Israel. The Temple offered physical and spiritual help in exchange for ritual offerings and the obedient practice of certain rites. We know that a percentage of the money collected was set aside for the priests who administered the system. The following question arises, therefore: Is this the role that "agencies," "parachurch" institutions and international mega-churches should play? Should they be in charge of redistributing the accumulated funds for the poor?

In short, there are four kinds of decision-making processes (supposedly in all societies) which rule any social response to the problem of poverty, each with its own particular characteristics. Although each is different in terms of its pattern of interaction and distribution, in "real life," decision-making mechanisms often use more than one of these models at the same time.

If we may continue with the presupposition—which, in my opinion, clearly emerges from the biblical text—that poverty is the consequence of injustice—whether that injustice be individual or social, of a citizen or of the State, personal or structural—then we can imagine the kinds of moral and political arguments that any society could consider, on the basis of these models, as a reaction towards this poverty:

1. People may have a strong sense of mutual identification and communal solidarity. This would lead them to believe that they must help and protect each other when the need arises. Perhaps they perceive that providing help is normal and natural when one belongs to a family or community group which is united by kindness, compassion and love. In societies of this kind, people should care for each other. Poverty is a threat to all; therefore, each person "feels" a need for his brother or sister. What is a loss for one is a loss for all. This would be the moral response in terms of *communal sharing*.

2. At the same time, people may consider that a response to the condition of poverty must be based on a conviction of justice and reciprocity. All people, and especially friends, deserve equal security. It is unfair that some have in excess while others experience a crushing poverty. Everyone should receive the same assistance. This represents a call to moral action based on *equality matching*.

3. Another alternative may be that the ethical response to poverty that springs from the community will have originated in the word of an authority or "being." Perhaps they seek guidance in the Scriptures. If not, they may seek wisdom from a "teacher" or "guru" with a special gift. In this case, the community would

gravitate towards an authority, sacred or secular, whose knowledge was trustworthy. In this relational situation, the community would accept the plan of action proposed by the leader. This moral reasoning is based on the model of *authority ranking.*

4. The fourth option is for the people of the community to respond to the problem of poverty from a stance of freedom: everyone is free to choose whether he or she wants to be committed or involved in the dilemma of the poor. Each individual makes a rational decision as to whether to take action or not. In this scenario, "institutions" or "agencies" are created to provide assistance. The individual then decides whether to take advantage of the opportunities that these agencies provide for personal involvement. These arguments are implicit in terms of *market pricing.*

Fiske is correct when he maintains that in every current debate, whether political, moral or ideological, we can find all of these arguments interwoven in complex ways. Of course there are situations, which Fiske calls "asocial," in which all ethical standards are abandoned. In these cases, terror, torture, sexual enticement, etc., are used to try and convince the community. He concludes by stating that such actions that are carried out by force are not based on the model of *authority ranking*, because those that have been coerced do not accept the authority nor do they accept the hierarchical coercion as a legitimate social relationship. But if a poor person accepts his suffering as an appropriate consequence of his disobedience, then the punishment is legitimized.[25]

---

[25] *Op. cit.*, p. 6.

In short, Fisk submits that the different understandings of social relationships are sustained by these four kinds of moral and political arguments. The "ideology" or "theology" of the group will determine the choice of one model over another.

Furthermore, Fiske suggests that there is a fifth possibility: it is feasible to conceive of an approach to the problem of poverty which is completely anarchic.[26] In a scenario of this kind there would be no social responsibilities. People could approach the problem of poverty without coordinating their efforts with others. If a fire broke out in a city, for example, people would worry about putting out their own fire without paying any attention to the problems of those around them. This can be seen in some cities where people don't apply any structured social mechanism to deal with a given problem. In these situations, complete apathy exists; in other words, the lack of any personal motivation generates a chaotic conflict where social relationships no long make any sense.

Lastly, Fiske tries to demonstrate how the victims in any given human group can use each of these basic models to find meaning for their unfortunate situation. In other words, in light of these relational models, the victims of poverty could explain their situation using any of the following options:

1. Beginning with the *communal sharing* model, people could suggest or question whether their condition of poverty is not a violation of the unity, solidarity and integrity of the community. Their answers may range from the acceptance of an inevitable situation to an intrinsic rejection of the situation.

---

[26] *Ibid.*, p. 7.

2. Victims of poverty could use the model of *equality matching*. The initial proposal would be: "It's not fair." "Why does this happen to me and not to others?" Why poverty affects some and not others is an enigma. Many perhaps will conduct an "inner search" to see if they have done something bad to deserve poverty. Theories are propounded on the basis of good or bad "luck."

3. When it comes to the model of *authority ranking*, the victims of poverty would try to understand why God would have done this to them. This is Job's dilemma: "Haven't I been faithful and loyal? I have not worshipped any other god." This understanding of poverty seems to be present in Jesus' agony, when he shouts: 'My God, my God, why have you forsaken me?" The underlying presupposition here is that a superior authority, God or someone else, is the cause of my suffering or of my punishment. People consider that they have done something to bring upon themselves the wrath of the supreme being.

4. The victims of poverty could explain their situation of injustice in terms of the *market pricing* model. In a free market context, risks are taken in the midst of desired profits. In this social relationship model, the poor may try to understand their situation or accept it, if they understand that the possibility of making a choice is desirable but, at the same time, includes risks that must be taken. The person must accept the consequences.

Preliminary Conclusions

In the first place, we want to state that the biblical proposal is clear and final with regard to the need for and the priority of integral mission. The evidence offered in this paper, though incomplete, shows clearly that a reductionist, partial and dualistic mission is not contemplated in the world view of the Holy Scriptures. The texts from the Hebrew Bible and the life and ministry of Jesus proclaim that the biblical-theological alternative restores people's dignity to their entire being.

Secondly, we put forward Fiske's model of social relationships as an alternative for reflection, discussion and analysis in order to discover how the Church of Jesus Christ, immersed in many diverse cultures and societies, can apply an integral mission. We suggest that a dialogue with the proposals made by social anthropology may uncover paths the Church has not yet traveled. Poverty is a cruel and oppressive reality. It dehumanizes people to such an extent that it is almost impossible to affirm that the image of God is reflected in them. Fiske's model is not the only one nor is it necessarily the best, but we do maintain that, in practical terms, it may be of great assistance in the task of implementing integral mission.

Finally, we submit that the biblical evidence and the present situation point to the lack of justice as the principal—and practically exclusive—cause of poverty. This does not mean that we wish to minimize the complexity of the different realities of poverty in the world today, but we do wish to propose, together with the prophets of ancient Israel, that injustice generates contexts of poverty. The Church can begin to offer a tangible integral mission by applying Fiske's models of social relationships and by taking seriously the deuteronomic mandate to be generous (be open-handed). Without the practice of justice from a biblical perspective there is no solution to the problem of poverty. If the Church works for justice by means of its varied social relationships, the image of God may one day be restored in the poor.

3

The Theology of Integral Mission and Community Discernment

Nancy E. Bedford

1. A Preliminary Look at Some Ideas Underlying the Theologal Bias of Integral Mission[1]

Although it is important to develop a *theological* perspective on mission—that is, a second order reflection born out of faith, but not identical with it—it is appropriate to note that mission carries a *bias* which is first and foremost *theologal,* that is, related to God himself. That is to say, it refers directly to God himself in the same way as do the godly virtues of faith, hope and love. Mission means *sending out,* commission, and refers in the first

[1] In this section, I take up some of the ideas sketched out in my contribution to "The River Plate Meeting on Mission and Evangelism. Scenarios Old and New: Challenges for the Mission of the Church in 2000. *Protestantism, Evangelicals and Mission in the River Plate Region*" , June 17-19, 2000, in Ward College (Buenos Aires).

instance to the sending of the Son by the Father in the power of the Spirit, and subsequently to the *sending* of those who have come to be sons and daughters in the Son. Therefore, a theology of integral mission, if it is also to be an integral theology of mission, will have to be, above all, *trinitarian*.

a. Sending and Incarnation in a Culture

Frequently evangelicals in Latin America have unquestioningly considered evangelization to be the objective of the missionary enterprise. The problem is that "evangelization" or, still more frequently, "evangelism" usually has an exclusively verbal connotation. So mission has often been understood as a basically oral communication of the gospel message: words about the Word. Of course, the verbal communication of the gospel message is good and necessary, but it must always be kept in mind that the Word of which we speak is the *Logos Incarnate*, as the prologue to John's Gospel reminds us. The Good News of God in Christ Jesus is disclosed as *Emmanuel*, as God with humankind, God involved right up to the final consequences with our corporeal nature and destiny. This involvement has a verbal element and another element consisting of concrete earthly activities which together make up a profile of life. And the word "mission," which means *sending*, testifies to this integral quality.

What, then, is the substance of this sending? In the Johannine *great commission* (unjustly obscured since the nineteenth century by the prominence given to the great commission in Matthew), the risen Jesus says: "'As the Father has sent me, so I send you.' When he had said this, he breathed on them and said to them 'Receive the Holy Spirit'" (Jn 20: 21-22). The sending or mission of the believers here is about participating in the vigorous dynamic of the triune God. The Father sends the Son in the power of the Spirit, the Son sends us in the same way that the Father sent him, and empowers us to live as he did, through the Holy Spirit. Unity among Christians derives from participating in the myriad forms of this commission, from this same trinitarian dynamic reflected in the evangelistic message that God loves the world in the same way as the Father loves the Son (Jn 17:20-26).[2]

It follows from this that the Church's evangelistic mission can be neither clearly understood nor properly practiced if we lose sight of its trinitarian nature. Though this may seem a bit abstract, it takes on vital importance, for example, in the decisions made by the Jerusalem Council, according to the book of Acts.[3] There it was decided what should be the parameters of the *sending* or evangelizing mission of Christians. Should every new Christian also become a proselyte to Judaism? The text states that, after hearing the testimonies of God's working among the gentiles, a model of mission which drew its inspiration from the *incarnation of the Son* seemed right "to the Holy Spirit and to us." Just as the Son was sent in the fullness of time to be born into a Jewish family from Galilee at the time of the Roman hegemony over Palestine, those who believe in the Son are sent to be incarnated in the culture in which they find themselves. The principle of mission is not the slavish reproduction of the religious norms that determined the cultural framework of Jesus' spirituality (circumcision, for example). It is, rather, to proceed creatively

---

[2] On the subject of mission understood as *missio dei* see also David J. Bosch, *Transforming Mission: Paradigm Shifts in the Theology of Mission* (American Society of Missiology Series, no. 16) (Maryknoll, New York: Orbis Books, 1991), pp. 389ff.

[3] The following paragraph is influenced by a conversation with Andrew Walls, a Scottish missiologist and Africa expert, during which he affirmed the importance of the text in question for current mission theology.

along the way in which the Son was sent, in the power of the Spirit. The text attributes to Peter the words "we will be saved through the grace of the Lord Jesus," not through the obligation to observe alien religio-cultural regulations, which become a burden for anyone brought up in a very different culture (Acts 15: 10-11). In the Council, as Luke and the echoes in Paul's writings describe it, a special hermeneutic is applied to the Old Testament and Jewish tradition, to extract what appears to be crucial to the situation and must be preserved: ethical correctness in areas which might otherwise give rise to a suggestion of tolerance towards idolatry (Acts 15: 29), and the unwavering commitment to the welfare of the poor (Gal. 2: 10). In this way, continuity with the history of God's posture of justice with the people of Israel is maintained while preserving the creativity of mission in the world of gentile cultures.

As the example of the Jerusalem Council shows, to speak of mission, understood as the sending of sons and daughters in the trinitarian dynamic of the Father, the Son and of the Holy Spirit, leads us inescapably to speak of culture. I am not speaking about the imperative to "evangelize the culture" characteristic of Christendom,[4] but about the fact that *incarnation* always takes place in the context of a particular culture and history: in the case of Latin America, in the *hybrid cultures* affected by globalization in ways that are currently the object of careful analysis by anthropologists and sociologists.[5]

---

[4] See the Santo Domingo document (1992) of the Roman Catholic Church.

[5] See, for example, Néstor García Canclini, *Latinoamericanos buscando lugar en este siglo* (Latin Americans Seeking a Place in This Century) (Buenos Aires: Paidós, 2002).

A crucial question for the *mission* of the churches is this: Exactly how should the gospel be incarnated in these hybrid cultures? Should we accept them in their entirety? Should we reject them wherever possible and, thus, create ecclesiastical ghettoes? The example of the Jerusalem Council suggests that it is necessary to incorporate some elements and to discard others that are not consistent with the essence of the gospel. So we have to look for symbols and metaphors that meaningfully address people in this culture, while at the same time challenging some customs, such as the practice of nepotism or the values of androcentricity[6] not only when they get into the churches, but also as they continue to operate in society. It also is necessary to see which elements of the ecclesiastical tradition, imported from outside the local culture, need to be discarded—customs analogous to male circumcision, which, in the context of following Jesus, would have become a yoke and a burden. Perhaps the most pertinent example would be fundamentalism in the interpretation of the Bible. *This task of incorporating and discarding requires a diligent process of discernment.* In the discernment process, the two principles of the Council of Jerusalem can still point the way for us: the rejection of complicity with idolatry (which confuses the ultimate with the penultimate) and the centrality of the commitment to the poor, marginalized, and socially excluded. Neither extreme, total rejection of the surrounding culture nor simply aping it, will provide a satisfactory way of carrying out the church's mission.

---

[6] I understand "androcentricity" to mean that cultural habit whereby men, or an idealization of the male, are seen, consciously or unconsciously, as the archetype of reality, including the reality of God.

b. The Sending and Globalized Structures

If the principal missionary paradigm is to be sent in the power of the Spirit to be incarnated in a given culture and situation, as the Son was sent, *there is no formula or methodology of mission which can be globalized in the sense of having universal application for Christians in every part of the globe.* This position disputes the claim of those who resort to a single globalized appeal in the church's mission and insist that this or that method is the only way to sustain and deepen the relevance of the Christian faith in current society. At the same time we have to avoid a fragmentation of Christian practice that renders communication between communities impossible. If that happens, the all-embracing logic of modern capitalism will reconstitute the fragments in its own way, a way totally alien to the spirit of the Gospel, with the precise aim of confusing God and Mammon (idolatry), and without any concern for the welfare of "the poor, the widow, the orphan and the stranger."

The churches, both at the level of the local congregation and at wider, more inclusive levels, need to take the economic and cultural processes of globalization seriously, because they affect the way that Christians live and see the world. For example, in many of our countries, programs of "adjustment," unleashed by the forces and dynamics of high finance at the global level, have affected the living conditions of the socio-economic middle classes. A theoretical notion of a nominal option for the poor has, for many, turned into a concrete experience of poverty, which has opted for them, excluding them from the labor market and denying them access to the accouterments of prosperity (home ownership, cars, holidays, etc.) which they had hitherto been able to take for granted. What does the mission of the church mean in this situation? A new sensitivity to the structural needs of the "always poor"? The exodus of the fittest? This change in the conditions of congregations in the middle sector of society is opening people's eyes to the social dimension of the gospel and to the demands of structural poverty and injustice on the Christian faith. To face this situation, within congregations there are emerging new initiatives that are as cooperative and participative as possible: micro-enterprises, barter systems, and support groups for vulnerable people.[7] Also, many people are rediscovering that hope which comes from living the life of faith and in the community of faith amid a culture of pessimism and depression, as reflected by the quest for a deeper and more integrated spirituality. It might appear that the current situation has brought about an unforeseen *kairos* in which the "social gospel" and the "gospel of the Word" can come together and overcome their absurd polarization. However, we still have to admit that the *metanoia* needed to stop being "stiff necked" in this way can be quite painful. The task of living as people sent by God is full of pitfalls and stumbling blocks, including an inherited hermeneutic which allows us to avoid the demands of obedience to love the orphan and the widow, the stranger, the poor and the enemy.

---

[7] These initiatives are not only taken by churches; they occur, too, in every type of non-governmental organization, as we were able to see in the *World Social Forum* held in Porto Alegre in January, 2001. See Carlos Gabetta, "Porto Alegre: activismo y propuestas para un futuro distinto" (Porto Alegre: Actions and Proposals for a New Future), in *Le Monde Diplomatique*, February, 2001, 4f.

c. Sending and Hope Based on the Mission of the Triune God

Our assignment, then, is to seek out a trinitarian way of life during those times when "the horizons are closed" (E. Támez): to be imaginative and not rigid; to live the love of Jesus among the brothers and sisters; to see God reflected in the otherness of those different from us; to be creative in the face of whatever concrete problems arise. Even though these tasks are far from easy, they are not overwhelming or beyond the capabilities of our communities. Rather, they are the kinds of activity that are bringing them to maturity and growth in the way of Jesus Christ. Put simply, each community, in a style determined by its own particular charisma within the wider family of faith, has to work out concrete forms of "*doing justice to reality*" (Jon Sobrino), *inspired by the Spirit of the God of life*. The resulting experience has then to be shared and communicated to form a huge network engaged with many different facets of our society. That, in a nutshell, is the mission: the sending of our churches. Faithfulness to the commission of the triune God will help us to discover particular ways of widening our horizons in matters great and small.

2. A Short Theological Checklist as a Framework for Well Tempered Discernment in Integral Mission: *notae missionis*

Traditionally, systematic theology has referred to "the marks of the church" or *notae ecclesiae*. The "marks" are intended as criteria whereby one can judge whether the church is true or false. There are four classical marks evolved by the Fathers: the *sanctity, unity, universality (or catholicity) and apostolicity* of the church.[8] In the same way, one could propose certain marks for mission, *notae missionis,* as confirmatory theological criteria for our task of discernment as followers of Jesus in the context of the church. I suggest *pentecostality, ecumenicity, inclusiveness and ubiquity* as indispensable marks of the *integral nature* of mission in a trinitarian dynamic, and as cardinal points to keep us orientated in our search for a route toward integral mission.

a. *"Pentecostality"*

Pentecostality is the counterpart in mission of *sanctity* in the church, though it implies more than is normally understood by the word "sanctity." It means the interpenetration of the Spirit in a whole range of dynamics. It is not a synonym for pentecostalism, though the emergence and growth of pentecostal movements during the twentieth century provide an example and a challenge to take seriously the crucial nature of the sanctifying, life-giving work of the *Ruach (Spirit)* of God.[9] Coincidentally,

---

[8] In light of the experience of the Radical Reformation, Yoder adds *suffering* as a *nota ecclesiae*, for, while the existence of martyrs does not guarantee the truth of a position, he considers that the whole church should learn from the Anabaptists the willingness to suffer persecution and, wherever necessary, martyrdom in the cause of following Jesus; see John H. Yoder, *Täufertum und Reform im Gespräch. Dogmengeschichtliche Untersuchung der frühen Gespräche zwischen Schweitzerischen Täufern und Reformatoren* (Zurich: EVZ-Verlag, 1968), pp. 195ff.

[9] Two important books that illustrate this point are Darío Lopez, *Pentecostalismo y transformación social* (Pentecostalism and Social

during recent decades there has been a rediscovery of pneumatology in the ranks of systematic theology. That personal Presence, who is at the same time impersonal, immanent and transcendent, who gives us birth into new life, who interprets our groans and those of creation, who intercedes for us before our maternal Father, is also the one who directs the mission so that it continues following in the way of Jesus Christ. Any missionary project that forgets that only the Spirit of God, with immense and mysterious freedom, can bring the work to fruition, and tries instead to quantify or project outcomes like some capitalist enterprise, distorts this mark.

b. ***Ecumenicity***

Ecumenicity is the mission equivalent of *unity* in ecclesiology. It is not to be understood as bureaucratic uniformity, but as unity which takes as its model the interpenetration of the three divine Persons. Integral mission cannot be a sectarian mission. It delights in the diversity of gifts that the *Ruach* (Spirit) of life has prepared for the church—gifts which are displayed both in the myriad personalities and talents of a local congregation, and also in the diversity of gifts which different Christian confessions and denominations bring to the universal church. This *ecumenicity* can be seen in structured, documented discussions on mission between formally elected representatives of the denominations, resulting in documents or declarations such as the Lima

---

Change) (Buenos Aires: Kairós, 2000), and Eldin Villafañe, *El Espíritu liberador: Hacia una ética social pentecostal hispanoamericana* (The Liberating Spirit: Towards a Latin American Pentecostal Social Ethic) (Buenos Aires: Nueva Creación, 1996).

Document[10] or the Lausanne Covenant.[11] The greatest treasures, however, can be found in simple down-to-earth relationships among multi-gifted Christians who, from different communities and traditions, and without denying their differences, commit themselves in *co-operative* response to concrete missionary challenges. Any mission project devised by and for one particular group, and undertaken with deep distrust of the *differences* of other Christian groups, and without any discussion with them, is seriously defective in this mark.

c. *Ubiquity*

Ubiquity is the counterpart in mission of *universality* or *catholicity* in the church. As local church, the church of Christ is present, in different ways, "on every side." No two local churches are the same. They are not present everywhere with an identical shape like a transnational hamburger chain. Every faith community, under God's commission, is distinct and individual, with its own character, and participates in its own way in the sending by God yet is united with all others by one Spirit. The world is encompassed by a great network of faith communities whose interaction and inter-relatedness weave a huge tapestry whose overall design is known to God alone. If we could begin

---

[10] *Bautismo, Eucaristía, Ministerio. Convergencias doctrinales en el seno del Consejo Ecuménico de Iglesias. Documento final de Lima* (Baptism, Eucharist, Ministry. Doctrinal accords in the meeting of the Council of Churches. Final statement of Lima) (Mendoza: C.E.P.A./F.E.C., 1983).

[11] This refers to the final statement of the International Congress on World Evangelization, held in Lausanne, Switzerland, in 1974. (Editor's note: This document is to be found on the internet at www.albchristian.com /english/lausanne.)

by accomplishing one tiny bit of "integral" action, we would be preparing ourselves in small things for faithfulness in large things, such as an occasion when civil society might ask us to offer concrete suggestions arising from our experience. On the contrary, a mission project aimed at maintaining an exclusive idea, using exclusive methods to achieve the "extension" of a kingdom that is more or less identified with the church, has not properly understood the significance of ubiquity in mission.

d. *Inclusiveness*

Inclusiveness in mission is the counterpart of *apostolicity* in the church. This inclusiveness works on two levels. On the first level, mission—if it is to be really integral mission, mission to the whole of life—has to include everything concerned with human, or even cosmic existence. There is no atom or constellation which is beyond the concern and love of the triune God and of his mission of re-creation and regeneration. His passion is human life in every facet. And so we need to adopt the watchword of John Wesley, "The world is my parish." That is not some colonialist or imperialist motto, but a recognition of the profound inter-relatedness of the whole of life on this planet and its involvement in God's redemptive dynamic, in which all of us may participate. The second level is the inclusiveness of the mission with respect to gender. This is directly concerned with that apostolicity in which *women and men* were witnesses to the resurrection of Jesus Christ and entrusted with the task of living and proclaiming the good news of Easter.[12] No mission can be founded on an

[12] Cipriano. *La unidad de la iglesia* (The Unity of the Church) (Ciudad Nueva, Madrid).

apostolic base that does not include the sending out of men and women, shoulder to shoulder, on an equal basis. This is not some minor detail; it represents a determination to renounce a structural sin which has profoundly damaged the church of Jesus Christ virtually from its inception. A mission program which does not explicitly enjoin the equal treatment of men and women has lost continuity with the program of apostleship initiated in the paschal commission of Mary Magdalene.

3. Toward an Integral Understanding of Discernment: The Contribution of Gender Perspective to the Hermeneutic Circle

Women who work in ordained ministry or other non-ordained forms of pastoral leadership have to use large quantities of discernment just to keep themselves from being overwhelmed by the pressures of androcentric structures. It follows then that they normally carry about, consciously or unconsciously, a great store of wisdom on the subject. That is why, when I was looking for a more adequate understanding of discernment, I asked a group of Latin American women pastors and church leaders what ideas they had on the subject. A very productive interchange ensued, whose main thrusts are summarized below. I have organized the material under the heading of the church tradition of each participant in the order in which it was presented.[13]

---

[13] Cf. Congregation for the Doctrine of the Faith [Ratzinger] *Dominus Jesus* Declaration. On the uniqueness and salvific universality of Jesus Christ and the Church (2000).

Pentecostal: In the Old Testament, the *Ruach* relates to the presence of God among the chosen people, and in the New Testament the *pneuma* makes me think about life, about vitality. God wants to infuse us with life. Since I moved to Pentecostalism as a young person, from having been a nominal Catholic, I have been secure in the presence of the Spirit of God in me. When I studied theology, I was aware that that presence was absent from the lecture rooms. I prayed a lot, alone at first, and then with others, about what to do with all the information that I was getting. I realized that I had to listen a great deal, to consider what the person was really trying to tell me, and then to decide what to do with the information. That is discernment.

Methodist: The one thing I am certain about with regard to discernment is that I want to be a Christian and I believe in all the gifts, but I get the impression that institutions like the churches or the seminaries are prejudicial to the process of discernment.

Disciples of Christ: I believe that these institutions do condition us, but I do not think that they necessarily impair our discernment. The protestant church "institution" has given me the freedom to be a person close to God, without being a nun as I had originally planned. And it has given me a certain stance, though I am no puppet. God has many ways to give us discernment, but we cannot discern whether something is good or bad without some familiarity with the analytical tools that the institutions give us. My theological training is pretty scholastic, so it is not easy to relate it to Pentecostal religiosity. However, through certain experiences, God enables us to change things which we could not change by reason alone. So we can be rational and still leave ourselves with some latitude for other expressions and symbols for people who need them. Discernment means opening ourselves up for God to work through us in the lives of other people, in ways and styles which may not be our natural ones, but without betraying our convictions.

Waldensian: Discernment does not play a large part in my vocabulary, but I believe that to attain wisdom requires both the rational and the non-rational, because wisdom embraces both. No one can say, "I am absolutely sure; this is how it is and there is no other way." That does not mean that I cannot make decisions and live with the consequences, while I go on searching. Is part of discerning living without complete certainty? If having discernment means living in total certainty, then I do not have it.

If we analyze the dynamic of this conversation, we can see the outline of a tentative hermeneutic circle. Discernment needs critical tools, which can support a good theology, while its conclusions have to be tested out in pastoral or ecclesiastical praxis.

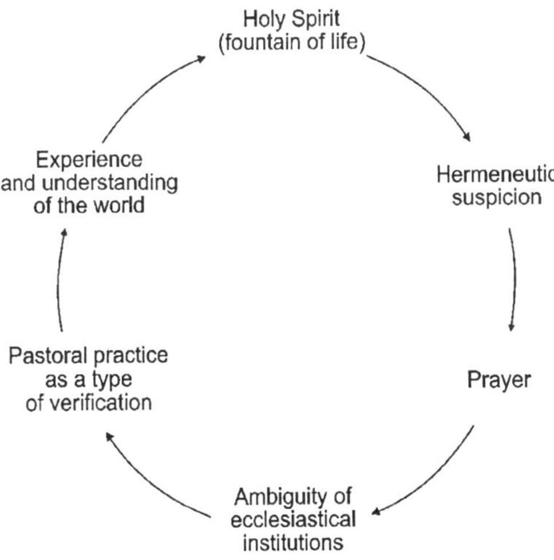

Theologically speaking, perhaps the most relevant element in the circle is the centrality of the Spirit in the discernment process. In the conversation summarized above, the Third Person of the Trinity was present explicitly in the discussion, while the Second

Person was there in an implicit way. That is the exact reverse of the dynamic which we normally encounter in western trinitarian discussions, where it is the Ruach-Spirit who is usually the statue at the dinner table. Observation suggests that the Ruach-Spirit, which of the three personal substances or *hypostases* is the one most often identified by feminine metaphors, has frequently been, as with women themselves, displaced by the church institution, typified and moderated by male clerics. The practice of discernment forces us to face the things of the Spirit clearly and explicitly, and that is a healthy corrective to communities that have been church centered, or "Jesus-only-ers," rather than practitioners of a *pneumatic christology*. The latter is vital if we are to discern the ways of integral mission. As José María Castillo maintains, while Jesus is the most perfect example of one who discerned wisely, the only means whereby we Christians can know whether we have discerned correctly is by the fruits of the Spirit (in the sense of Galatians 5:22), that is, through the concrete outworking of love in our social interaction. Given the complexity of the material nature of our life in society, we need cultural, historical, economic and socio-political tools to interpret the evident signs of the love of God and to discern them with wisdom.[14] This leads us to the point of looking for a flexible and adaptable, but structured process to guide a community of faith judiciously in its search for discernment, as it tries to deepen its experience of integral mission.

---

[14] Jose María Castillo, *El discernimiento cristiano. Por una conciencia crítica* (Salamanca: Sígueme, 1989), pp. 154-155.

4. Community Discernment in Integral Mission

The practice of discernment helps people in community, at a given time and place, to find out what actions appear to be consistent with their stand against evil, their desire to respond concretely to need, and their commitment to follow the way of Jesus Christ, amid the personal, structural and cosmic ambiguities of life in all its dimensions.[15] A way to provide some structure to this process of social discernment, in order to form disciples who want to please God in everything, is rediscovering the Christian tradition of *lectio, meditatio, oratio and tentatio.* Beginning with its search for integral mission, a faith community can follow these steps—which are nothing more than a hermeneutical spiral—to discover and engage in the trinitarian dynamic of the *missio Dei.*

The four "hours" are of medieval monastic origin. Martin Luther rescued for Protestantism especially the *oratio, meditatio* and *tentatio* as fundamental exercises and experiences for theology. From there they were incorporated into the Protestant pastoral tradition, where Dietrich Bonhoeffer took them and

---

[15] The use of discernment involves a hermeneutic of suspicion and redemption (Ricoeur). In other words discernment has a special value because it is a process that recognizes that all Christian practice and activity (including discernment itself) is "penultimate" and not "ultimate." I expand on this in more detail, and correlate it with the heritage of Latin American liberation theology and the experience of my own faith community, in "Little Moves against Closed Horizons: Theology and the Practice of Discernment " in D. Bass and M. Volf (eds.), *Practicing Theology: Beliefs and Practices in Christian Life* (Grand Rapids: Wm. B. Eerdmans Publishing Co., 2001).

placed them at the heart of the experiment of the confessing church clergy seminary in Finkewalde. Bonhoeffer envisioned a kind of hermeneutical circle of *lectio, meditatio, oratio* and *tentatio* which leads back into *lectio* and so on.[16] Here, I am freely adapting the "hours" as a possible method of structuring the search for the discernment of integral mission in the life of a faith community.

a. *Lectio*

In Benedictine spirituality, the *lectio divina* describes the practice of daily meditation on Scripture for the purpose of deepening the life of faith. Rediscovering the fecundity of these monastic disciplines is a most enriching ecumenical activity. The tradition of the free[17] churches as well can also shed much light on the practice of *lectio.* Among these traditions there is usually a prevailing shared conviction that the present faith community "is" also the primitive church community and the eschatological

---

[16] D. Bonhoeffer, *Vida en comunidad* (Buenos Aires: La Aurora, 1966). This work demonstrates Bonhoeffer's plan for the organization of the community of future pastors. In my judgment, when it comes to directions for an "intentional community," these proposals have much to offer to the lives of those free churches that also see themselves as intentional communities. In what follows in this section, a book I find very illuminating is Sabine Bobert-Stützel's *Dietrich Bonhoeffers Pastoraltheologie* (Gütersloh: Chr. Kaiser/Gütersloher Verlaghaus, 1995), pp. 140-185.

[17] I am referring here to those church communities more associated with the Anabaptist movement and its successors—churches like the Mennonites, the Brethren, Baptist, Disciples of Christ, many Pentecostals, and some Methodist and Adventist churches—than with the more Constantinian type, classical Reformation typified by Calvin, Luther and Zwingli. This *ethos* is not limited to Evangelicals: it also appears in other ways in some Catholic base ecclesial communities in which the popular reading of Scripture has flourished.

community too, so that when the biblical texts are read, not only are they linked to what was and what is to come, but also with what the hermeneutic community constituted in the church actually *is*. Without discrediting the meticulous work of exegesis, there exists a dimension of almost mystical immediacy due to the working of the Spirit, so that when a text is read it ceases to be ancient and remote and speaks to us today. In this way, the Bible stories that have a context different from that of the present shape the community of faith here and now. Expressed another way, the Bible narratives about the history of Israel, Jesus, and the early church are intimately linked with the basic foundations of life in our communities today, and Christians are to discern in what ways "that" shapes "this."[18]

Lectio has several important advantages at this point:

—Its starting point is a shared, communal, not individualistic vision (the faith community as *hermeneutic community*).

—It encourages a spirit-driven dynamic that is horizontal and not elitist (by virtue of the priesthood of all believers, everyone has the responsibility and the right to take part in the *lectio*).

—It means looking at one's own situation in all its richness, as well as relating it to its biblical context (what Barth described as having the Bible in one hand and the newspaper in the other).

The dangers of this tradition are well known: biblical fundamentalism, suspicion of everything that might seem intellectual, leading to ill-considered exegesis and the allegorical manipulation of texts, among others. However, the *freshness* of

---

[18] Here I am paraphrasing the ideas of James McClendon in the opening chapter of his magisterial *Ethics: Systematic Theology, Volume 1* (Nashville: Abingdon Press, 1986), pp. 27-41.

the *lectio* tradition and its capacity to allow the text *to read us,* questioning us and educating us, mean that we cannot ignore it, any more than we can ignore the critical importance of the private, family and community Bible reading that are typical of our communities.

b. *Meditatio*

Meditation on what has been read must accompany the reading. It is about *ruminatio,* ruminating on what comes from the *lectio* until a "knowing" and an "understanding" begin to crystallize, which, although they are provisional, point the way forward. In the faith community, the *meditatio* takes the form of dialogue and conversation. Discussing the sermon over the family lunch after the Sunday morning worship is a way of practicing *meditatio.* When we talk to a child about the Bible story we have read, we are doing *meditatio.* When something that happens in the street brings to mind the passage we read that morning, that is part of our "ruminating." You could say that in total contrast to "transcendental meditation," Christian *meditatio* is *immanent* meditation, immanent in the daily calling of Christians and in their integral mission, their sending or commission. And then, as we take time for the *meditatio* we meet the reality of our suffering world, which constrains us with new questions and new awareness with which to engage the *lectio*. Meditation also functions as *active listening* to the Spirit of God. That is why it is closely linked with *oratio.*

c. *Oratio*

Oratio, prayer, grows out of meditation on Scripture, but it also underlies and anticipates the personal and communal reading of the Bible and of reality. It is not emergency action to be undertaken when all else fails, but rather is dialogue with God, which belongs at the very center of the Christian life. The demand is *to live in conversation with God.*[19] This conversation might take the form of a supplication, an accusation, a demand, a request or a cry of pain or anguish. At other times, it can be an expression of thankfulness and of the peace which passes all understanding. When God seems to be unresponsive, or when the pain and anguish are overwhelming and we scarcely feel able to frame any prayer—that is the time when prayer in its community form becomes especially important, as our sisters and brothers pray for us and with us. This is one of the reasons why following Jesus—and the consequent Christian mission—are not meant to be heroic individual actions, but the activity of a community.[20] Prayer is a conversation that flows naturally out of the experience of confidence in God, but it also is a habit that we are taught by the model prayer of Jesus, the "Our Father," by the insistent petitions for the healing of the sick in a period of congregational prayer, by a family member's expressions of thanks to God for his love for us at the table before we eat. Good conversation is an art. It assumes a sympathetic interest in the person with whom we are talking and an effort to understand their perspective and put ourselves in their place. That is how we

---

[19] The phrase belongs to Dorothy Sölle, to be found in her essay "Gebet," in *Atheistisch an Gott Glauben* (Otten: Walter-Verlag, 1968, Sixth Edition), pp. 109-117: 113.

[20] It is worth adding that the saying attributed to Prospero of Aquitania, "the rule of prayer sustains the rule of belief" (*lex orandi, lex credendi)* is also valuable for discerning ways in which to respond in faith to God's sending or commission. Prayer is the inhaling and exhaling of the *Ruach*, the Spirit-breath of God who speaks in us and intercedes for us (Rom 8:26) and causes us to glorify God in our speech and actions.

begin to see things not only from our own standpoint, but also begin to seek to understand God's own viewpoint. We can ask, for example, not only what the cross means to us, but also what it means to God (Moltmann); not only what injustice and sin mean to us, but also what they mean to God; not only what the violent premature death of a child means to us, but also what it means to God; not only what integral mission means to us, but also what it means to God.

d. *Tentatio*

"*Tentatio*" means "trying out" what we believe we have discerned about our *sending* from our *lectio, meditatio* and *oratio.* Put negatively, *tentatio* means what we do about the temptation not to put into effect what we have discerned or, at least, to put it into effect only partially and not completely. Or, perhaps, it is the temptation to deceive ourselves into believing that we have discerned something, when we are really looking at some idol. More positively, *tentatio* is about "putting to the test" what we have perceived or presumably discerned.[21] Being "stiff-necked" was not only a problem for the people of the Covenant after the Exodus. It is a still a factor in many faith communities today. There are communities that are reluctant to act upon things that they know they should do. In other words, there are times when we discern clearly, but then shy off from putting into

---

[21] A text of John Wesley might be useful here. "A Process of Self-Examination," *Obras de Wesley* (Works of John Wesley) Volume IX *Espiritualidad e Himnos. Notas al Nuevo Testamento* (Spirituality and Hymns. Notes on the New Testament;) Part 1 (Franklin, Tennessee: Providence House Publishers, 1998), pp. 101-104 (translated by A. Zambrano and F. Pagura) as a reflection on the four *notae misionis.* (Only Spanish available to the author.)

practice what we have discerned, because it seems too painful or costly. But the injustices suffered in our countries continue to cry out for redress. That means that our being situated geographically and metaphorically on the margins of global power places us in a situation where the pressing need for what we call integral mission behaves like the importunate widow of the parable, drumming on the door of our church, however imperfect and unjust it might be.

5. The Formation of Disciples in Discernment

How then are disciples given formation in discernment in order to seek ways of pursuing integral mission? The possibilities are legion, as are the spiritual gifts in the church and the special charismas of each congregation. However, following the dynamics of this essay, we should emphasize that, as a community of faith, we should understand that the formation of disciples in these ways is an objective inherent in the gospel. That implies, first, a process of *lectio* and *meditatio* which involves the whole faith community, reflected in Bible studies, sermons, spiritual retreats, Sunday school curricula or catechism classes, and so on. A second and simultaneous priority is persistent prayer to God (*oratio*) that he provide us as a community with opportunities to serve together in one or two concrete projects which would suit both the gifts that our church possesses and the needs of the community to which we belong. Then, a third emphasis would be the actual embarking, albeit modestly to start with, on a response to the need toward which we see the Spirit guiding us, by carrying out a critical analysis using the criteria provided by our *notae missionis (tentatio)*.

Let us imagine, by way of example, that a small urban church has an opportunity to organize some Saturday activities for the neighborhood children, something in the style of the traditional "kids' club" held by evangelical churches. If the faith community is immersed in a faithful *lectio* and *meditatio* and committed to regular *oratio*, it will have its ears open to the needs of those children. It will soon discover among them, for example, symptoms of family dysfunction, malnutrition, alcoholism among parents, lack of employment opportunity for the adults, sexual abuse or incest, child neglect, domestic violence, unwanted pregnancy and so on. So what to do? Suppose a mother who has invested her trust in the group and discovered the self-esteem that the gospel brings to women, appeals for help to the group leaders, because her partner is beating her and the children. The leaders, faced with the situation, have to seek help from people close by, particularly other church members, in praying, befriending, seeking help about what to do in cases of domestic violence, and so on. Step by step, the faith community may discover that the most comprehensive way to respond to the needs they have discovered may be to organize a family counseling center, or it may be to put in place some simple mechanisms for cases like that of the abused mother to be referred to suitable professionals in the field. All of this will be part of the *tentatio*. What is certain is that Bible reading will be subtly but definitely different, because the community has been directly affected by domestic violence. Likewise, the children of the family in question will have learned something about the comprehensive, integral nature of the message, which is not limited to sharing picnics or telling exciting Bible stories, but which provides concrete, life-giving ways of putting into practice today the wonderful things that Jesus said and did. The other children in the group are going to feel more emotionally secure, even though they may not be able to put it into words, and the adolescents and adults involved will have taken a concrete step towards the kind of service that is characteristic of the mercurial trinitarian dynamic of the God who is sending us out into the world.

When a church takes even a few modest steps in this direction, that is to say, when it abandons that spiritual/material dualism that creates a false dichotomy between "spiritual gospel" and "social gospel," and responds, in the most integrated way it can, to the needs of both its members and those within its sphere of influence, then possibly—even probably—some members will get upset by the complications associated with that kind of ministry. In every system, whether family or church, there is normally some resistance to change, even positive change. Recognizing this means that the "stiff neck" syndrome, whether one's own or somebody else's, should not be a reason for anxiety and paralysis. It is the Spirit of God who impels integral mission and he is persistent. As the old refrain says: the mills of God grind slowly, but they grind finely. Discernment and the practice of integral mission are not to be achieved without *ardent patience* and *profound compassion.* After all, these are God's own attributes that he is instilling into us, his disciples. Developing them without giving up is a normal part of following Jesus in the power of the Spirit.

The process of discernment for those who earnestly want to get involved in integral mission is a trinitarian activity. The Ruach/Spirit/Wisdom who guides the discernment process is not a spirit of ambition or power, but the Spirit of the incarnate Son, who has demonstrated in historical reality how to resist evil and live in righteousness. As Christians, we take his sending, his commission. upon ourselves, and we make his mission our own; discernment within the faith community helps us to find out in what concrete ways we can and should pursue this mission in our reality. Effective Christian discernment necessarily involves a trinitarian vision of the world, in which the three divine Persons, who are One, invite the whole of creation to find imaginative ways to participate in the integral dynamic of love, justice and equality. We, then, come to be engaged and enabled by the Spirit until the *missio Dei* becomes our mission too. Such a mission can only be integral.

4

The Church as Community

Samuel Escobar

In carrying out its integral mission, the Latin American evangelical church faces two challenging realities. On the one hand, the multiplicity of human needs and situations tests the churches' ability to direct all their resources—from the clamorous joyfulness of their worship to their proven ability to gather huge crowds—into organizing and equipping people for voluntary community service. On the other hand, in Latin America it is quite a challenge to get people to put together concerted actions, even within the realm of local churches, due to strong individualism and the tendency to fragmentation and division which seem innate to evangelicals.

This chapter examines the main thrusts of apostolic teaching on the growth of the people of God into fullness of life in Christ. It is about growth to achieve "maturity, to the measure of the full stature of Christ" (Eph 4:13): growth of the individual persons who make up the church, as well as that of the church as a whole, which implies growth in the quality of relationships within the church, the community of faith and life that has been called to carry out the mission. The great variety of human needs of society becomes a multifaceted challenge to Christian mission that may only be met by the growth of the community into fullness of life. While the challenge of the Latin American situation brings many pastors and leaders to cry with Jesus, "There is so much to be done and so few resources" (Mt 9:37), the word of God is insistent about the wealth and variety of gifts that the Lord has bestowed on his church for that purpose. Those gifts start to operate when the church is a community growing toward maturity in faith, hope and love.

1. Churches and Integral Mission in Latin America

Despite all their present shortcomings, the evangelical churches of Latin America are getting on with their task of providing service in response to the missionary challenges with which the continent confronts them. Churches are becoming homes to the uprooted, families for those who have no family, especially in an urban society hungry for fellowship and belonging arising from anomie, family disintegration, and secularization. My own pastoral experience has taught me that many come to the church in search of community, and when they are received with acceptance, understanding and warmth, they stay. The love of Christ reaches them first through the acceptance of the Christian community; that is, *koinonia* in action. Sociologists might disparage what they see as the church's role as a refuge, but there are people whose deepest and most obvious need is for a refuge, a home, or a family. This stems from a fundamental human need to get back into communion with the Creator as Father.

The demise of ideologies, the rise of globalization with its bombardment of consumerism, and the decline in the few values which shaped social life, are leading many people to wonder if human life has any meaning or if there are any guidelines to direct our humanity and prevent it from simply descending into bestiality. People desire to hear truths that ring with certainty, and this is what many find in the preaching and teaching of the Word of God. For these seekers after truth, God's message takes form in the Bible stories, the prayers of the psalmist, the charges of the prophets, the parables of Jesus, or the letters of Paul or John. Even in this age when words are devalued and people are looking for mystical experience, the proclamation of truth, the preaching of the *kerygma,* is still what attracts and holds many.

Poverty has increased on the Latin American continent and many governments have reduced their programs of support for the poor in areas such as education and health care. The problem of abandoned children has grown to enormous proportions, and new plagues such as HIV-aids infect a growing number of people. All this has presented the churches with new challenges to be faced in a spirit of service and with creativity. Following the Lausanne Congress of 1974, service organizations have multiplied in the evangelical world, organizations such as World Vision, Bread for the World, Tearfund, Care International, and MAP International. Many churches have discovered new ways of practising *diakonia* either through the opportunities provided by these agencies or by creating their own projects. It is my pastoral experience and observation that these aid programs are only possible where there are disciples of Christ ready to dedicate their talents and their caring spirit to the disinterested service of others. So the first contact that thousands of people have with Christ is the glass of water, the plate of food, the blankets, the scholarships, or the urgently needed medicines offered in Christ's name.

The new century is a time of intensified religiosity. While it is true that many have abandoned their traditional catholic religiosity, it is also true that many, including people from the middle and upper classes, have been drawn in by the singing, the praise, the prayer and even the experience of healing in the popular evangelical churches. This opening up to the supernatural and to the uninhibited expression of the human need to give homage to the Creator does not always bring people to the knowledge of Jesus Christ; sometimes it leads into strange and dangerous paths. However, this spiritual dimension of opening up and responding to the sacred, of thankfulness and worshipping God, of *liturgy* as joyful praise in the face of the revelation of divine mystery, has been part of the life of Christians since the foundation of the Church. It is that dimension that provides the way whereby some people come to a personal knowledge of Jesus Christ as Savior and Lord of life.

All these dimensions of the life of the church are ways of responding to the challenges to integral mission posed by the world. The very existence of the church as the community in which an effort is made to live out the values of the Kingdom of God, even when they challenge and enter into conflict with the surrounding society, is the *witness* which sometimes leads to suffering and *martyrdom*. By simply existing as an alternative community, the church becomes a judgment on those values that are opposed to the will of God and that so often hold sway in society. As an element of her task of proclaiming the gospel, the church often has to speak out in criticism and denunciation—that is, a *prophetic* message—which derives from her own experience. In a racist, class-ridden society, when the church as a body, as a community, incarnates the brotherly love that crosses all human barriers, it becomes a question mark for the rest of the world. And the church sometimes has to raise a prophetic voice based on her understanding and practice of the Word of God.

Thus it is possible to see the multiple challenges that integral mission faces, and also to understand clearly why all the gifts that God has bestowed on his Church are vital, valid, and necessary. There is a need for *pastors* capable of guiding God's people to growth in mutual love, a role that needs specific gifts of leadership, judgment, guidance, teaching and vision for the future. There is a need for *teachers and communicators* of biblical truths with the creative skills to make themselves understood inside and outside the church, who can use not only verbal communication, but also art, drama, music. There is a need for *activists and servants* to help bring to the needy the resources that the church either has or can access, people with administrative and entrepreneurial talents, or with simple faithfulness in the practical tasks of service. In different countries I have seen an army of humble women, dedicated to God, serving community breakfasts to thousands of children, helping elderly people, or ministering to victims of HIV-aids. I have seen simple men and women with astonishing managerial skills planning aid projects, developing small industries to provide work for young people, and organizing credit to help peasants who had been victims of loan sharks. However, I have also seen pastors who, though great teachers of the Word, failed as directors of projects by monopolizing the management and not recognizing other people's gifts and talents, especially those of the lay people in their own churches.

It is precisely here, faced with the multiple challenges of integral mission, that we see the need to create community and help the church to grow into the fullness of life in Christ. The foundation of this construction work, the resources available, and some practical examples, are clearly and explicitly set out in the teaching and practice of the apostles, especially Paul of Tarsus, who occupies a key position in the exercise of mission in the New Testament.

2. Community Life and Mission

In the very essence of Christian existence there is a community dimension. This is to be seen, for example, in the biblical teaching on prayer, crucial to understanding the relationship between human beings and God. When the disciples asked Jesus to teach them how to pray, his teaching was unequivocal and it has demonstrated its validity for all time (Mt 6:9-13; Lk 11:2-4). Jesus teaches us to address God as Father, as "our Father," because the relationship between God and human beings exists always in the context of community, a people. In a book on the spiritual life, Justo González reminds us that this attitude permeates the whole of the prayer known as "The Lord´s Prayer" or the "Our Father," so when we address God, we do not say, "give me this day my daily bread," or "forgive me my trespasses," or "do not lead me into temptation." This model prayer of the Church is always uttered from the heart of the community: "give us our bread. . . forgive our trespasses. . . lead us not into temptation." González has this to say:

> In sum, the Lord's Prayer can never be prayed in absolute isolation. It is always the prayer of the community and for the community—even when you say it in the privacy of your room as part of your personal devotions.[1]

This truth needs to be stressed in any reflection on Christian mission, because the evangelical tradition has placed great emphasis on the personal relationship between the human being

---

[1] Justo L. González, *When Christ Lives in Us* (Nashville: Abingdon Press, 1995), p. 23.

and God, mediated through Jesus Christ. The Reformation of the sixteenth century held the conviction that the human being had no need of the mediation of an institution, especially when that institution had become corrupt; we are free to approach God through Jesus Christ. The pietistic movement—to which both the Latin American Protestantism that grew out of the missionary movement and the Pentecostal movement owe a great deal—was a current of renewal within the Protestant establishment, calling it back to stressing the personal experience of salvation. As time passed, this evangelical emphasis on the personal dimension gradually turned into an excessive individualism. As such it has often undervalued the importance of the communal aspect of faith which is to be seen in the practice and teaching of Jesus and the apostles who, in turn, were deeply rooted in biblical revelation. Bible scholar H. H. Rowley expressed this with striking clarity with reference to the Old Testament. While acknowledging that prophets such as Jeremiah and Ezekiel give prominence to the idea of individual responsibility and response to God, Rowley recalls us to the profound community consciousness in the teaching of the Old Testament, and concludes:

> In no period of the life of Israel do we find extreme collectivism or extreme individualism, but a combination of both. Some writers or some passages emphasize the one side of this dual nature of man more than the other, but both sides belong to the wholeness of biblical thought in all periods.[2]

---

[2] H. H. Rowley, *The Faith of Israel* (Philadelphia: The Westminster Press, 1956), p. 100.

The passage in Matthew's Gospel in which Jesus calls twelve disciples to send them out on their missionary task is preceded by an outline of the wholeness of the mission which the Lord undertook: "Jesus went about all the cities and villages, teaching in their synagogues, and proclaiming the good news of the Kingdom, and curing *every* disease and *every* sickness" (Mt 9:35). In the verses that follow, the names of those sent out appear in groups of two: Simon and Andrew, James and John, Philip and Bartholomew (Mt 10:1-4). Another account of Jesus' sending of the missionaries specifies that the missionaries were sent "two by two" (Lk 10:1). This could also be related to the fact that Jesus promised his permanent presence and assistance to help them fulfill their mission wherever there were two or three gathered together in his name (Mt 18:19-20). These actions and this promise of Jesus are echoed in the essence of his high priestly prayer in the upper room (Jn 17). Here Jesus asks the Father to work in us so that we become a community deeply united by a bond like the one that unites Father and Son in the Trinity. Mission, then, grows out of fellowship and community. It should never be a solitary exercise undertaken by an individualistic anchorite, because the salvation to which God calls us through Jesus Christ, and which comes into being through the power of his Spirit, brings the human being into membership in that community called the Church. As the *Lausanne Covenant* clearly states:

> ... evangelism itself is the proclamation of the historical, biblical Christ as Savior and Lord, with a view to *persuading people* to come to him *personally* and so be reconciled to God. In issuing the Gospel invitation, we have no liberty to conceal the cost of discipleship. Jesus still calls all who would follow him to deny themselves, take up their cross, *and*

> *identify themselves with his new community.* The results of evangelism include obedience to Christ, incorporation into his Church, and responsible service in the world.[3]

In the italicized phrases the understanding of the dual nature of the evangelical position is spelled out. People come to Christ personally; but those who do come to Christ come to a community as well, and are incorporated into the Church of Christ.

The account of Paul's conversion or calling demonstrates how he grasped this profound truth in a dramatic way in his encounter with Christ. Zealous to put an end to what he considered a dangerous sect, Saul hears the voice of someone whom he addresses as "Lord," recognizing it as a divine voice. When he asks who is speaking to him, the voice replies, "I am Jesus whom you are persecuting" (Ac 9:5). In that way, Saul discovers the identification between Jesus and his people, that incorporation into the community called *Church.* And his first experiences following this encounter with the Lord are precisely those of incorporation into the Church through baptism and the fraternal embrace of the meal with Ananias (Ac 9:17-18).

When Saul becomes the apostle Paul, this unity between Christ and his people, which he grasped in his conversion experience, comes to be a foundation stone for his theology and missionary activity, a principle that generates community. His exhortation to the believers in Rome, for example, expresses it forcefully: "May the God of steadfastness and encouragement grant you to live in harmony with one another, in accordance with Christ Jesus, so

---

[3] *Lausanne Covenant.* Final Document of the International Congress on World Evangelization, held in Lausanne, Switzerland, 1974. A copy of the Covenant is to be found on the internet at www.albchristian.com/english/lausanne. Author's italics.

that together you may with one voice glorify the God and Father of our Lord Jesus Christ" (Ro 15:5-6). That common life, that living together in harmony, has a starting point, to which the apostle refers in the lines that follow in his letter: "Welcome one another, therefore, just as Christ has welcomed you, for the glory of God" (Ro 15:7). Let us locate this passage in Romans in the context of the whole epistle and note that this is a missionary context. Paul wants the believers in Rome to join him in the new missionary enterprise that he is planning: to go to establish the Church in the extreme West of the Empire, that is, in Spain (Ro 15:23-24, 28-29). The church that sends him will have to be a united church, a church in which Jews and gentiles—divided in society for so many historical, cultural, linguistic, and religious reasons—find in Jesus Christ a deep indestructible bond of unity, because mission is born out of community.

The images that Paul uses to describe the church convey an image of a living community, growing in love, providing mutual help and support. Peter's message also refers to the relationships among members of the Christian community, using the image of hospitality. The author of a commentary on the First Letter of Peter has entitled his book *A Home for the Homeless*. The idea of the church as a community where strangers finally discover a home and a family also indicates the nature of the mutual relationships: "Once you were not a people, but now you are God's people" (1Pe 2:10). In contrast with his idea of belonging to the people of God, the faithful are "aliens and exiles" (1Pe 2:11) in relation to the surrounding society, the Roman world with a culture hostile to faith in Jesus Christ. For Peter, brotherly love is the immediate consequence of the purification that the truth effects in the lives of people: "Now that you have purified your souls by your obedience to the truth so that you have genuine mutual love, love one another deeply from the heart" (1Pe 1:22).

When we look at John's writings in both the Gospel and the epistles we also come across references to real brotherly love that must be demonstrated by serving our sisters and brothers. We already referred to the priestly prayer of Jesus in John's Gospel. Pedro Arana reminds us, with nearly forty references, that John's text is constantly using "one of the most important titles given to Jesus in the Gospel, which has an intrinsically missionary character: Jesus is the One who is Sent."[4] Jesus is the missionary whom God sends into the world, and in turn Jesus is the one who sends: "As you have sent me into the world, so I have sent them into the world" (Jn 17:18). Interceding for those he sends, he prays that their life together should be distinguished by their unity, on the model of the union between himself and the Father: ". . . that they may be one, as we are one;" and he continues: "I in them and you in me, that they may become completely one, so that the world may know that you have sent me and have loved them even as you have loved me" (Jn 17:22-23). The First Letter of John is marked by its critical stand against Docetism, that is, against a form of spiritualism that denies the human body of Christ, and which consequently denies the importance of brotherly relationships in the life of the community. "How does God's love abide in anyone who has the world's goods and sees a brother or sister in need and yet refuses help?" (1Jn 3:17).[5]

In all these references to relationships within the Christian community there is something that we might call pastoral realism.

---

[4] Pedro Arana-Quiroz, "*Misión en el Evangelio de Juan*" (Mission in the Gospel of John), in C. René Padilla, ed., *Bases bíblicas de la misión* (The Biblical Foundations of Mission) (Buenos Aires: Nueva Creación, 1998), p. 283.

[5] On this issue see Justo L. González. *Mañana* (Nashville: Abingdon Press, 1990).

Relationships within the community do not just happen automatically: they have to be nurtured. In some cases, the apostolic exhortation gives direction to pastors about nurturing the quality of relationships, while in other cases the advice is directed towards the whole congregation to develop certain attitudes and to behave in certain ways, as a part of the process of discipleship. It is at this deepest level of the quality of relationships that we need to understand certain teachings, like those on spiritual gifts and stewardship, that are vital to the missionary undertaking. Both of these, in practice, are prone to dangerous corruptions. The diversity of gifts and the excessive value accorded to some over others can lead to a situation where the exercise of people's gifts in the church can turn into an arena for competition and rivalries. We have the most explicit teaching on this in the epistles to the Corinthians, especially in the image of *the body*. And then, too, stewardship of money, when it is misconstrued, can turn a question of resources into an issue of status and superiority. In the development of integral mission both the variety of gifts and the understanding of the nature of stewardship are important, so we need to give them special attention in our reflection on missiology.

In the apostolic teaching about the life and mission of the church, a correlation between the fullness of Christian living and the complexity of integral mission can be established. This teaching sees the church as a community in process of continuous growth. It is a process of metamorphosis through which the Holy Spirit enables believers in Christ to be continuously transformed in conformity with the image of Jesus Christ. This dynamic of the Christian life is seen, for example, in 1 Corinthians 3, with reference to the ministry of the Word and of the Spirit. The description of the action of the Spirit, according to this passage, is correlated with Romans 12, where the emphasis is on the continuous surrender of the disciple, in a state of vigilance and readiness to be transformed. In Ephesians this process of transformation has a communal dimension as well as a personal one. The whole body that is the Church is in a process of growth and transformation into the measure of maturity that is the stature of Jesus Christ. Evangelical pastoral ministry and theology have emphasized conversion and sanctification as realities experienced by people individually, but very few have given the same emphasis to the corporate dimension. In Ephesians, however, it is clear that harmonious growth to fullness includes a recognized and respected array of gifts, all of which are essential to the missionary work of the church. In their variety there is unity and growth into fullness. The apostolic teaching testifies to this fact, and it also exhorts us to find ways of demonstrating it.

The work which God does in his Church through people equipped with the gifts Christ has provided includes setting up new communities (apostles), the communication of the gospel (evangelists), sharing the riches of Christian truth (teachers), the wise analysis of the times so as to apply the Word in their own situation (prophets), and the pastoral care of the community (pastors). All of this is directed towards *service*, the daily activity of the whole people, what all the members of the community are doing in the world. The presence of God's people in the world presents them with daily challenges which require the resources of faith to come up with appropriate responses. This variety of challenges, all demanding a response, makes up the agenda and the content of integral mission. The teaching of Scripture repeatedly shows that growth into the fullness of communal life in the church is a prerequisite for the undertaking of integral mission.

3. The Recovery of the Apostolic Practice of Discipleship

A valuable recovery of our biblical and historical heritage is taking place in recent studies of the forms of initiation in the Christian life practiced by the New Testament church. Sociological studies of the present day church have led to a new understanding of the biblical material.[6] We are now aware that in the process of evangelism and formation of disciples by the apostles there were at least three key elements whose importance we have rediscovered through the questions that have emerged from this sociological study. The three elements are *belief, behavior, and belonging.*

In the previous section, we have sketched out the substance of the apostolic teaching on the communal life of the church. The various figures of speech (body, building, family) present us with a dynamic vision of that common life which should characterize the disciples of Jesus. This life is rooted in the very being of Jesus Christ, the One sent by God, whose truth brings us into the Church, which is his body, through the power of the Holy Spirit. This is the *content of belief.* When this truth acts effectively in our lives through faith, it transforms us into the likeness of Christ, in such a way that we acquire *personal and social behavior* conformed to new standards, those of the Kingdom of God.

---

[6] On this subject, a most valuable book is the study by Mennonite scholar Alan Kreider,*The Change of Conversion and the Origin of Christendom* (Harrisburg: Trinity Press International, 1999).

Christian life, then, is not just new information accumulating in our memory. It is an imperative bringing us to a new way of life. This emphasis on the truth which shows itself in a new life should provide a corrective to the superficial evangelism that appeals exclusively to such emotions as superstitious fear or transient enthusiasm, easily manipulated by any clever orator or communicator.

In addition to *belief* and *behavior*, there is *belonging.* Those who put their faith in Christ's message and decide on a change of life and accept Christ as Lord and model also experience becoming part of a community, belonging to a body, not living isolated in a private relationship with God. Life in the warmth of the Christian community brings with it an awareness of belonging, in place of alienation; of family life, in place of an orphan life; of hospitality, in place of hostility; of feeling oneself to be somebody, in place of being a nobody. Sociological studies have observed the joy and the sense of finding oneself that coming into membership of a community brings to the new believer. Middle class evangelicals generally have not experienced the full healing force of this sense of belonging. But the socially marginalized, especially those in the cities, experience this life in the church as a consolation, a refuge, and a place of integration. And this experience has the power to transform and reorient their existence.

In the light of these realities, we can better understand the New Testament language describing life in the primitive church. For example, these words in Acts: "They devoted themselves to the apostles' teaching and fellowship, to the breaking of bread and the prayers. . . . All who believed were together and had all things in common. . . . They broke bread at home and ate their food with glad and generous hearts. . ." (Ac 2:42-46). The vocabulary of Paul or Peter, referring to ideas such as having become a people, having overcome divisions, coming to mutual acceptance, and being a new people distinguished by mutual love, is not simply metaphorical. It graphically describes the reality of this sense of belonging to a new community. The figures describe an ideal, and the exhortations of the apostles make it clear that pastoral activity should aim at turning that ideal into communal reality.

In what follows, we will briefly examine two examples of Paul's missionary practice that illustrate the pastoral ministry that intentionally seeks to create and strengthen the sense of Christian community. The first example is taken from his work with a particular church, and the second concerns what could be called his long-term missionary strategy.

4. The Affective Infrastructure of Mission

In Philippians 2:25-30, Paul refers to Epaphroditus in the following terms: "My brother, and co-worker and fellow soldier" (v. 25). The passage opens a window on the private life of the apostle, the depth of the relationships he cultivated, and his efforts to strengthen them. We find ourselves looking at what we might call "the affective ground of mission." Paul is old and in prison, and the church of Philippi, as a mark of the affection they have for him, sends him Epaphroditus as their messenger to accompany and encourage him. The affection between the missionary and the church he founded is mutual, as Paul writes to them: "God is my witness how I long for you all" (1: 8). From the time when Lydia, the founding convert in Philippi, first opened her home to the missionaries, the church inaugurated there had practiced generous financial stewardship to help Paul (Ac 16:15 and Php 4:15-20). Now, by sending Epaphroditus, they display generous *stewardship of their affection*, which is just as important for mission.

As he served Paul, Epaphroditus "came close to death…risking his life" (v. 30). The church at Philippi received the news and became anxious, so Paul sent their messenger back, this time to comfort the Philippians. Thus, sympathy and compassion came to be an important missionary asset. The generosity of the Philippians and the dedication of Epaphroditus were enabling factors in Paul's mission. The apostle responds with warmth expressed repeatedly in this epistle. That same warmth also provided the grounding for his message. This kind of *affective infrastructure of mission* has been revealed over and again during the twenty centuries of the Church's history. The bearer of the message of Christ is no cold communicator of intellectual ideas, but someone who really comes to care for the people with whom he or she shares the gospel and the teaching. For this style of caring there is a christological model, because it is the kind of care that was incarnated in Jesus himself during his earthly ministry. Paul displays generosity and consideration in his missionary style. To avoid prolonging the anxiety of the Philippians over Epaphroditus's health, and to discharge his pastoral concern for them, he sends back to them the messenger of their love (v. 27-28). His letter makes it clear that he himself is sending Epaphroditus, and that Epaphroditus is not leaving his service in some irresponsible fashion. Maybe it was Epaphroditus himself who took the letter, and Paul exhorts them to "Welcome him then in the Lord, with all joy, and honor such people" (v. 29).

In this epistle, the idea of an affective basis for mission is linked with a reference to the new attitude that should be a distinguishing mark of believers. Some Spanish translations of the exhortation in Philippians 2:5 rendered the word *phronein* as *sentir* ("feeling"), which in Spanish makes sense as referring to a basic motivation for action. Most English translations render the Greek word as "mind." This is the case with the NRSV, "let the same mind be in you that was in Christ Jesus." Today´s NIV says, "have the same attitude of mind Christ Jesus had." So, I ask, is it about feeling (affection) or about thinking (intellect)? Paul Rees recalled classic English translations such as Moffatt, "Treat one another with the same spirit that you experience in Christ Jesus," and Weymouth, "let the same spirit which was in Christ Jesus be in you also." Reed comments that "the word mind speaks not of our Lord´s *intelligence* but of his *disposition.*"[7] In other words, a combination of the intellectual and the affective which moves to Christ-like action.[8] The story of the relationship between Paul, Epaphroditus, and the Philippians is a telling illustration of this Christian attitude. Such human integration in Christ makes mission possible. Life in community in the churches has to be nurtured by positive actions, large and small.

5. Liberating, Non-manipulative Pastoral Ministry

At a time of great religiosity such as ours, what we have said about pastoral endeavors to nurture the community life of the church requires some clarification. *Belonging* to the body of

---

[7]Paul S. Rees, *The Adequate Man* (Revell, 1999), p. 42.

[8]Ralph P. Martin, *Philippians, The New Century Bible Commentary* (Grand Rapids-London: Wm. B. Eerdmans - Marshall, Morgan & Scott, 1976).

Christ as a way of experiencing the Christian life, and also what we are calling the *affective infrastructure of mission,* could be understood in a way very different from the biblical sense. For example, in some Pentecostal churches as well as in some of those called charismatic "megachurches" the idea of "apostleship" comes to be associated with strong charismatic personalities, who exercise a more or less total control over the faithful. That then leads to an authoritarian style of leadership followed by the regimentation and control of the people. The leaders speak as God's anointed, always in the right, and accept no differences of criterion or opinion. Sometimes they justify their capricious interpretations of the Scriptures with some notion of a "gift of prophecy" or "discernment" which a competent exegesis of the biblical text would not admit.

Two passages representative of the teaching of Paul and Peter, respectively, provide us with keys to correct these tendencies. In writing to the Philippians, Paul provides a valuable line of teaching on spiritual life, or *spirituality,* calling for a mature, independent spirituality. Philippians 2:12-13, which follows the beautiful hymn on the humbling and exaltation of Jesus Christ, says, "Therefore, my beloved, just as you have always obeyed me, not only in my presence, but much more now in my absence, work out your own salvation with fear and trembling; for it is God who is at work in you, enabling you both to will and to work for his good pleasure." Having just made reference to the contemplation of Jesus Christ, he now calls for action: "Work out your own salvation." The action is not some human activism, but rather it is a response to an initiative from God himself that springs up in them *with fear and trembling.* Verse 12 also alludes to the presence and absence of the apostle. The whole epistle is an invitation to move toward maturity, and a part of that maturity is that the Philippians have grown to the point where they no longer need the close supervision of their spiritual father. Even though Paul offers himself as a model to the Philippians (3:17) and attests to his deep affection for them, it is clear that he does not want their spirituality to be dependent, needing the constant oversight of other people. Here we have the basis for the criticism of a certain practice of intensive and detailed pastoral supervision, adopted these days by some charismatic leaders, that makes people dependent to the point where they can no longer make any decision without consulting their counselor or pastor. It is no surprise that the counselors and pastors then give in to the temptation of authoritarianism. That, in turn, leads to dangerous trends of spiritual tyranny and abuse imposed on disempowered people no longer capable of finding their own way, making judgments, or thinking for themselves. If we can follow Paul's pastoral style, reflected in these lines to the Philippians, it will provide a valuable antidote to such deviations.

The pastoral approach that Peter recommends in his first epistle is also explicit on this issue. He advises the leaders "to tend the flock of God that is in your charge, exercising oversight, not under compulsion but willingly, as God would have you do it—not for sordid gain but eagerly. Do not lord it over those in your charge, but be examples to the flock" (1Pe 5:2-3). The sheep belong to no leader or director, but to the Lord; it is God who has put them under their care. So they have to care for them in a spirit of service, not exploit them with domineering attitudes. It is illuminating that in referring to himself Peter describes himself as "a fellow elder" (NIV) and claims no hierarchical priority or superiority in the Christian life. On the contrary, he invokes the sufferings of Christ, which play a very important part in this epistle as the model of a kind of humble service. With Paul and

Peter we are miles from that manipulative despotism with which some of today's charismatic leaders aspire to "construct" community by force or "mobilize" the flock for mission. It is worth noting here a few lines by Lesslie Newbigin, the great mission theologian:

> The supreme gift of the Spirit is not the spectacular power by which an individual might gain pre-eminence, but the humble self-effacing love by which the body is built up and knit together. It follows that a decisive mark of the Spirit's presence will be a tender concern for the unity of the body, a horror of all that exalts some human leader or some party into the place where Christ alone can occupy.[9]

6. Money and the Construction of Community

Practically all Paul's epistles refer to the collection which the apostle organized among the gentile churches for the poor in Jerusalem (see, for example, Ro 15:25-29; 1Co 16:1-4; 2Co 8–9; Gal 2:10).[10] A key passage in which Paul summarizes the methodology of his mission is Romans 15:17-33. Here, he powerfully spells out his apostolic vision for the evangelization of Spain, a distant area as yet untouched by the gospel. At the same time, he makes an extended reference to the journey on which

---

[9] Lesslie Newbigin, *The Household of God* (London: SCM Press, 1953), p. 104..

[10] In this section I am using material I have developed in "A Pauline Paradigm in Mission," chapter 4 in Charles Van Engen et al, eds., *The Good News of the Kingdom* (Maryknoll: Orbis Books, 2003).

he was currently engaged to take money to Jerusalem. Despite his sense of urgency for the evangelization of Spain, Paul still ascribes a great deal of importance to this voyage of economic assistance to Jerusalem. The juxtaposition of these two very different aspects of his missionary task demonstrates the apostle's integral mission in action. Biblical theologian Paul Minear points out that

> financial drives are so routine in our modern churches, that we readily overlook the strategic importance of the first collection. It was a startling innovation. *Gentile* Christians in Macedonia and Achaea had been asked to send money to poor *Jewish* Christians in Jerusalem. Earlier appeals had been resisted; Paul's authority had been rejected. There were rumors that the whole business was graft.[11]

It is important to keep in mind the missionary context in which the apostle was organizing the collection. The Gentile churches were the result of the evangelistic actions of the apostles, who had come from the world of Judaism. And the New Testament reveals that the move from the Jewish world to the Gentile world brought about a crisis of continuity and discontinuity. Many of the Jerusalem faithful, including several leaders, believed it important that gentiles should take on Jewish customs as they received the gospel, beginning with circumcision. Paul was the champion of freedom for the Gentiles and was teaching that they could receive the gospel while remaining culturally Gentiles. He believed that the imposition of a Jewish way of life was a violation of their Christian freedom. This is the force of his

---

[11] Paul Minear. *The Obedience of Faith* (London: SCM Press, 1971), p. 3.

argument in the epistles to the Galatians and to the Romans. However, Paul was also keen that there should be a mutual recognition between Jews and Gentiles since they were one in Christ, and the walls that had previously separated them had been broken down.

This explains Paul's terminology with regard to this financial project of bringing economic assistance to the poor. In effect, the vocabulary he uses reveals the missionary importance that he attributes to the project, and allows us to see his pastoral goal, namely that the collection should contribute to the creation of community among the young churches of his day. For example, in Romans 15:26-27, Paul describes the money in question as *koinonia*, a word which, as we have seen, has deep spiritual and missiological echoes. Australian Bible scholar Leon Morris says this implies that "the money was not a soulless gift but the outward expression of the deep love that binds Christian believers in one body, the Church (it is used similarly in 2Co 8:4; 9:13)."[12]

We also notice Paul's insistence on the voluntary nature of this offering. Twice he uses the phrase "have been pleased" or "they were pleased" in referring to the attitude of the believers in Macedonia and Achaia (Ro 15:26-27). It would not be beyond the bounds of supposition, as several scholars have claimed, that some of the Jewish believers in Jerusalem should have misunderstood the nature of the offering, regarding it as some sort of tax or tribute that the Gentile churches were obliged to send to the mother church in Jerusalem. Paul's teachings in regard to the offering are aimed at emphasizing its voluntary character. The action had been undertaken "as a voluntary gift,

---

[12] Leon Morris, *The Epistle to the Romans* (Leicester: Inter-Varsity Press, 1988), p. 520.

and not as an extortion" (2Co 9:5). Nothing was further from the apostle's mind than the idea of creating a religious tax, or some kind of franchise payment similar to that demanded by the parent companies of foreign subsidiaries!

What theological basis does Paul use to underpin this action? By locating the collection in the context of God's plan for the salvation of humankind, the apostle implants the idea of an element of correspondence and reciprocity between those who first received the gospel and the people with whom they shared it. The sense of commitment and urgency with which the apostle's evangelism is imbued springs from the deep wellspring of Christ's love, not from some institutionally regulated obligation: "the love of Christ urges us on" (2Co 5:14). And, in the same way, the spontaneous gratitude to God for the gift of salvation provides the impetus for the gift of the gentiles to the poor in Jerusalem.

With this background, we can understand the passage in Romans 15:27: "for if the Gentiles have come to share in their spiritual blessings, they ought also to be of service to them in material things." In this mutual sharing, the spiritual blessings that the Jews shared with the Gentiles are put on the same level as the material blessings that the Gentiles shared with the Jews. Implicit in this is the demolition of a cultural barrier, vital for the progress of the mission among the Gentiles. As Leenhardt says, "The collection is a manifest sign of the unity of the Church. It shows in concrete fashion that the young shoots were firmly linked to the old trunk."[13]

---

[13] Franz J. Leenhardt, *The Epistle to the Romans: A Commentary* (London: Lutterworth Press, 1961), p. 375..

There are two elements in this integral perspective on mission. One is the empirical fact of a certain amount of money, gathered, in many instances, with some sacrifice, that is an expression of the concern of the Gentile believers for their poor Jewish brothers and sisters in Judea. The other is the sign of maturity, of the culmination of the evangelistic process, which is embodied in this offering. In giving, the giver grows and receives a blessing, and the beneficiary is blessed with the practical help provided for the relief of his or her affliction. The transaction itself acquires a "eucharistic" dimension (2Co 9:12). The missionary exerts himself in building up the church as a global community, because mission springs from real community in Christ. As many scholars have observed, the aid operation that Paul organized was something new in the Gentile churches. Its missionary originality provides a great example of the kind of creativity that we need in our times, because from now on, we are looking at missionary cooperation on a world scale.

If Paul's practice inspires us in some way, we must recover his theological basis for the countless missionary programs for economic assistance in our own day. In that way, we can correct the harmful elements that have crept in during the churches' historical journey. The Christian contribution to the relief of the poor and the elimination of the causes of poverty should be channeled through those conduits of mutuality and reciprocity that only the common commitment to faith in Christ can provide. That would reinforce the bonds of Christian unity and help to overcome the barriers of culture, politics, and even ideology. In place of paternalistic attitudes, borrowed from state welfare systems with their bureaucratic apparatus, we need to cultivate a "eucharistic" focus, through which those who provide assistance and those who receive it become fellow workers, and at the same time agents of their own development and liberation. That would be the outworking of a truly integral focus, in which the proclamation of the gospel and service in response to human need are harnessed together, without difficulty and without any need for explanations. The truth is that real mission springs out of a church that lives as a community in brotherly love.

5

The Priesthood of All Believers and Integral Mission

Alberto Fernando Roldán

There can be no "ecclesiastics" and "lay people," there cannot be one church that simply "instructs" and another that is "under instruction," because no member of the church exists who is not all of that in their own right.
Karl Barth

The power behind unity is love.
The power behind diversity is freedom.
Jürgen Moltmann

One of the New Testament doctrines rediscovered by the Protestant Reformation—along with *sola scriptura, sola gratia* and *sola fide*—which became of prime importance for the life of the church was "the universal priesthood of all believers." Its formulation not only broke with the medieval ecclesiastical schema, with its powerful hierarchical structure; it also had a profound practical influence on the fulfilment of the mission of the church. When this doctrine is related to the question of mission, understood in the sense of integral mission, a number of unavoidable questions arise: What is the significance of the priesthood of all believers for our understanding of the church? How does that understanding affect the life and mission of the church in the world? How does the practice of universal priesthood relate to our undertaking of what has come to be called "integral mission?" These basic questions provide the direction for reflection on the following fundamental hypothesis: *only the unyielding and coherent exercise of the priesthood of all believers can make integral mission possible in today's world.*

1. Universal Priesthood: "From Saying to Doing"

Of all the doctrines recovered by the Reformation, "the universal priesthood of all believers" is still far from becoming historical reality. With its roots deep within some passages of the New Testament such as 1 Peter 2:9-10 and Revelation 1:6, this doctrine entailed a revolutionary change from the Old Testament situation in which only members of Aaron's family were given the right to exercise priesthood in Israel. Today, in and through Christ all Christians, all believers, without exception, are priests, qualified to serve as priests in the church. However, this stupendous truth has often been obscured through history by a range of ecclesiastical and clerical practices.

With the institutionalization of the church in the early centuries of Christianity, a sharp differentiation began to appear between clergy and laity.[1] The former were those who specifically and

[1] For an analysis of the word "laity" and its relevance for the mission of the church see Catharine F. Padilla's study, "Los 'laicos' en la misión en

exclusively undertook the ministry of the church. The latter included the people in general, understood as the *laos* of God. It is impossible to escape the contradictions implied in this dichotomy. If the *clergy* is differentiated from the *laity* understood as "members of the people of God," what, then, are the clergy? Are they not members of the people? Are they part of the people? Or outside the people? Or above the people? The Protestant Reformation recovered this doctrine and the inclusive understanding of the doctrine of priesthood. Martin Luther can be singled out as the particular leader who provoked the rupture in the understanding of the nature of the priesthood by critically reinterpreting the reductionist perspective that held sway in medieval Catholicism. In his treatise, *On the Liberty of a Christian,* Luther responds to the question of the difference between "priests" and "lay people," by affirming that all Christians are priests. He says:

> The reply is as follows: the words "priest," "curate," "ecclesiastic" and such similar expressions were robbed of their true meaning when they were applied uniquely to a reduced number of men, who separated themselves from the main body and took on what we now know under the title of "the priestly state." Holy Scripture does not differentiate between Christians, except the learned and dedicated people given such titles as "*ministri,*" "*servi,*" "*oeconomi,*" which

---

el Nuevo Testamento," in C. René Padilla (ed.) *Bases bíblicas de la misión* (The Biblical Foundations of Mission) (Buenos Aires: Nueva Creación, 1998), pp. 405ff. There the author reveals that the word *laity,* as such, does not appear in the New Testament. It is first used by Clement of Rome in his First Epistle to the Corinthians. As an adjective it is derived from the word *laos* which, as we note above, signifies the whole church seen as the "people of God."

> mean ministers, servants, administrators, whose vocation was to preach to their fellows about Christ, the faith and Christian freedom.[2]

What is it that makes Christians priests? According to Luther, Christians become priests through baptism. We are all baptized into Christ and, consequently, recruited into service for God's world. There is an important and practical implication here for the life of the church. As Norberto Bertón has pointed out, it means that "the responsibility for the *governing* of the church is the responsibility of all of them [i.e., all Christians]"[3] and he goes on to say: "Luther affirms a definite militant commitment for *all*, an evangelical calling without exclusions or exclusiveness.... All are *priests*; a real ecclesiological revolution."[4]

What then, in Luther's thinking, has universal priesthood to do with the mission of the church? In a well documented work that shows the importance that Luther accorded to mission, Sidney Rooy states categorically that, "every Christian is an agent of mission by participating in the universal priesthood of all believers."[5] The task of proclaiming the word of God is not reserved for a few. It is the responsibility of the whole church.

---

[2] Martin Luther, *La libertad cristiana* (Christian Liberty) (Buenos Aires: La Aurora, 1983), pp. 61, 62. Only the Spanish translation available to the author.

[3] Norberto Bertón, "El sacerdocio universal de los creyentes" (The Universal Priesthood of Believers) in Daniel Arcaute *et al.*, *Lutero ayer y hoy* (Luther Yesterday and Today) (Buenos Aires: La Aurora, 1984), p. 75, original italics.

[4] *Ibid.*, original italics.

[5] Sidney Rooy, "Lutero y la misión" (Luther and Mission), in *ibid.*, p. 239.

The accomplishment of the work needs neither ordination nor ecclesiastical regulation. Rooy summarizes the relationship between universal priesthood and integral mission in Luther's theology in the following way:

> The execution of the mission is founded on the universal priesthood of all believers and is nourished by it. Every Christian has his or her own sacred vocation. Within this framework preachers serve as representatives of the Christian community through their specialized vocation. But they do not constitute a class with greater powers than those of every other believer. The responsibility of disseminating the love and message of Christ is laid upon all believers in the whole of life.[6]

However, there is a lot of truth in the popular adage "It's a long way from saying to doing."[7] Luther's ideas were undoubtedly revolutionary. The great German reformer was breaking with the hierarchical ideas that had existed in the church, as they had grown within Catholicism. But the crucial question is: to what extent did Luther manage to put his ideas into practice? In his analysis of the subject, David Bosch weighs up the positives and negatives:

> It is true that Luther is to be credited with the rediscovery of the notion of the "priesthood of all believers." In his thesis that "the Christian . . . congregation has the right and power to judge all teaching and to call, install and dismiss teachers" (quoted in Pfürtner 1984:184), Luther most certainly broke with the dominant paradigm. However, when Luther's

[6] *Ibid.*, p. 303.

[7] In Spanish, *"Del dicho al hecho hay mucho trecho"*.

> understanding of church and theology was under assault from Anabaptists (some of whom had jettisoned the idea of an ordained ministry altogether) and Catholics alike, he reverted to the inherited paradigm. In the end, he still had the clergyman at the center of his church, endowed with considerable authority (cf. Burrows 1981:104).[8]

As Bosch suggests, it was the Anabaptists, with their insistence on "believers' baptism" based on personal testimony of faith in Jesus Christ and on life together in a democratic community, who best succeeded in the practice of the universal priesthood of all believers.[9] At this point, it would be worthwhile to take a critical look at the factors conspiring against the actual practice of such an important doctrine.

2. Universal Priesthood and the Exercise of Authority

The problem of putting universal priesthood into practice starts with the area of authority. Regardless of the type of church

---

[8] David J. Bosch, *Transforming Mission* (Maryknoll: Orbis Books, 1991), p. 469.

[9] For historical information about the Anabaptist view on the church and its practice, see Donald F. Durnbaugh, *La iglesia de creyentes. Historia y carácter del protestantismo radical* (The Church of Believers. The History and the Nature of Radical Protestantism) (Guatemala: Ediciones Semilla-Clara, 1992); William R. Estep, *Revolucionarios del siglo XVI. Historia de los anabautistas* (Revolutionaries of the 16th Century. A History of the Anabaptists) (El Paso: Casa Bautista de Publicaciones, 1975); and John H. Yoder (comp.), *Textos escogidos de la Reforma radical* (Selected Texts from the Radical Reformation) (Buenos Aires: La Aurora, 1976).

government in existence, one fact is clear: sooner or later, either secretly and deviously or plainly and openly, some kind of differentiations will emerge and stand in open opposition to the universal priesthood of all Christians. It is true that Protestantism adheres to the axiom of *sola scriptura*, claiming that the Bible is the only rule of faith (some would add "and practice"). This is not the place to examine this principle in depth, but we refer the reader to the careful and profound study of Wolfhart Pannenberg, "The Crisis of the Scripture Principle."[10] While the Reformation promulgated the belief in the final authority of the Scriptures, in practice various pressures militated against it. We cannot give an exhaustive treatment of the topic, but simply offer a demonstration of how—in the explosive growth of Protestantism in Latin America—churches have adopted models that stand in direct opposition to universal priesthood. Before briefly describing these models, however, it is necessary to recall the historical and theological perspective on the question of authority and its exercise in the church. The key question, which we are not always disposed to ask, is: Where, in the end, does authority lie in the church? It is useless to go on saying, "In the Bible, because the Bible is the final authority on matters of faith (and practice)." Everyone should be aware that in practice it just does not work that way. Inevitably, problems in the interpretation of Scripture come into play. Roman Catholicism has less trouble in this area because it recognizes two sources of authority, the

---

[10] Wolfhart Pannenberg, *Basic Questions in Theology* (London: SCM Press, 1970). In this essay, Pannenberg analyzes the cultural and theological context in which this principle was developed, and the problems it began to face in the light of the application of modern critical-historical methods to the Bible.

Bible and tradition. And both depend, in one way or another, on the final arbitration of the church's teaching. For Protestants, interpretation is more difficult, for various reasons. First of all, because they do not accept—at least in theory—tradition as a source of authority. Secondly, because they do not recognize any single body of teaching which could from time to time resolve certain questions. And, more recently because, in a determined way, certain hierarchies have set themselves up as supreme authorities, in the form of self-appointed leaders claiming to be the sole arbiters and repositories of divine truth. Luther's critique of the Catholic position and his option for the collective exercise of authority are germane:

> Word and human doctrine arranged and determined that decisions about doctrine should be delegated exclusively to bishops, scholars and councils. . . . The power and the right to judge what is Christian and what is heretical resides with them. . . . Whereas Christ decrees the very opposite, and takes from the bishops, scholars and councils both things, both the right and the power to judge on matters of doctrine, and gives them to everybody, to Christians in general.[11]

This view proved revolutionary whenever it led to a fundamental change in ministry, vocation, and profession. Luther was urging that final authority be removed from the hierarchies of the church, in order to "democratize" that authority and distribute it throughout the church as community (*Gemeinde*). Karl Barth's

---

[11] Martin Luther, "Foundations and Motivations" quoted by Martin Volkmann, "Teologia Prática e o Ministerio da Igreja" (Practical Theology and the Ministry of the Church), in Christoph Schneider-Harpprecht (org.), *Teologia Prática no Contexto de América Latina* (São Leopoldo: Sinodal-Aste, 1980), pp. 89-90. Only the Portuguese available to the author.

keen perception is that this is in keeping with the very essence of the church. He says: "The concept of Church is the concept of a *dynamic* reality."[12] He goes on to add: "The existence of the Church is the event in which that unique human 'one another' is possible and takes on reality."[13] So, in light of these guiding principles, we must understand that, beyond the necessary and important elements of organization and institution, the church is—above all things—a community, a dynamic reality, and an event, something that *happens*. And it happens, precisely, whenever authority resides in the community, and not in hierarchies that claim to have the last word or to be the final arbiter of what should be believed and practiced. These are "interpolations of human pride and authority (that) can only get in the way, and never enhance, the free flow of the word and the Spirit of God."[14] Because, as the church is first and foremost an event, the Word of God, beyond its "materialness" in the Bible, it is an event which, as Paul Tillich notes, "depends not only on the preacher, nor only on the hearer, but on both together." [15]

A careful look at the ecclesiastical vocabulary of evangelicals in Latin America—especially of some that consider themselves part of what are called "neopentecostalism" and "renewal

---

[12] Karl Barth, "La Iglesia: Comunidad Viva de Jesucristo, el Señor que Vive" (The Church: Living Community of Jesus Christ, the Living Lord"), in *Ensayos teológicos* (Theological Essays) (Barcelona: Herder, 1978), p. 192. Only the Spanish translation available to the author.

[13] *Ibid.*, p. 193.

[14] *Ibid.*, p. 206.

[15] Paul Tillich, *Teología sistemática* (Systematic Theology) (Barcelona: Libros de Nopal-Ariel, Vol. 1, 1972), p. 203. Only the Spanish translation available to the author.

movements"—reveals how they have tended toward authoritarian practices that cannot be glossed over or ignored. There are some extreme examples in which the word of the pastor is equated with the word of God. Despite the fact that "infallibility" is a Catholic dogma reserved for the bishop of Rome in his role as head of the church, in practice some evangelical churches apply it to their current ecclesiastical leaders, who claim the title of "Bishop" or even "Apostle" for themselves, with all the connotations that those titles convey.[16] In his systematic ecclesiology, Moltmann has pointed out in a powerful way how the social environment of the church exerts a marked influence on the way it exercises authority. He says:

> Every human community corresponds to its environment and reflects it. The church is no exception. In its concrete form it corresponds to its social environment and reflects the conditions which govern the society in which it lives. Most of these are not in dispute but are considered "self-evident." Most people find them self-evident because, as they say, "there is no other way of doing things."[17]

The problem is serious and raises questions beyond what kind of church government exists in any given protestant church or denomination, because authoritarianism can infiltrate into every form of ecclesiastical governance, whether it is "episcopal government," "representative government," or even "congrega-

---

[16] For a critical analysis of the subject, I would direct the reader to my book, *Para qué sirve la teología? Una respuesta crítica con horizonte abierto* (What is Theology For? A Critical Response with Open Horizons) (Buenos Aires: FIET, 1999), pp. 181-197.

[17] Jürgen Moltmann, *The Church in the Power of the Spirit. A Contribution to Messianic Ecclesiology* (London: SCM Press, 1977), p. 105.

tional government." It is a question, in the end, of avoiding hierarchies, authorities without limits, which by their nature have no point of reference other than themselves. It is necessary, then, not only to warn about these dangers, but also to provide church life that involves the practice of community in which authority is expressed in terms of love and service in practical ways, not in terms of tyrannies that have so often marked he character of government in Latin America.[18]

The exercise of gifts and ministries and, in the end, the way the mission of the church takes shape, all depend on how authority is exercised in the church. For this reason the topic has been given priority. Now we turn to other related themes.

3. Universal Priesthood and the Gifts of the Spirit

The universal priesthood of all believers should be reflected not only in the exercise of authority, but also in the exercise of the different gifts of the Holy Spirit. The key passages in the New

---

[18] In this respect, we would mention the work of the Argentine historian José Ignacio Garcia Hamilton, *Los orígenes de nuestra cultura autoritaria (e improductiva)* (Buenos Aires: Albino y acociados, eds., 1991), which analyses the difference between Catholic and protestant influences on the ways of working out democratic and republican values. The author looks at the protestant *ethos,* which favored the countries where it had influence and where, typically, the democratic processes were more current than in the countries influenced by Catholicism. The North American researcher Nicolás Shumway made the same point, in introducing the second edition of his book *La invención de la Argentina* (Buenos Aires: Emecé, 2002). Introductory lecture, Universidad de Palermo, Buenos Aires, May 6, 2002.

Testament that address the subject are Romans 12, 1 Corinthians 12, and Ephesians 4:11-12.[19] The focus moves between pairs of opposites such as natural gifts and supernatural gifts, temporary gifts and permanent gifts, and gifts of speech and gifts of action. The important thing to realize is that there will be neither ministry nor mission without an explicit recognition and integrated employment of these gifts. The gifts of the Spirit make possible the life and the mission of the church. The gifts are skills bestowed by God, the "equipping of the saints" to bring ministry into being and build up the body of Christ and its service in the world. John Driver says:

> The church will be truly the body of Christ to the extent that all the gifts of the Spirit are recognized and exercised in the community. The plurality (whereby more than one person can exercise a single gift), and the universality (whereby every member has a gift or gifts to use) are part of the very essence of the church.[20]

It is more or less universally agreed that, of all the metaphors used in the New Testament to describe the church, there is none richer or more apposite than that of the body of Christ. As Smedes says: "Paul could not have found any more important words than these to convey that our union with Christ is to be found in community, and in no other way. Union with Christ is a corporate reality."[21] Speaking of the "body of Christ" means

---

[19] To these Pauline texts we could add 1Pet 4:10-11.

[20] Juan Driver, *Comunidad y compromiso* (Community and Commitment) (Buenos Aires: Ediciones Certeza, 1974), p. 30. Only the Spanish version available to the author.

[21] Lewis B. Smedes, *Todas las cosas nuevas* (All Things New) (Buenos Aires: La Aurora, 1972), p. 197. John A.T.Robinson accorded so much

that we are talking about Christ himself and the community founded in his person. This is represented visually in the Eucharist or the Lord's Supper. Paul says that when we eat the bread we have communion with the body of Christ. The bread symbolizes the very body of the Lord, while, at the same time, (like a sort of play on the word *soma)*, it also signifies the oneness of the church as a body, which is expressed in the one bread. Paul says, "Because there is one bread, we who are many are one body, for we all partake of the one bread" (1Co 10:17). The idea of the church as the one and only body of Christ leads us to consider it as the means whereby Christ—now in glory—reveals himself in the world, without, however, implying that the church is some kind of "extension of Christ." The Son of God remains active in the Father's world through the action of the Spirit, but for that very reason the church, constituted in Christ as a body, furnishes the means whereby Christ continues to do his work on earth. Therefore the church has to take seriously its communal essence, its corporal nature, and work with a common mind in service to society and to the world. It is in the employment of the gifts of the Spirit that the multi-faceted wisdom and grace of God find expression.[22] Only the recognition of the rich diversity of spiritual gifts in every Christian and in all the members of the body will make it possible to carry out integral mission in service to the world. To this end love and freedom are also fundamental. It is love that makes it possible to accept brothers and sisters in

---

importance to "body" as representing Pauline theology that he entitled his book on the subject *The Body* (London: SCM Press, 1952).

[22] It is interesting to note the echoes and nuances between the texts of 1Pet 4:10 and Ephesians 3:10. The Greek word is *poikilos* ("varied," "colored," "marbled") which is then intensified in Ephesians to *polupoikilos* ("multivariegated," or "multimarbled").

the church as different and necessary. Love prevents the growth of hierarchies which accord special importance to one ministry over and against another. There is no "essential difference between the various spiritual gifts and their functions. The widow, doing works of mercy, is working just as charismatically as the 'bishop'."[23] On the other hand freedom makes it possible to create an ambience in which it is possible for people to express themselves in accordance with the gifts they have, whether of speech or action. Both spheres of ministry need a variety of ways of expression. All people are necessary to one another and must help in the growth of the body of Christ, to the end that it accomplish the mission that God has entrusted to it. Those in positions of pastoral leadership have a responsibility to create space for the exercise of all the spiritual gifts. It is in the community of faith in Jesus Christ, where the Spirit operates and consequently there is freedom, that the gifts of the Spirit take shape and their development should be encouraged. Conversely, where freedom is not allowed, where spontaneity is stifled, where creativity is not encouraged, the church body is likely to fall into spiritual paralysis and loss of vision. Peter's words describe this type of church, when he describes the Christian who has amnesia and myopia: ". . . nearsighted and blind, and. . . forgetful of the cleansing of past sins" (2Pe 1:9).

The way of love and freedom is not easy. If it were, it would not be necessary to talk so much about these values. We talk a great deal about love, but are far from putting it into practice. Freedom, however, we often do not even discuss as a virtue in church leadership circles. In fact, the *ethos* of evangelicals has been characterized for decades by a set of micro-ethics pointing

---

[23] Moltmann, *op. cit.*, p. 298.

out "what one should not do." So it is not uncommon for a new member joining a church to be given, explicitly or implicitly, in words or in writing, a set of rules that, in many cases, have nothing to do with the essence of the gospel of Jesus Christ. In these ways, we are slipping into a new kind of pharisaism, condemned in the Bible and by Jesus himself.

As for the lack of freedom in the exercise of spiritual gifts, churches often have a thousand rationalizations that take the form of explanations for why they should not be allowed: "We don't have that kind of ministry here." "The brother who would like to exercise this ministry is not mature enough yet." "What you want to do just isn't needed in our church." Sometimes these reasons are valid; these comments are not intended to create some kind of ecclesiastical anarchy. Freedom, however, is always risky, and sometimes we are unwilling to take risks. That leaves us with nothing but the way of authoritarianism and the restriction of freedom. Moltmann relates these two virtues, which are fundamental to the fulfilment of the ministry and mission of the church, in the following way: "The strength of unity is *love.* The strength of diversity is *freedom*. The communion of the Spirit is the space in which we can awaken and grow the myriad gifts of the Spirit."[24] So the question now is, what is the relationship between spiritual gifts, universal priesthood, and integral mission?

[24] J. Moltmann, *O Espírito de vida. Uma pneumatologia integral* (The Spirit of Life. An Integrated Pneumatology) (Petrópolis: Vozes, 1999), p. 186. Only Portuguese available to the author.

4. Universal Priesthood and Integral Mission

To speak of the church is to speak of mission and viceversa. Such is the inextricable relation between the two that, as Emil Brunner has indicated in his remarkable simile, "the Church exists for mission as fire exists for burning."[25] The mission of the church can only be understood in light of the Kingdom of God and the ministry of Jesus of Nazareth. But we must avoid falling into an "ecclesiocentrism" that might lead us, in a sort of synecdoche, to confuse the part with the whole, overstating the parameters of the church at the expense of the Kingdom. As Pannenberg lays out clearly, "The doctrine of the church begins, not with the church, but with the Kingdom of God."[26] Apart from its relationship to the Kingdom of God, the church practically has no real raison d'être, because it is not an end in itself. When the church becomes an end in itself, it quickly encloses itself in its own narrow limits and abandons the mission of the Kingdom for which it was given existence in Jesus Christ. In a clear and categorical fashion René Padilla states: "The mission of the church can be understood only in light of the Kingdom of God."[27] The dangers of "ecclesiocentrism" are not easily recognized. We could even say that it is only in recent decades

---

[25] Cited by C. René Padilla, *Mission Between the Times: Essays on the Kingdom* (Grand Rapids: William B. Eerdmans Publishing Company, 1985), p. 129.

[26] Wolfhart Pannenberg, *Teología y Reino de Dios* (Salamanca: Sígueme, 1974), p. 49. Only the Spanish translation available to the author.

[27] C. René Padilla, *op. cit.*, p.180.

that the danger has been recognized at all. Perhaps the images that Howard Snyder uses in his book *The Community of the King* can help us to understand the correlation between the Kingdom and the Church. Commenting on some Pauline passages on reconciliation, such as 2 Corinthians 5:17-21 and Romans 8:21, Snyder says:

> The redemption of persons is the center of God's plan, but it is not the *circumference* of that plan. Paul switches from a close-up shot to a long-distance view. He uses a zoom lens, for the most part taking a close-up of personal redemption, but periodically zooming to a long-distance, wide-angle view which takes in "all things"—things visible and invisible; things past, present and future; things in heaven and things on earth; all the principalities and powers—in the cosmic-historical scene.[28]

More exactly, the cosmic view which derives from the Pauline vision of a *cosmos* reconciled in Christ is a reference to the consummation of the Kingdom of God, which, because it is integral by nature, includes the whole created order which is suffering until now the effects of its corruption and waiting for its final redemption. As the same author points out, "Evangelicalism today needs a Kingdom consciousness—an awareness of the Kingdom of God—similar to that of earlier American Protestantism, but one with more biblically based."[29] When we lose the vision of God's cosmic plan, we separate the creator God from the redeemer God and fall into dichotomies such as church *versus* world, soul *versus* spirit, present *versus* future, evangelism *versus* social action and so on. The biblical paradigm which

---

[28] Howard A. Snyder (Downers Grove: Inter-Varsity Press, 1977), p. 48.

[29] *Ibid.*, p. 29.

enables us to overcome the dichotomies and bring together the plan of the one God—who is both Creator and Savior—is, precisely, the Kingdom of God. When we lose sight of the Kingdom, the church loses the frame of reference and the eschatological *telos* of God revealed in Jesus Christ. This loss of perspective has brought out ideas and movements which, despite the best of intentions, do not measure up to the breadth of God's purpose for his creation. Expressions such as "salvation of souls" and "church growth" are examples of this kind of reductionism. This is not to say that church growth is of no interest. We should be interested in the growth of the church: not in the growth of the church *per se*, but rather in the proclamation and extension of the Kingdom of God through the mission that the church carries out. Put another way, it is one thing to talk about growth as a *goal* in itself; it is something else to speak of growth as a *consequence.* "Ecclesiocentrism" has conspired against the fulfilment of the mission. J. C. Hoekendijk has criticized:

> The ecclesiocentric conception which, since Jerusalem 1928 seems to have been the only dogma hardly disputed on the theory of mission, has tied us so firmly, has entangled us in such a dense web, that we scarcely can realize the extent to which our thought has been "ecclesified."[30]

The only way to overcome "ecclesiocentrism" is to recover the theology of the Kingdom, which is simply to recover the message and the *praxis* of Jesus of Nazareth. The "ultimate" for Jesus was not simply "God," nor the church, nor even himself. As Jon

---

[30] J. C. Hoekendijk, in *Evangelische Missions Zeitschrift.* January, 1952, p. 9, quoted by José Míguez-Bonino in *Faces of Latin American Protestantism* (Grand Rapids: William B. Eerdmans Publishing Company, 1997), pp. 136-137.

Sobrino has pointed out, *"the ultimate for Jesus is the Kingdom of God."*[31] He goes on to explain: "What I am affirming is that the ultimate for Jesus is God in relationship to human history, understood as kingdom. . . ."[32] How does the church fit into this perspective? It is there as part of a project which reaches beyond itself—the project that God has for history and which has already been anticipated in the life and mission of Jesus—which is none other than the promise of the Kingdom of God and his justice in every order of life and existence.

When we speak of the Kingdom, we have to make it plain that we are speaking precisely of the Kingdom *of God.* Human beings cannot produce it—regardless of our good intentions and good will—in the way that theologians like Albrecht Ritschl proposed in his day. He maintained that the Kingdom of God was the society that people were creating through the inspiration of love. Our position is very different. We must emphasize, with Sobrino, that "the Kingdom of God can not be established by people. It will not come about through the planning of goals for the future. It is vitally important that it remains the kingdom *of God,* whose path through history has come to be understood in the majority of instances through the downfall of human pride."[33] In addition to demolishing human pride beyond the frontiers of the church, it is also possible that the Kingdom of God may need to demolish the pride of Christians as well. There is always a tendency—very typical of human nature, or if we prefer Stanley Jones's neologism "human antinature"—that draws us, if we are not

---

[31] Jon Sobrino, *Jesús en América Latina* (Santander: Sal Terrae, 1982), p. 135.

[32] *Ibid.*, p. 134.

[33] *Ibid.*, p. 56, original italics.

careful, into feelings of pride: "We are the church of Jesus Christ; this makes us superior to unbelievers and to the world in general." Every tendency to identify the church with the Kingdom, as well as signaling a theological derailment, leads almost inevitably to pride and self sufficiency. To this end, and even though it might appear exaggerated to us, it is good to remember once again, with Pannenberg, the transitory nature of the church: "The church is necessary so long as the social and political life of man does not provide the ultimate human fulfilment that the Kingdom of God is to bring in human history."[34] The Kingdom of God is eternal even though it is manifested in history. The church, on the other hand, is an historical entity formed around Jesus of Nazareth to proclaim and embody the values of the Kingdom of God: fundamentally love, peace, and justice. Thus, we could say that the church has no mission other than the *missio Dei* that is expressed paradigmatically in Jesus, the Christ. Along with the essential link between the church and the Kingdom, we have to establish the link between the church and the life and work of Jesus of Nazareth. As we affirmed in a conference in Brazil:

> It is impossible to define mission without making reference to the kingdom. The church has a mission, and that mission has its objective, its paradigm, its model, in the Kingdom of God. It is in the light of the Kingdom as God's utopia that the church can function in the world and carry out the mission which God has granted it.[35]

---

[34] Pannenberg, *Teología y Reino de Dios*, p. 49.

[35] Alberto F. Roldán, *Missão, Unidade e Identidade da Igreja,* Regional Reflection Process for the Fourth General Assembly of CLAI (Latin American Council of Churches), Quito, 2000, p. 85. This document draws

The historical pattern for the mission that the church has to undertake has been given to us, once and for all, in the person and life of Jesus of Nazareth. We could summarize this by saying that the mission of the church is defined by the Kingdom of God and given exemplary reality in the life of Jesus of Nazareth. Mission cannot be limited to the transmission of a message, but must also include concrete action. Passages such as Matthew 10:7-8 and Luke 4:16-19 demonstrate clearly that both Jesus and his disciples preached the gospel of the Kingdom, healed, liberated, and showed compassion for the poor, marginalized, and rejected. "Just as Jesus proclaimed the *kingdom of God* to the poor and the *power of God* to the sick, he also brought the *righteousness of God* to the 'tax-collectors and sinners,' that is, the righteousness of grace."[36]

When the church limits its mission to the speaking of the gospel, it diminishes the mission to which it was called in Jesus Christ, which is nothing less than mercy, compassion, solidarity, activity, liberation, and the restoration of people, families, and society. Just as there are no limits to God's care for his creation, so there should no limits to the mission the church carries out in God's world.

When we apply this to the context of our Latin American societies it means that the churches have to be sensitive to the serious problems that beset individuals, married couples, families in their different conditions, the unemployed, the excluded, single mothers, abandoned children, and others. We live in a society

---

together the contributions made to the Consultation held in Londrina, Brazil.

[36] Jürgen Moltmann, *O Caminho de Jesús Cristo* (Petrópolis: Vozes, 1993), p. 159. Only the Portuguese translation available to the author.

built on the foundation of insensitive individualism and a market economy that daily offers human sacrifices on its altar. Faced with this, the Lord's church finds itself with an enormous responsibility. It is not the responsibility to enter the political arena; that is not the church's task. But it is the churches' task to be responsive to human needs, including the provision of assistance, in an integrated way, from the resources that congregations have in their membership, and to train their people to engage in the concrete provision of help, nourishment, education, and solidarity. We need to understand that activities like these are not some kind of appendix to the mission of the church, to be done because the government fails to do them. They have to be done because they are part of that integral mission given to the church as the community of the Kingdom of God. It is precisely to this end that the church is endowed and energized by the Holy Spirit. As Moltmann says, "The charismatic community is a *unity in diversity* and a *diversity in unity*. Each one as the Lord calls them, each one as the Lord endows them."[37] The variety of gifts has been created by the same Holy Spirit, simply to equip every Christian to perform a particular function in response to the diversity of real human needs. These mission activities poured into society become, in the metaphor of René Padilla, "'bridges' over which the Kingdom of God penetrates into the life of the people and gives them new meaning."[38]

It follows naturally that the church can only respond to the challenge of integral mission when it exercises the priesthood of

---

[37] Jürgen Moltmann, *O Espírito de Vida,* p. 185. Only the Portuguese translation available to the author.

[38] By e-mail, Buenos Aires, July 18, 2002.

all its members. For integral mission that includes—among other ministries—evangelism, baptism, teaching, counseling, liberation, restoration, compassion, and social action, there is no other way but by mobilizing all its members. It is time to move beyond those "pastorcentric" models in which the whole ministry of the church rests in the hands of one or two people, while the others are "stone guests." It is also time to move beyond hierarchies of ministry, as though being a pastor were superior to showing compassion for the needy or providing food for the hungry. At this point, the maxim of Barth which serves as an epigraph for this essay takes on obvious relevance, since in the church there cannot be "ecclesiastics" and "secular" (lay) people, "because no member of the church exists who is not all of that in their own right."[39]

A final question arises from the present world-church context, and, in our case in Latin America, from the modern movement of "churches with cells" and "cellular churches,"[40] which in a way

---

[39] Karl Barth, *Ensayos teológicos* (Essays in Theology), p. 209. Only the Spanish translation available to the author. Leonardo Boff makes the same point in his possibly most critical work on the Roman hierarchy. He says: "Being *discens* and *docens* is something that derives from the exercise of two functions in one and the same church, not as two fractions of the church or in the church," in *Iglesia: carisma y poder. Ensayos de eclesiología militante* (Church: Carisma and Power. Essays in Militant Ecclesiology) (Santander: Sal Terrae, 1982), p. 221. Only the Spanish translation available to the author.

[40] The distinction is that "churches with cells" are churches which have, in addition to their normal program, cells which meet weekly for the purpose of communion and testimony, while "cellular churches" are congregations which work only in cells. We should add that in addition to the word "cells"—an appropriate metaphor when speaking of the body of Christ, which grows and multiplies—there are other expressions such as

is a reworking of models already tried in the past, like the *colleges of piety*[41] and the "Methodist classes."[42] The question is whether these models provide a suitable instrument for putting the universal priesthood of all believers into practice.

Following the example of the primitive church, today's cells and house groups are seeking to mobilize all the members of the

---

"florets" or "arks," etc. On the ministry of cellular churches see the works of Ralph W. Neighbour, *El manual de siervo* (The Social Service Manual) (Houston: Touch Outreach Ministries, 1989) and William A. Beckham, *The Second Reformation, Remaking the Church for the Twenty-First Century* (Houston: Touch Publications).

[41] The *Collegia Pietatis* grew and developed in seventeenth-century German pietism. On this subject , Christina Bucher discusses the ideas of Jacob Spener, author of the influential work *Pia Disideria*: "Even though Spener maintained that the clergy were responsible for public worship, he held that the laity could minister to each other in Bible study groups, where they offered one another support, welfare and instruction." ("People of the Covenant Small Groups Bible Study: A Twentieth Century Revival of the Collegia Pietatis," in *Brethren Life and Thought*, 1998, p. 49, quoted by Daniel Bruno, "*Ecclesiola in Ecclesia:* Criticism and Renewal of the Church. Seventeenth Century Pietism and Base Communities," in *Cuadernos de Teología* (Buenos Aires: ISEDET, Vol. XX, 2001), p. 323.

[42] Methodism used various names like "societies," "bands" and "classes." Quoting J. S. Simon, Bruno notes that Wesley borrowed some arrangements from the Moravians in the organization of his early meetings. The faithful "met weekly to 'confess their faults to each other,' to pray for each other to be healed" (*ibid.*, p. 328). Emilio Monti says: "Each class is formed of twelve persons and conducted by a leader. People are assigned to a class by virtue of where they live, in order to further relations between them. They meet at least once a week. According to Wesley himself, 'all who seek the power of holiness' are invited to participate in these communities. That is 'all who fear God and wish to be saved from their sins'." "Llamó Jesús a Doce" (Jesus Called Twelve). Unpublished article, Buenos Aires, 2002, p. 3, kindly provided by the author.

body of Christ to testify to the love of God, to spread the Word in a spontaneous way—through contacts and friendships—and to live out a zealous and visible *koinonia*. Those of us who have pastoral experience in this mode of ministry can testify that the members of a cell do develop greater levels of friendship and care for each other. The weekly meeting provides occasion for sharing thanks and praise for blessings received, matters for prayer, and study of the Word of God, with everybody working together to find practical, concrete application for people's lives. Members all feel part of the body and support each other spiritually. In many cases, because of the explosive growth of some churches, the cells prove to be the only way of providing pastoral care for the whole congregation, as members of Christ's body are encouraged to participate more profoundly in the life of the church, beyond attending Sunday worship and joining in various church activities.

However, we still need to be clear that this form of church life does not guarantee the application of the universal priesthood of all believers, nor do cells ensure the practice of integral mission. We have always to take into account the cultural and social environment in which various programs have developed and recognize that they cannot always be simply transplanted into other contexts. Put another way, "cells" and "florets" and "arks" will not automatically and magically turn the local church into a community where universal priesthood is exercised and the church is dedicated to the practice of integral mission. It all depends on the motivation with which the project was set up, and also on the theological understanding on the part of the pastors and leaders who are directing it. If these people see the mission of the church only in terms of the total numbers of those making "decisions of faith" and "accepting Jesus as their personal Savior" without implications for the society and culture in which the church is located, it is doubtful that the church is living out the universal priesthood of believers in the practice of integrated mission. To sum up, the model of churches in cells can be suitable for the effective implementation of the universal priesthood of all believers in integral mission, with two conditions: first, an awareness on the part of all the members with regard to the different elements implicit in integral mission; and second, enough free space for all believers to develop the abundant variety of the gifts of the Spirit for the well-being of the whole body of Christ.

Conclusions

An integral church for integral mission is one that uses authority, not in terms of hierarchy, superiority, or control, but rather in terms of service, following the example of Jesus of Nazareth. We are referring to a church that lives out freedom in love and uses all the gifts of the Spirit in the appropriate spheres of ministry; a church that pours itself out for the world, in recognition that its mission is none other than to love the world as God loved the world in Jesus Christ; a church that values all the gifts of the Spirit that enable the members of the body to cultivate a mission that has both diversity and wholeness; a church whose goal is not to proclaim itself but rather the proclamation of the Kingdom of God and his justice in every area of life—spiritual, personal, family, social and political. However, for all this to happen the church must give priority to making the practice of the universal priesthood of all believers a reality. In concrete terms, that means creating space for ministerial and missionary freedom in love, in order to respond to the needs of the people that the church is called to serve. It is essential that the church be, above all, a community of love and service, faithfully and courageously following Jesus of Nazareth and his liberating, redemptive *praxis*. Only when it is a community that lives in the freedom that love brings will the church be able to become what Jesus called, in his expressive metaphors, salt of the earth and light of the world. In order to avoid seeking easy solutions or becoming autocratic, we need to remember that becoming a community of service to the world is not something that comes by spontaneous generation, since "a community does not become such until all its members share in a sense of the urgency of its mission."[43] May the Holy Spirit, Maker and Giver of life, engender in us that sense of urgency!

[43] Jean Vanier, *La comunidad. Lugar del perdón y de la fiesta* (Community. Locus of Pardon and Celebration) 2nd Edition (Madrid: PPC, 1998), p. 100. English version: *Community and Growth* (London: Darton, Longman and Todd, 1979).

6

Integral Mission in the Framework of Grace, World, and Church

Pedro Arana-Quiroz

It is my conviction that if something does not happen in the local church, it does not happen anywhere. The purpose of this essay is to share a few reflections on the integral mission of the church, as I have experienced them in the local congregation. It is the local church that is challenged to cooperate to bring about a more holistic, more determined, more effective, and more biblical missionary effort.

In the first place, I will present briefly both the context of the rediscovery of integral mission in recent decades and also my own process of personal discovery. Then, I will formulate the question of integral mission in three "moments" that are theological in tone, emphasizing the ecclesiology of integral mission. Essentially it is my conviction that integral mission springs from the very *grace* of God, it challenges us to get involved in our own *world* understood as a particular "theological situation," and it requires an integral *ecclesiology*, with a trinitarian basis, in which the community of faith experiences the tension of being called out as it is also being sent out, consequently recognizing the need to embody creatively those images and tasks of the church that are to be found in scripture.

1. The Rediscovery of Integral Mission

Since the 1950's, the life and mission of the church have been obligatory themes in international church gatherings. During the last three decades, missiology—the science of mission—has enjoyed a great boom in Protestant and evangelical circles. The curricula of a large percentage of Christian seminaries in six continents confirm this. The impact that organizations with missiological goals have had and still have in the world is remarkable. And, since Vatican II, missiology has found its place in the Roman Catholic Church too.

The Christian church has often had to remind itself of the terms of its existence; that mission is the real essence of its nature and identity; that "the Church exists for mission as fire exists for burning,"[1] and that "the church exists insofar as it is living its mission."[2] It does not exist as an end in itself, and it does not exist if it is not living its mission. As it recalled that fact, a painful controversy about the nature of the church's mission has became more acute, especially during the second half of the last century.

---

[1] Emil Brunner, quoted by Martin Conway in *The Undivided Vision* (London: SCM Press, 1966), p. 65.

[2] Karl Barth, "El mensaje de la libre gracia de Dios" (The Message of the Free Grace of God), in *Ensayos teológicos* (Theological Essays) (Barcelona: Herder, 1978), p.158. Only the Spanish translation available to the author.

Gradually, the church has been overcoming the misunderstandings that were prevalent in the 1970s. When faced with the question "What is the mission of church?", the more conservative evangelical confessions would reply, "Evangelism! To do mission is to evangelize, only evangelize, and nothing but evangelize!" Other more liberal churches replied, "Social service! Mission is social service!" Some progressive groups within the Roman Catholic and Protestant Churches replied, "Liberation! Mission is setting free." Consequently, they set about mobilizing their parishes for political action. Still other Christian groups recognized the power of worship, and that became the focus of the life and mission of the church. "Mission is worship!" They repeated (and still repeat), "The letter kills but the Spirit brings life!" And so the Bible is neither read nor expounded during worship. Personal testimonies to the power of God in the lives of believers abound—something very significant and valuable to hear—but in this context testimonies that usurp the place of the Word. More recently, for some Christian communities, the church's mission consists of promoting prosperity among the membership: "Mission is to prosper materially!"

We believe that in each of these conceptions of the mission of the church there are elements of truth, but this reductionism does not do justice to "the whole counsel of God" contained in the biblical revelation. During the last twenty years, however, we have seen how evangelical leaders and believers in general have been opening up to a more biblical (and therefore more comprehensive) understanding of the church's mission, which many sectors of the world church have christened "*integral mission.*" This more comprehensive understanding has born generous fruit through the presence and involvement of Christians in Latin America and other parts of the world, who have mobilized themselves in the great mission field of human need—spiritual and emotional, physical and material—among our neighbors in the subcontinent and in the world.

2. A Personal Discovery of Integral Mission

I committed myself to the integral mission of the church during my time as a student, thanks to the intellectual and practical guidance of my teachers James Mackintosh, Sam Will and Donald Mitchell. The first of these brought me to understand the value of human beings, loved by God, who have no business card to introduce themselves other than their needful humanity. Out of the blue one time I came across a man from the Peruvian jungle, wrapped in dirty rags and evil smelling, victim apparently of intestinal cancer. And there I was, a student with no money and no idea of what to do. Back in the classroom that day, my face betrayed something of my problem, and so Mr. Mackintosh asked me what had happened. I told him the story. Without a second thought, he said: "Bring him to my house." Also without thinking I replied, "He is infectious and smelly." His surprising, kind, yet firm response was, "Pedro, he is a human being!" And straight away, he took care of him in his home.

Sam Will was the first to take our youth group, called "Onward Christian Youth," to visit the nascent "shanty towns" that were beginning to encircle the city of Lima: "El Agustino," "San Cosme," "El Ermitaño." In these places we began to get to know poor people. Their poverty was not the result of laziness, but because a centralist political structure prevented them from making a living in their places of origin, and because a covetous and usurious oligarchy manipulated the nation's politics and economics.

Donald Mitchell, a New Zealander, was the first to put a Bible commentary in my hands: *Epistle to the Romans,* by Clifton J. Allen. I still keep the copy. The book was part of a unified course of study for all members of the Baptist church. But he was Presbyterian. With him, we enjoyed holiday camps by the Pacific on the beaches of Mala, expounding the Word and making friends. In 1957, recognizing my interest in reading, Mitchell opened an account for me in the evangelical bookstore "El Inca," so that I could buy books worth up to a hundred *soles* a month. When I asked him, "Donald, how am I ever going to repay your generosity?", he replied, "Once you have a job, do the same for some other student."

The value of the human person, the church, the poor, understanding the situation in the country, having a positive attitude toward other denominations, the rightful enjoyment of life, leadership training, and the practice of generosity were the first components that accompanied my understanding of the integral mission of the church. I am thankful to the people who lived in grace and for grace, and shared their lives and gifts of grace with me.

During my time in university, the theory and practice of integral mission were instilled in me through the books by Juan A. Mackay and Martin Luther King, and later found expression in the evangelistic Bible study group of which I was a member and in my participation as student delegate on the Council of the Faculty of Chemistry in the University of San Marcos. Later on, serving on the staff of the International Fellowship of Evangelical Students, I agreed with Samuel Escobar and René Padilla that our training courses for Christian student leaders for Latin

American universities should emphasize the Latin American situation, combined with Bible study, theological reflection, and methodology of practical action. We recognized the context of our mission to be of primary importance.

Later, as a lay elder in my congregation, and as a citizen, I was elected to the Constituent Assembly of Peru 1978-1979. It was then that I was able to incorporate into my Christian witness the challenges of political involvement and the church's prophetic function. Still later I served as pastor in a Presbyterian congregation that joined evangelism and discipleship with practical service among our sisters and brothers of the marginal community "Luis Pardo." In 1983, a group of us organized the "*Paz y Esperanza*" (Peace and Hope) Commission under the auspices of the National Evangelical Council of Peru (CONEP), for the purpose of helping the victims of the terrorist violence initiated by the *Sendero Luminoso* (Shining Path) guerrilla movement.

In 1987, with another group of Christians, largely Presbyterians, we set up the *Misión Integral Urbano-Rural* (MISIUR) to assist poor families and communities with both spiritual and material nourishment. Shortly after that, in that same context, the *Instituto Cristiano de Estudios Sociales "Juan A. Mackay"* (ICES) (Christian Institute for Social Studies) came into being. Its goal was to see, feel, and join in the realities of Peruvian life with the light of God. For six years, the Institute has taught the course, "Christian Worldview and Peruvian Reality," in two theological seminaries in the city of Lima. In 1991, we began the first integral projects of the Peruvian Bible Society, which were later adopted by the United Bible Societies in their General Assembly held in South Africa in 2001, as part of their world ministry.

3. Grace & Mission

My proposition, which is fundamental from biblical, theological, and missiological perspectives, is this: *The mission of the Church is to testify, in the world, to the God of grace and to the grace of God.*

The hymn with which the Holy Scripture begins is the confession of the faithful about this eternal free and living Being, whom they call God, and who takes the portentous initiative of making his sovereign power and bounty known, who creates out of nothing all that exists, and from chaos produces the cosmos (Gen 1). Creation, in all its manifestations and dimensions, is the work of the God of grace. All spiritual and material reality, the whole universe known and unknown, the macro and the micro, the world and all that lives in it, especially human beings, are the work of the God of grace, and the expression of the grace of God.

The author of these mighty works, to which the same Holy Scripture bears direct, authentic, and complete testimony, is he who in his sovereign freedom chooses "Abraham and no other, Isaac and not Ishmael, Jacob and not Esau, David and not Saul,"[3] to be, in his incomparable grace, the God of all Israel. Fulfilling his promise and covenant with Abraham, God breaks down, in Jesus Christ, the wall of separation between Jews and non-Jews and offers his blessing on all nations. He is good and almighty; he acted in the *exodus* (departure) and in the *eisodos* (entry); in the virgin birth of Jesus, in his life and miracles, in his vicarious death and his glorious resurrection; in his visible

---

[3] *Ibid.*, p. 146.

ascension and in the celebration of the birthday of the Church at Pentecost. He is the God of grace. And salvation history is no more or less than the eloquent landmarks of his grace.

The God of grace is the one, living, free, and sovereign God who spoke to the prophets and apostles, and through them, gave his message to the Church, the gospel, of which the Church itself is part. The joyful news is that, in Jesus of Nazareth, the Uncreated "lived among us. And we beheld his glory, glory as of the only begotten of the Father, full of grace and truth" (John 1:14). Not only did he live with sinners, he saved them. He charges the Church with the task of inviting the world to receive "the abundance of grace and the gift of justice" (Rom. 5:17). He is the God whose purpose, plan, and design—that is to say, *mission*—is "to unite all things in him (in Christ)" (Eph. 1:10). The supreme and final accomplishment of this mission is the establishment of the Kingdom of God, when humanity and the entire creation fulfil their essential nature and the purpose of their existence, and share in the glory of the One whose glory we have already begun to see in Jesus Christ. From eternity and unto eternity, including this parenthesis that is human history, we have the awesome unfolding of grace, called Emmanuel: "God with us."

Seen in this way, both the world and the Church originate in the grace of God and are constantly the objects of that grace: "God so loved the world, that he gave his only Son"(Jn 3:16); "Christ loved the Church and gave himself for her" (Eph 5:25). The Church is the handiwork of the God of grace, and its members administer "God's grace in its various forms" (1Pet 4:10, NIV). It is grace that establishes the essential difference between the world and the Church, in the act of mission. *The*

God of grace has given to the Church the mission of testifying to his grace in his world.

4. Living the World as a "Theological Situation"

Today's world comes to meet us in terms of a particular "theological situation." Paraphrasing the title of José Míguez-Bonino's book *Doing Theology in a Revolutionary Situation,*[4] what we need today is an essay titled: "Doing history in a theological situation."

In the seventies there were some of us who spoke, without a shadow of a doubt about its biblical foundations, of God as liberator, but there were also others speaking of "the death of God" and "the absurdity of life and the universe." While some of us were affirming the action of God in history, others were seeking to exile him from his creation. It is said that Newton exiled God from nature by unravelling the laws that governed it; that Darwin exiled God from life, by reducing the whole biological process to the struggle for the survival of the fittest; that Freud exiled him from the human soul, by explaining human conduct as a function of the libido and ego system; and that Marx exiled him from sovereignty over history by postulating that the real driving force was the class struggle.

In the 1980s, Protestant and Catholic theologians tended to exile God from the Church, by considering the worship of God not so much as an authentic act of homage, as liturgical actions

---

[4] José Míguez-Bonino, *Doing Theology in a Revolutionary Situation* (Philadelphia: Fortress Press, 1975).

which exercised a therapeutic function, useful for relieving the tensions of stressful existence in the great cities. The progressive theologians ascribed a political function to Christian worship, seeing it as the celebration of the poor and oppressed peoples of the earth in their long and painful struggle for freedom.

In 1992, a Japanese North American, Francis Fukuyama, published his book *The End of History and the Last Man.* The author claims to have discovered another key to the interpretation of human life and history, the desire for recognition. He writes:

> An understanding of the importance of the desire for recognition as the motor of history allows us to reinterpret many phenomena that are otherwise seemingly familiar to us, such as culture, religion, work, nationalism, and war. . . . A religious believer, for example, seeks recognition for his particular gods or sacred practices, while a nationalist demands recognition for his particular linguistic, cultural, or ethnic group. Both of these forms of recognition are less rational than the universal recognition of the liberal state, because they are based on arbitrary distinctions between sacred and profane, or between human social groups. For this reason, religion, nationalism, and a people's complex of ethical habits and customs (more broadly "culture") have traditionally been interpreted as obstacles to the establishment of successful democratic political institutions and free-market economies.[5]

It would seem that Fukuyama is somewhat unaware of the history of his adoptive country. It is well known that Protestants,

[5] Francis Fukuyama, *The End of History and the Last Man* (Toronto: New York Free Press, 1992), p. xix.

who escaped persecution for their faith in Europe, settled in the United States. Presbyterianism was so predominant there that some Britons called the North American Revolution the "Presbyterian Revolution." At least fourteen of the signatories to the Declaration of Independence were Presbyterians, including Pastor John Witherspoon.

According to Fukuyama, religion and God will be exiled from the society of the future in favor of a democratic state and a free-market economy. According to Fukuyama, this ideology is insurmountable; it therefore represents the end of history—the universal liberal state.

However, contrary to the landmarks mentioned here, which appear to indicate that "man is God," Marxism has passed away, the Berlin wall has fallen, and the Soviet Union has been dismembered. The market economy has arrived, but the poor are even poorer, and the life of the majority of the people of the world has deteriorated.

The results of all the efforts to exile the divine and the spiritual from human existence are now apparent in our world. Alongside scientific and technological progress, fear and anguish are increasing. Man is incapable of controlling his knowledge and directing it only toward just and noble ends. The existential vacuum in human life "has the shape of God." There is an irrational force that comes into play in our historical pilgrimage. The apostle Paul calls it "the mystery of lawlessness" (2Thes 2:7).

Therefore, we can now say that, in this first century of the new millennium, the globalization of the economy finds itself in a *theological situation*, and that the Church needs to do its theology reflecting on the special revelation within the real historical situation: namely, an economically globalized world. *It is vitally important that Christians and the Church remember that the achievements and setbacks produced by human beings in the development of our culture and history are marked by our sin, and that they take place in a theological situation. Likewise, the key to human life is theological.*

Over against *human speculation*—which presupposes the effort to remove God from the historical process, to install human beings as the measure of all things, and to look to human knowledge in the search for the meaning of life—God offers us his *special revelation* in the person and work of Jesus of Nazareth, to whom the Holy Spirit and the Holy Scriptures bear witness. *Progressive revelation* is a historical manifestation of the God of grace. But we must also refer to a *progressive enlightenment* whereby the Spirit illuminates the special revelation in Jesus Christ so as to enable the church to respond to current issues. The struggle against slavery and racial discrimination and, now, the discussions about the role of women in the Church are examples of this.

5. The Ecclesiology of Integral Mission

Its Origin in the Word

The Word of the God of grace—essential for understanding the world as the *theological context* of mission—is the foundation of the Church and integral mission. Word and Church are inseparably united. The Word of God which called the world into existence is the same Word that calls believers to faith in Jesus Christ (2Cor 4:6). The Word that called Abram "to leave his lands and his ancestors" and become Abraham "father of many nations" is the same Word as the one that calls believers of all nations to constitute the Church though their faith in Christ, making them descendants of Abraham (Gal 3:25-29). The Word that is creator of the cosmos and of the human community is also the creator of the community of faith, the Church. The Word proceeding from the God of grace is the very expression of that grace.

The Church recognizes the Bible as the Word of God, but the Word of God is the foundation and origin of the Church. The Word of God calls, nourishes, directs, establishes, and inspires the Church to fulfill its mission. Without the Word and the Spirit, there would not be a single believer in the God and Father of our Lord Jesus Christ. There would be no Church and no mission.

Regarding importance of the Word, the reformers of the sixteenth century affirmed the principle of *sola scriptura.* Today, from the perspective of integral mission, we must add—*and of the whole of Scripture.* Both Testaments are the Word of God and our study has to be faithful to both, recognizing, of course, that the triune God is the central character, and that the primary theme is the salvation which the Father God has brought into the world in Jesus, the Christ, his only Son, promised, begotten, sustained and restored to life by God, the Holy Spirit.

Integral mission synthesizes a way of reading the Bible. We read it as the Word of God, and, therefore, as the final authority on matters relating to the faith, life, and mission of Christians in this world. Both tradition and teaching—and creeds, confessions, catechisms, and covenants—have to be brought under the final supreme authority of the Word.

It is of particular importance that the Church that reads the Bible understands *what the mission of that Bible is.* In the biblical account of the history of salvation, the covenant and the Kingdom of God stand out as interpretive keys. They mark the beginning and the final destination of the community of faith, hope, and love, beneath the sovereign action of a God, who blesses it and makes it a blessing for all the families of the earth during its historic pilgrimage. During the time of "God's patience" which comes between the resurrection and the coming of Christ in glory, the community of the Living One is called to bear a whole-life witness to him who lives and reigns, enlivened by the Spirit of life, in the midst of a world branded by death. The Church has to demonstrate that love is the law of life.

The mission of the Bible is one of salvation and practical guidance (2Tim 3:14-17). What is the wisdom contained in the Holy Scriptures? It is *the knowledge of salvation.* The Bible is a soteriological text. It is not a scientific or philosophical book; it is a book of salvation. This does not imply that it is unscientific or antiscientific, but that it was written before the modern scientific revolution began. Its message is the historical action of the God of grace, who takes the initiative and comes to seek out sinful human beings, to offer us his salvation. And that salvation is to be found, not in a religion, nor in a Church, nor in a philosophical system, but in Jesus of Nazareth. God's salvation always was, is, and shall be through Christ.

How do we receive the salvation that is in Christ? The answer that all the New Testament writers give is unequivocal: by faith in Christ. It is in this faith that we pass through the soteriological fields of evangelism, and invite people to become Christians. Then the text immediately leads us to the soteriological fields of discipleship. The purpose of the Scriptures is useful and practical and its function is to make us good people, prepared for every good work. The soteriological goal of the Bible is to make people

Christians, to make them saints. And its practical goal is to render them of service to others.

The Church comes to know and recognize its mission through the Bible. So knowledge and understanding of *mission in the Bible* are prerequisites of responding to the demands of history with the eternal message. The pilgrimage of God's people through the centuries has meant seeking God's will in order to serve each generation in accordance with the divine plan. The overall policy of the mission of the Church is set out in the Bible. The Church is an agent of the Kingdom of God,[6] and its historic and eschatological purpose is to glorify God. However, it still has to discern *the times of mission* through the promptings of the Spirit, attention to the Word, and reading the "signs of the times."

The mission of the Church always takes place in a particular space-time-culture-sin *context*, of which the Church is a part and to which it must give a "reason for its hope." This *context* questions the Church and requires of it a Word from God, that is to say, a Word that has authority, *a text* that brings light and liberation, and that expels darkness and demons. It is this Word of God, and not of man, that enables the Church to discern and "put everything to the test and hold fast to that which is good" among the human words (anthropology, sociology, psychology, economy, politics, management, and so on). This Word of God allows the Church to enlighten and give direction to the human condition.

---

[6] An excellent work on the mission of the Church in the light of the Kingdom of God is to be found in C. René Padilla, *Mission Between the Times* (Grand Rapids: Wm. B. Eerdmans Publishing Company, 1985).

These encounters between text and context guide the Church in its missionary practice. The church begins its mission *ideologically* with revelation—with the text, with the Word—though *chronologically* it begins with the situation—with the context, with human need. And out of this meeting between the God of *grace*—mediated through his Word—and human beings in their disgrace—evidenced by the multiplicity and complexity of their needs—the possibilities for the Church's mission are born. Thus, the importance of considering *the role played by the Bible in the integral mission of the church.*

A Community Called Out and Also Sent Out

Once and again the Church has to discover its collective vocation as a witnessing community drawn from the world and set apart by God for mission. *The Church lives in the tension between being called out and being sent out.* It is the grace of God that produces this tension. The calling out and the sending out are two aspects of its vocation to be the witnessing community, which implies two movements: one *centripetal* and the other *centrifugal*. The former is that of the worshipping community, brought together in communion with the triune God to share in the means of grace: the Word, prayer, the sacraments, giving and receiving teaching, in order to grow in the grace of Jesus Christ and learn how to face up to the challenges of its particular situation. The latter is that of the Church dispersed in its evangelistic, prophetic, and diaconal mission.

However, being called out and being sent out also carry with them two dangers. The first of these is to regard the calling out as an end in itself, which leads to a "chapel mentality:" the unfortunate expression of a narrow denominationalism, a ghetto religion that cuts off all contact with the sinful world, the pharisaical, self-righteous attitude of belonging exclusively to "the saved." The other danger is that of succumbing to the slow, insidious process of assimilation, whereby the people of God lose their identity and take on the life style of the pagan, secular culture in which they live and breathe. "Israel conquers Canaan, but the Baals conquer Israel; the Church conquers the Roman Empire, but it becomes a secularized Church, salt that has lost its savior."[7] This process of conquering and being conquered is repeated throughout the history of the Church, but the God of grace always intervenes, to prune the vine and cut out the dead branches, to preserve the stem without which the redemptive plan would fail.

Trinitarian Mission, Trinitarian Ecclesiology

There is no definition of the Church in the Bible, but it is seen in different guises. Sometimes the church is seen as relationships: people of God, family of God, community of the Spirit; other times, as pictures and metaphors: body of Christ, bride of Christ, temple of the Holy Spirit, "salt of the earth," "letter of Christ," "fishers of men," "branches of the vine."[8] It is only when we take them together, and examine their mutual connections that these

---

[7] Suzanne Dietrich, *The Witnessing Community* (Philadelphia: Westminster Press, 1956), p. 17.

[8] Paul Minear, *Images of the Church in the New Testament* (Philadelphia: Westminster Press, 1960). Minear offers a list of some ninety-six different images and analogues of the Church to be found in the New Testament.

images constitute a description of the nature and character of the Church of Christ.

Since integral mission is founded on the mission of the triune God, I propose an ecclesiology of integral mission from a trinitarian viewpoint, that is, as people of God, body of Christ, and community of the Spirit.

People of God: The people of Israel were witnesses of the mighty acts of God, and especially that of the Exodus. (cf. Isa 43:10; Lev 26:12). Christ's disciples, the new Israel of God, were witnesses to the mightiest act of God: the resurrection of Jesus from the realm of the dead (cf. Acts 1:8). The two groups of people manifest the historical unity and missionary continuity of the people of God in their task of witnessing to the one, living, free, and sovereign God. The Church is a *witnessing people* and people who witness.

The covenant relationship between God and his chosen people is deeply rooted in both Testaments (cf. Ex 19:4-6; Lev 26:12; 1Pet 2:9). The outstanding feature in the similes of witness and covenant is that of *building community*.

The people of God are also called to be both a *servant people* and people who serve. The liberation *from* Egypt was *for* the service of Yahweh (Ex 8:1; 9:1; 10:3). The same emphasis is to be found in the New Testament: just as Jesus is the Servant-Lord, so his community is to be *a servant community* and composed of *servants* (Mk 10:45; 2Cor 4:5). The servant-church is called to serve God and God's world (Mt 20:25-26).

Body of Christ: The image of the body stresses the *organic* nature of the relationship between Christ and the church and among the church's own members. The body is the means of communicating with the world around. To reveal the will of God on the earth, Christ took on a body (Heb 10:5-9). To say that we are the body of Christ implies that the church is the place where the will of God is revealed, where the life of Christ is manifested in words and actions, and where the presence and mighty works of the Spirit are to be seen. The image of the body of Christ means that the Church has to bring with it the voice of Christ, his healing hands, his steadfast feet, and also his character marked by love. Christ has chosen to work through the Church, and has entrusted to it the message, the power, and the style of mission that he received from the Father (Jn 20:21; Lk 10:16; Mt 18:18).

The body is an organic unity, and whatever divisions it suffers damage the whole organism. Christ is the head of the body, and life flows from the head to the members. A member cut off from the body ceases to live. Therefore, belonging to Christ means belonging to the Church. In the New Testament, a lone or isolated Christian is inconceivable.

Furthermore, the life of the body includes diversity in unity (Rom 12 and 1Cor 12–14). God is the donor of the gifts of the different members of the community. There are many gifts, each with its own function, and nobody should become arrogant about his or her gift, or disparage or envy the gifts of others. Leaders should see themselves as those who serve with humility and with love (cf. 1Pet 5:1-4; 1Cor 12:4-31; Lk 22:26). Believers have to be constantly aware that the greatest of all the gifts, whose absence invalidates all the others, is love. This priority is found in Jesus and in the apostles (Jn 13:34; 1Cor 13; Phil 2:1-8; 1Jn 3:14-18; 4:7-12). The Christian life is one in which we learn to love—a most exacting apprenticeship. The continued emphasis of the apostolic letters on exhortations on love and good fellowship demonstrates in an unequivocal way that the primitive Christian communities had enjoyed scant success in seeking to carry out the law of love. But, at the same time, it also showed that the life of love was one of the proofs of discipleship. The total health of the body is achieved only when all the members of the body are wholesome and contribute with their gifts to the building up of the life of the community in love. This organic image of the church assumes a mutual dependence on the part of all the members of the community.

In Ephesians 4:1-6, church unity is seen as both something given and something to be achieved. Unity is of the essence of the Church. *Christ has only one body.* Its unity originates in the Holy Spirit and is to be preserved by the members of the community by means of the practice of love (Eph 4:1-3). At the same time, the church continues to be built up "until all of us come to the unity of the faith and of the knowledge of the Son of God, to maturity, to the measure of the full stature of Christ" (Eph 4:13). If it really wants its mission in the world to bear fruit, the Church has to demonstrate its unity in real terms (Jn 17:21,23). That is the only way it will achieve adulthood or maturity. Are we really aware of the huge obstacle that our divisions have put in the way of the progress of the gospel and mission? Unity has a missionary purpose (Jn 17:21,23). How are we to present it adequately?

The Community of the Spirit: In order that there be unity among us, the God of grace has marked us with the seal of his Spirit (Eph 1:13). In our negligence and our fears, with our knowledge that "puffs up" and our lack of the love that "builds up" (1Cor 8:1), "the Spirit helps us in our weakness, for we do not know how to pray as we ought, but that very Spirit intercedes with sighs too deep for words." He only helps those who are aware of their weakness. Is the failure of Christian unity one such weakness? Are we listening to the intercession of the Spirit? It is "according to the will of God:" "That they may all be one. . . so that the world may believe" (Rom 8:26-27, Jn 17:21). This will show the *otherness and the unity* of the church as a community governed by the Spirit; it is this that marks the quality of its fellowship and convinces a sceptical world of the reality of God's grace.

The Church is the habitation of God in the Spirit. It is the Christ-bearer, as are its members. This is the reality that distinguishes its character and that of its members: to be like Jesus. The church sealed, "empowered," and guided by the Spirit is God's "new creation," the first sign of the "new humanity" which God is creating in Christ Jesus. It is the "first fruits" of the new age, witnessing and serving not only with its words and works, but also with its very life.

The Church is the "alternative community," an alternative to race, gender, class, and religious hatred, because it is called to live the freedom with which Christ has freed it (Gal 3:28). The Church is the community where both the stranger and the foreigner are welcomed, where power is exercised in the service of others rather than the service of self, and where life in the Spirit means self-giving in the common good, not ascendancy or the accumulation of wealth.

As the community of the Spirit, the church celebrates and waits in hope. Here and now, in the fellowship of the Spirit, it has a foretaste of the joy of its new life. In this way the Church comes to be a sign of the Kingdom of God.

Integral Ecclesiology in a Globalized World

Today, a more biblical view of integral mission is gaining acceptance, a view that ascribes to the church a whole range of functions—ecumenical, liturgical, soteriological, diaconal, prophetic, as well as those of stewardship and *koinonia*—each of which has an evangelistic dimension. All these activities flow from the Word of God and are subject to it, and represent the permanent dimensions of the mission of the church for the historical future.

In the history of the church, however, different ecclesiastical currents have emphasized some of the functions to the detriment of others. Some Christian confessions such as the Roman Catholics, Orthodox, Episcopal, and Lutherans have had a strong liturgical tradition. Others, like almost all the evangelical churches, have sounded evangelism as the dominant and, sometimes, only note. Christian fellowship (*koinonia*) has been the mark of the Quakers and Mennonites and some charismatic communities. The Reformed and Presbyterian Churches are known for the predominant place they have accorded to the teaching ministry. In the past, it has only been among evangelical churches that there has been opposition toward social engagement, or at least a suspicion of the threat of slipping into the "social gospel." However, these churches understand more clearly these days that the practical outworking of love in practice is part of their task.

We have to overcome this partiality in our appreciation of the church's functions. In fact, they all need to be exercised and to complement each other in the realization of an integral ecclesiology. There are functions that have been pushed into the background, but that represent challenges that must be taken into consideration in the formulation of such an ecclesiology. We will present three functions of church life that are so pertinent that they demand to be incarnated in today's globalized world.

Function of *Koinonia*: The early Christian community was a fellowship before it was a congregation. It was a *koinonia* (communion, community) before it was an *ecclesia* (assembly). The Church is a local, global, and trans-national brother- and sister-hood, made up of people who have the same Father, the same one Lord and Saviour, and in whom the same Spirit is living.

The existence of such a community opens up unlimited possibilities for service in the context of the current globalization. To have *koinonia* is to be part of the life of the one and triune God, the Foundation of Christian community, and to become conscious of the essential importance of our brothers and sisters. It means purifying the heart of all egoism, resentment and competitiveness, and opening ourselves up to know and be known, without masks, without self-sufficiency, without formality, and without superficial reactions. *Koinonia* includes helping one another, confessing our sins, building up those who are weak, face-to-face exhortation, hospitality, and financial help for those in need. *Koinonia* means affirming community over individualism, which is its negation; over collectivism, which is its corruption; and over elitism, which is its temptation. How can the local church practice *koinonia,* with all that it implies, at a global level?

Ecumenical function: The word "ecumenical" comes from *oikumene*, which means "the inhabited earth." The most ecumenical, most global organism, in geographical terms, is the church of Christ, in as much as it includes representatives of the whole inhabited earth. To speak of the "ecumenical function" is not to talk about church unity at the institutional level, but about the missionary vision of every community of faith. From its own small corner, the local community of faith knows and senses that it belongs to a world family. At the same time it prays for, and feels responsible for, the whole well-being of the inhabited world. This kind of unity among Christians has a missionary and evangelistic goal, and should be part of equipping every Christian confession and every individual Christian.

One of the tragedies of the evangelical Christian communities in today's world is that, ignoring the possibilities of integral mission for people's well-being, they have become an archipelago of small fiefdoms concerned with their own domestic interests, with sectarian achievements and impossible expectations. The proclamation of the gospel and loving community service should call us to join together in unity: not *institutional* unity, but one to be expressed in new forms of cooperation, an *essential* unity.

"That they may all be one…so that the world might believe" (Jn 17:21) is one of the challenges of the contemporary globalized world. It is the greatest demand that Christians hear, and it is coming from all countries and all races, from all languages and all cultures. The whole inhabited earth needs the united presence of Christians to bring them salvation instead of isolation; a sense of community instead of confusion; dignity instead of distraction.

Prophetic function: The church needs to carry out its prophetic function, to become the moral and spiritual conscience of nations and their governments. Armed with the Word of God, it must address its own situation, its governments, those foreign governments that directly or indirectly abuse other nations, and all their citizens. Among the rich nations, the church needs to assess whether their government has any strategy for the reduction of poverty, both within its own borders and among poorer nations. And, if it finds that its only strategy is for its own economic growth, it has to denounce it. In the poor countries, the church and the Christians need to know not only where the poor people are, but also uncover why they are poor, by stripping away the masks of both ideologies and utopias.

In its prophetic function the church should be the defender of the life and the rights of all human beings, especially those who are poor, destitute, marginalized, and excluded from their society. To that end, it should urge the governments to invest in social aid programs, placing great emphasis on the capabilities of local solidarity, both on the part of local churches and civil society, in bringing help to the poor. Love, service, and the cross are the permanent triad, so that Christians and the church perfectly join together their prophetic and their diaconal functions. This enables them to find ways to overcome their total dependence on international solidarity. The defense of the poor needs to begin with the affirmation of their dignity and the development of their potential, to enable them to engage in justly rewarded work, and thus, to overcome any culture of dependency. Finally, the church should cultivate a relationship with the poor that will encourage them to set up programs that will change their own situation. Governments should be made to feel moral pressure from the churches and Christians to stop avoiding their responsibility to set up and maintain a more just economic order in their respective societies. The prophetic function of the church must be to declare a new order that is more just, more cooperative, and more human.

The church should propose a new life-style that is able to contend with a way of life that offers only consumption, squander, envy, and waste. The church needs to be the moral conscience for stewardship of resources in our creation. Simple life-style is no longer a challenge only for Christians in the rich parts of the world; it has become an inescapable necessity, if the testimony of Christians in the poor world is to have any credibility. Like the biblical prophets of old, the church has to present its message with actions and signs that carry its message of judgment and hope.

Conclusion

Today, as in every period of history, we have to exercise the necessary discernment so that integral mission, which comes from the grace of God, takes concrete form in our globalized world, understood as a "theological situation," by means of an integral *ecclesiology* that is its vehicle. In this way, the ecclesiology will resound in a doxology, through its missionary faithfulness, to the God made flesh. *Soli Deo Gloria.*

7

Church Structures: The Perspective of Institutional Psychology

Hugo N. Santos

In this essay I would like to raise some important questions on which institutional psychology, in dialogue with theology and other human sciences, can make useful contributions to the church's understanding and practice of integral mission. Integral mission assumes an integral vision, which welcomes different viewpoints and strategies that will extend the range of our perception and action.

1. The Church as Organization

An oriental master, impressed by the spiritual progress of his disciple, allowed him to live alone in a shack by a river. Every morning, following his prayer time, the disciple washed his shorts—his sole possession—and hung them on a tree. One day the rats tore them to shreds and the disciple had to go begging in the village for the money to buy new ones. But the rats quickly tore them up too. So, when the disciple got another pair of shorts, he decided to get a cat to put an end to the rats.

The disciple then ran into a new problem that he had not foreseen. Now, as well as begging for his own needs, he had to beg for milk for the cat. After a while, he decided to acquire a cow so that he would have a permanent source of milk for the cat. Quite soon after that, he realized he would now need fodder for the cow. Then, with the ever-increasing demands of the animal, it dawned on him that all this was using up the time he should be spending on his spiritual life. So, he decided to cultivate the land surrounding his shack. Since he did not have the time or patience to do it himself, he arranged for two peasants to do it for him. But the peasants needed supervision, so he decided to get married and leave that task to his wife. Some time later, making one arrangement after the other, he was the richest man in the neighborhood.

One day, much later, the master came by and discovered that, in place of the old shack, there now stood a stately mansion. He went up to one of the workers to ask him if he knew anything of his former disciple. But the disciple, who had already spotted him from high up in the house, ran down to meet his master. When he was face to face with him he could only manage to cry out with veneration: "Master!"

The master, lost somewhere between astonishment and reproof, stammered to his disciple, "But what's this?" And the disciple replied, as if it were the most natural thing in the world, "Though it might seem hard to believe, master, it was the only way I could preserve my shorts."

I have no idea whether the author of this story intended it to be used as a parable about organizations, or whether he just left it for people to make their own interpretations. However, the bizarre picture it presents can teach us something about a phenomenon that is common within organizations: the specific purpose for which they are created is always at risk of being pushed into second place, leaving as the primary objective the survival of the organization itself.

So often, we see organizations in which the activities actually carried out have little or nothing to do with their stated purpose; we see the maintenance of inoperable and useless organizational systems, the use of resources (both material and human) in ways that disregard the priorities of their stated aims, and irrational procedures that harm the people they are supposed to benefit. In a word, organizations often polish their image in a halo of rationalizations that grossly deceive the simple perceptions of those who will believe, without question, their claims. Just like people, organizations can also become sick. Every social analyst knows that organizations are one thing, and what they say they are is often something else.

The church is an organization, but not just any kind of organization. It has its own distinctive features. From a theological point of view, with its concomitant faith stance, we can make a number of relevant affirmations; but from the point of view of institutional psychology we can state that the church, in addition to its unique characteristics, also shares in a series of phenomena which are common to all organizations, and which need to be considered when we are analyzing our communities.

Weick has defined organizations as solutions in search of problems. Perhaps the definition seems strange, but the author is getting at an important function of organizations, the preservation of what has been learned. Resolving problems and managing the tasks an organization faces are the result of a process of trial and error, advance and retreat, and adequate and inadequate responses to conflicts. Every church, like every individual, has its history recorded, passing through local, regional, and denominational levels.

Churches are the result of the historical process of learning solutions, which creates a set of behavioral patterns that enable it to reproduce the solutions in the future without the need to go through the whole difficult process again. This creates a practical memory that preserves solutions, although frequently and unfortunately without necessarily being aware of their origins, and generates a strong system of norms and culture. It should be clarified that solutions to present problems are justified by the extent to which they are efficient in practice. With what has been said, we are referring to the institution-preserving pole on an organizational continuum, in contrast to the institution-creating pole, which tends toward change and which is present, whether perceptibly or only potentially, in all organizations, even those that seem most conservative.

Consideration of these institution-creating / institution-preserving poles will provide us with a parameter for an institutional analysis. In effect it poses a question that will alert us to the potential danger that the organisation of the church consume or sap the energy from the event that gives it meaning. The church channels, but it also influences, the experience of the believer's encounter with God.

Organizations usually come to stay, and—like people—they fear and resist the idea of their own death. If the "preserving" pole is very strong, the organisation becomes bureaucratic and makes its existence its primary objective. It becomes an end in itself.

Every organization is born out of certain events that determine its nature. From that point, with the passage of time, they develop the processes that we have referred to above. Usually when people invoke traditions they are not referring to the founding events, but to later ones. It is not without reason that revolutionaries of every sort will commonly invoke the original event that brought the institution into being. That explains why Christian movements, which at their inception have a revolutionary impact through their preaching of the gospel, and expand rapidly, later become organizations turned in on themselves, with little evangelistic power. It explains too why movements which had, as part of their initial discourse, a strong critique of evangelical fragmentation become, in the course of time, groups who set themselves up as superior to other Christian bodies.

In the historical beginnings of the churches there is usually a statement, explicit or implicit, "We are turning to Christ," or at least to the beginnings of their original denomination. This constitutes not only an affirmation; it is also a criticism of the current establishment.

For this reason, if we talk of the need for renewal of the believer, we should also talk of the need for renewal of the church throughout the years. For the believer to be integrated into the church, both processes must be related. That means that the church should have a dynamism and flexibility in its structures, activities, spiritual disciplines, leadership, and personal relations, if it is to be all that it should be.

An important aspect of the church's being the church is the struggle against the tendency to bureaucracy, the hardening of roles and structures, and resistance to genuine renewal. These are the evils that all too often transform means into ends, confuse form with content, and personal needs with the will of God. When that happens, instead of being a therapeutic community for other people and for itself, the church becomes the opposite; it becomes a place that encourages rigidity, personal suffering (not that of bearing the cross of Christ), and the rationalization of pathologies (sometimes even looking for theological justifications) which alienate it and cause it to lose sight of its mission.

2. Church and Culture

Organizational culture is understood to mean the way people think, believe, and act within a system, whether explicit or not. These kinds of socially directed behaviors relate not only to the given task of the organization, but also to the type of communicative interaction transmitted and maintained by the group, such as the system's own idiom, internal leadership, and shared preferences. The culture is a group's shared frame of reference that indicates the accepted way of thinking and behaving in concrete situations. This frame of reference denotes the priorities and overall values that direct the activities of the organization. The cultural norms include models of behavior that stem from the social environment, as well as norms that belong to the organization's own culture.

The organizational culture is made up of the following elements: a) characteristics of its surroundings which the organization, as an open institution, shares; b) technology, the habits and forms of behavior learned in the life of the organization; c) social evaluation of work locations and functions, and their stratification; d) roles that are developed to ensure the cohesion of social groups; e) symbolic actions such as rituals and ceremonies which, official or not, are repeated and may become routine; f) communication networks which connect their participants for affective and emotional reasons, not necessarily technical or bureaucratic ones; and g) the system of values, myths, and beliefs shared by the work group. As part of the culture, mechanisms for the legitimation and establishment of organizational power also exist.

The culture is an active and dynamic component of the organization. Even where the norms are shared, it does not necessarily follow that they are unanimously accepted; that would attribute a stable and monolithic character to the organization, which is far from the case. On the contrary, the culture is created and modified in the daily reality of the organization's internal and external relations. The culture is never totally accepted or totally rejected. The dominant forces never establish themselves completely, and the radical elements are never able to generate instantaneous radical changes to the culture's defining features. This means that, in the organization, cultural components are in continuous flux, and emerge from a synthesis of opposites. In the culture, in addition to rational and tangible aspects, emotional factors appear in the social group as dramas, crises, or dilemmas.

Culture does not exist independently from the person. Personality develops in the midst of cultural networks that shape it. Culture happens as the result of imitation, interaction, and learning. The ideals of the culture connect with the subjectivity of the person, in close relation with the ideal ego and the ideal of the ego. Then, people attempt to make the ideals absolute. When the ideals become naturalized, they threaten to exclude individuals who resist them.

Obviously, there is a multiplicity of cultural ideals, including some that may be contradictory. People not only share one global culture, but are part of subcultures, which in certain areas may reinforce or may contradict certain aspects of it.

Culture leaves its imprint on people through the mediation of groups and institutions, the basic one being the family group, which mediates the relationship between the person and the culture. However, this does not apply only to a person. Institutions themselves are molded by the same culture. The culture carries its ideals and its idols, which subtly find their way into the institution.

Any analysis of the church must make use of this information. If we are to follow the apostle's injunction, "Do not be conformed to this world. . ." (Rom 12:2), we first need to understand that we do not choose whether or not we want to be involved in the culture, because we already are involved in it. Then, we need to look at how the culture works itself into our institutions and our lives. In that way, we will then be able to engage with it critically.

An example might demonstrate this phenomenon. Authors who have analyzed post-modern culture have indicated that the collapse of ideologies and a determinative understanding of history has engendered an idea that what may be axiomatic today is, nonetheless, something fleeting and ephemeral. This has had a conditioning effect on every aspect of people's lives, and has led to an image of a God who responds to the need of the moment as the person conceives it. Not long ago, in a church during a time of pastoral intercession for the personal blessing of some of the members, I heard the minister ending every petition for the needs of the person coming forward with the word "now!"

On the last day of the last millennium, Marita Carvallo, president of Gallup Argentina and a member of Gallup International, published in the newspaper *La Nación* the results of the millennium survey on aspects of religion. The survey took place in sixty countries and processed the opinions of 1,250 million adults. In Argentina, 93% of the population claimed to belong to some religion (at world level it was an average of 87%).

The survey investigated how important God was in people's lives. To measure this, there was a scale from 1 to 10 (from "not at all" to "of maximum importance"). The average 7.2 rating (at world level), according to the author, demonstrated the "high esteem" in which God was held in people's lives. This average rose to 9 in Argentina, noting that the importance of God increased in proportion to the decrease in the socio-economic and educational levels among women in the 50 to 64 group in the interior of the country.

Belief in God increased significantly from 89% in 1994 to 96% in 1999.

In another published work, the same author emphasized the growth in the importance of religion in people's lives, manifested not only by belief in God, but also by church membership, belief in life after death, and in devotional practice. Of course, there is also an increase in esoteric practice as well. According to the World Association of Parapsychologists, there are fifty thousand witches, seers, and astrologers in Argentina.

In his book *Imágenes de una iglesia en misión: Hacia una eclesiología transformadora* (Images of a Church In Mission. Toward a Transformational Ecclesiology) Juan Driver takes readers on a journey through the pages of Scripture and church history. According to him, from time to time the church used models taken from the culture of the day, which often contradicted the very essence of the gospel. By way of conclusion, Driver says this:

> If the church is to recover the integrity of its life and mission, it will have to use appropriate images, capable of commanding its attention and inspiring its "imagination." Models taken from secular society invariably have ended up delivering the church into the hands of the enemy. Even biblical images many times have not served to reorient the church onto the path of apostolic faithfulness, because their meaning has been interpreted by the predominant values of the society of which it is a part.[1]

He continues in another paragraph:

> In the Bible, the end to which God's saving purpose is directed is the transformation of the whole of creation. But, according to the biblical vision, it is in the people of God that this new reality is first demonstrated. The corrupt, life-negating systems that characterize our egocentric, violent societies with their desire to dominate and their unbounded avarice can only be overcome through the existence of an alternative, radically different society.[2]

He then extends this idea:

> Throughout its history the church has constantly been tempted to interpret the New Testament from the perspective of its own level of commitment. It is astonishing to see the way in which the church, in its Biblical interpretation, has continually reduced the most obvious significance of the primitive witness, simply because it was not willing to take the evangelical message seriously.[3]

---

[1] Juan Driver, *Imágenes de una iglesia en misión. Hacia una eclesiología transformada* (Images of a Church in Mission: Towards an Ecclesiology in Transformation) (Bogotá: Clara-Semilla, 1998), p. 13.

[2] *Ibid.*, pp. 13-14.

[3] *Ibid.*, p. 14.

The question which in various ways has already been asked must be faced: Do we need to take the matter really seriously? Has this numerical growth in the churches, which we are beginning to see, brought with it clear and visible transformations in the society we inhabit? Is there more justice, less drug traffic, less violence, less crime? Are people happier? Should we just go on concentrating on "religious" questions, and let others look after the worldly things? Can we continue to ignore the way of life of a whole culture that profoundly conditions individuals, groups, and institutions, when we have a message that ultimately affirms a new way of being?

We live in a special time in the history of the evangelical movement. To the very obvious growth among evangelical churches, taken all together, can be added a vision of the unity of the church, new in the last few years. We recognize the presence of the Spirit and we are happy and thank God for it. However we should not fall into an unthinking triumphalism, which could prevent us from seeing that not every "success" is synonymous with obedience to the Lord; that we live in a world in which, alongside evangelical churches, other forms of religion, which are not in accord with our view of the faith, are also growing; that the very culture we live in produces such a state of malaise and hopelessness, that it leads to severe personal crises, which in turn are fertile ground for all kinds of "conversions."

3. The Health of Organizations

As stated before, organizations, like people, can become sick (and can recover). And so, just as everyone brings both healthy and unhealthy qualities to bear upon his or her faith life, every church brings its therapeutic elements and others that work negatively.

The issue of mental health is no small matter. The message that comes from the gospel incarnated in the person and words of Jesus is the greatest single contribution to the well-being of human existence. If the church claims to be the "body of Christ," it must be alert and active so that in its words and actions the presence of Christ be reflected, in the clearest possible way.

Mental health should be central in the life and mission of the church, because it relates to its fundamental objectives. Spiritual health and mental health are intimately connected, even more so when it is realized that each local congregation has a tremendous opportunity to work preventively and therapeutically in the various aspects of people's lives. In a world which is suffering, distressed, sick and insecure, the church should provide a place for promoting health and wholeness. Every activity should contribute significantly to people's growth and to their capacity to live creatively. It should advance their ability to love more fully, so as to be able to love God and neighbor. The church has a rare opportunity to promote face-to-face relationships within society. Karl Menninger has said that "religion has been the world's psychiatrist down the centuries."[4] Many have found in the church a place of support, recognition, guidance, integral personal nourishment, and the inspiration to grow and live. But, admittedly, people can also find, cloaked beneath a dubious Christian spirituality, the promotion of everything from neurotic guilt, denial of reality, stimulation of fear, depreciation of self-esteem to pseudo-theological postures that border on dementia.

---

[4] Karl Menninger, *Man against Himself* (New York: Harcourt, Brace and World, 1998), p. 449.

It is important, therefore, to state that health, both personal and institutional, is not a *goal* that we can achieve once and for all; it is preferable to consider it a *task*, a construction that is being carried on with advances and setbacks. The Apostle Paul's words about striving to reach a target apply to the life of the church. The church needs to carry out this *responsibility* for the health of the whole person and the whole community through all its ministries and activities.

The issue really demands a more extended treatment than we are able to give it here, because it has many facets, especially if we were to deal with each ministry separately. Making use of institutional psychology, I will simply outline some of the characteristics of healthy organizations, applied to the church context. These are concepts for a local congregation, but could be applied more generally to the church at large.

a. The objectives are appropriate, defined, and progressive. To achieve this, we need to be clear about why the church exists. The concrete objectives for specific tasks will provide a starting point for congregational projects. There are three facets of the life and mission of the church that are closely related and must be taken into account: a) *The church exists to worship*, which implies affirming and celebrating the creation and the Kingdom of God; b) *The church exists to be a community*. That is, to make apparent the "body of Christ" and the "family of God" through a network of personal relationships which help toward holistic growth in love and commitment of one for the other, leading to an anticipation, albeit imperfect, of God's new creation; c) *The church exists to be and to exercise mission*, which carries the responsibility—in being, word, and action—of participating in God's action in history. The church has to be enabled to be committed to and in solidarity with the world, the object of God's love. It has to discern the signs of the times in which it lives, and the will and action of the Lord of history. The church should make clear its stance for love, truth, justice, peace, and hope. With other organizations whose objectives it can share it has a unique role to play.

The shaping of specific objectives has to be congruent with the church's being, and they need to be clearly defined so that they can be periodically reviewed. Their progressive nature is to be found in their temporal aspect, and that demands a step-by-step appraisal of how the church is progressing in the pursuit of its goals.

b. The organization reacts to the needs of its surroundings. This means that, to the extent that it offers integral service, it is an organization that is necessary for potential members as well as for its current members and for the local community. If the church is not an end in itself, it will be attentive to the needs of people inside and outside. This is important, because the church so often fails to devote enough time to facing such questions as: What are the needs of people who belong to the church? What are the needs of the people in the church's neighborhood? Or even more boldly: If this congregation were to disappear, would the life of the neighborhood and its inhabitants change for the worse or not? Integral mission has as a premise that it addresses the whole person. Sometimes this premise has been considered not sufficiently religious, but it is just the opposite: everything is part of God's concern and salvation. Every obstacle, unsatisfied basic need, or illness can, at least potentially, conspire against the spiritual health and fullness of the person, or, to put it in another way, against that new human being that the Spirit seeks to create in every believer. Unfortunately, sometimes the church not only ignores the needs, it even tries to get the person to adjust to obsolete and bureaucratic forms that militate against his/her growth.

c. The distribution of roles and functions is really directed towards the achievement of the objectives. The objectives guide the development of the action, but we have to find ways of structuring the church that will be enabling to both. There are certain aspects of ecclesiastical structures that have come to be part of the church's identity, or that perpetuate themselves, even when they have functional problems that hinder the achievement of the overall objectives.

Organizational inertia, if it is not assessed and analyzed, militates against the development of the potential of the community, or at least severely limits it. What practical lessons we could learn from passages like 1 Corinthians 12:4-31! All the functions, defined and given equal status, are made subject to a single head as parts of a body whose members are intimately related and coordinated.

d. Paying attention to the quality and nature of leadership. This relates to the previous point. Within a group or organization, leadership is associated with the notion of influencing, inspiring, bringing together, directing, encouraging, motivating, improving, mobilizing and activating others in pursuit of a common goal, stimulating commitment, drive, confidence, courage, healthy communication, and growth. Leadership includes the job of organizing resources, energy, and human contacts in a productive environment for the achievement of stated aims.

Different ecclesiastical structures and even different theological positions tend to produce their own type of leader. The quality and nature of the leadership will leave its mark on the organization and the life of its members. Every role presupposes its counterpart (there is no son without a father, no employee without an employer, etc.). In that way, carrying out any role brings one into a dynamic relationship with the role of the other. Democratic leaders and paternalist leaders and autocratic leaders and *laissez-faire* leaders are not going to exercise the same kind of influence or produce the same outcomes.

To take one problematic situation, we would warn against authoritarian leadership that concentrates in itself the power of decision and definition of group norms, which ultimately promotes narcissism in pastors and leaders. Sometimes, the authoritarian stance takes on a paternalist guise by seeking its own way, but getting it done voluntarily, with an over-protective, spoon-feeding attitude. "I go to. . ." or "I'm from So-and-so's church" is a common phrase spoken by people from churches where it is pretty clear who the boss is!

The exercise of authoritarianism and the consequent submissiveness to it does not nourish the maturing of some basic aspects of the personality, even if people might appear to be spiritually stronger. The authoritarian tends to produce people with immature personalities who are indecisive and insecure. Authoritarians like to appear better than they really are in everything. Authoritarianism is not the same thing as authority. And the authoritarian leader is not normally inclined toward self-criticism or accepting criticism from other people or, even less so, the help or pastoral accompaniment of a pastor or therapist.

Christian leaders need to be those who are concerned for their own growth, encourage the preparation of new leaders, and contribute to a climate and style of relating which is liberating for people and the community, so that they too can nourish growth.

e. The aims are understood and, in large measure, shared by all who are involved. To achieve this it is vital to encourage participation of all members, so that they feel part of the church and its project. Sometimes aims are known only to the leaders. All the various ministries should be involved in fostering a sense of belonging and participation.

f. The efficiency of the organization is satisfactory. This element is related to the achievement of objectives. Objectives are never completely fulfilled, but they indicate the targets to be achieved, and in this way they act as a kind of road map. The church has to be what it says it is, and this will be so to the extent that what it claims is consistent with what it does. Some obstacles are unresolved personal conflicts, explicit or hidden aggression, lack of motivation, lack of planning, and conscious or unconscious sabotaging of projects.

g. The organization is flexible enough to adapt to change. There are three types of changes in the structure of organizations: 1) *conservative* (changing something that does not alter anything substantial); 2) *innovative* (important structural change); and 3) *destructive* (changes that affect the identity). These definitions are not meant to imply whether the change is good or bad; they simply refer to the type of change. The church has to be flexible enough to make changes whenever they are necessary, but recognize the need to make them wisely and sensitively.

We need to remember that people have invested their identity in the organizations and that they act toward them like those who have deposited in them their very personality. Some changes can reawaken basic anxieties that were previously limited and controlled. Those anxieties then produce resistance and distress. The renewal of the church, then, has to be accompanied by a renewal of its members in a type of person-community dialectic, all of which implies a process, a maturing, and a clarifying of objectives.

h. Conflicts are resolved creatively. Conflicts are inherent in the human condition. No organization is free of them. It is assumed that in the church the members share a common faith, values, and basic life situation. Nevertheless, they come from different histories and they have their own ways of locating themselves in reality, and often think quite differently. The differences can become mutual enrichment that empowers the community, but they can also bring difficulties and conflicts. We must look for ways to move forward and encourage dialogue. Depending on how these difficulties are approached, they can either develop a maturity that enables us to confront new conflicts or the differences will become deeper. It is essential to work at learning to listen and to express ourselves, at overcoming prejudices and eliminating "labeling" people—often present in personal relations—and above all at fostering peacemaking within the community. Peacemaking will not eliminate the conflicts, but it will engender *shalom*, which implies seeking the greatest good in the life of each person. Conflicts can encourage growth or create divisions in the life of any organization.

i. The quality of personal relationships in the organization is a crucial factor in its life and work. The church is called to produce significant human relationships. Jesus said, "By this everyone will know that you are my disciples, if you have love for one another" (Jn 13:35). If this is true, love is the primary characteristic whereby the church should be recognized. But, as Dietrich Bonhoeffer said, the fact that two believers in Jesus Christ are together does not mean that they will spontaneously feel and act like brothers. Love—not in theory, but in feeling, thought, and action—proceeds out of meeting, recognition, acceptance, and mutual respect. The community is in process of becoming, and that means building and effort.

j. Finally, the organization has a clear vision of its future. This element is necessary. Vision is about the institutional dream. It is about goals, but assumes the ability to imagine a future in motion. The imagination is an important psychological function in creating the future. In the case of the church, the future refers not only to eschatology, but to a vision of the future it is striving towards. It refers to what the church wants to be in the coming years. The vision is the picture of what the church members think it should be, or might come to be. What do we want the church to be like in the next two, four, or ten years? The steps we take should be taken in the light of that vision.

A vision of the future has consequences for motivation and action. For example, three builders were working on the same job when a casual passer-by came up to them. He asked the first one, "What are you doing?" The first builder responded with an unkind gesture to a question that he perceived to be stupid, because the reply was obvious: "Can't you see? We're laying bricks!" The traveller repeated the question to the second builder. This one's reply did not take up too much of his time. He replied, "Putting a wall up!" The third answered the same question, but with a broad smile of satisfaction, "We're building a hospital for the village children!" Many activities in the congregations are carried out with the same narrow focus as that of the first and second builders. The vision of the future has consequences for motivation and action.

In summary, I believe that the human sciences are useful instruments for the analysis and operation of the community of faith. Furthermore, they help us unpack many elements that are already in the Bible. A church that wishes to be the faithful, obedient body of Christ must not neglect the need to take into consideration and continually examine the questions of organization, the relationship with the culture in which it lives, and the promotion of health.

8

Servant-leaders, Facilitators of Integral Mission

Alberto Guerrero

What are the characteristics of the leaders of a local church that, in the power of the Spirit, is fulfilling its responsibility to be "salt of the earth" and "light of the world?"[1]

It is impossible to approach an issue like this, so vital to the life of the church, without making reference to concrete personal experiences and inherited patterns and models. In our case, there are inherited models to which have been added different responsibilities with interdenominational evangelical organizations that have contributed to the discussion with church leadership. This leads to the affirmation that there is an enormous diversity of criteria and understanding about what a leader is and how a leader should act, from those that are

[1] I should like to point out here that I am not keen on the word "leader", because it comes from a context and idiom that are associated with authoritarianism and a concept of direction that pays no attention to the ideas of others. So from this point on I shall use the composite expression "servant-leader," which, in my opinion, is more in accord with the New Testament thinking.

exemplary, valuable, helpful models, to others that are perverse, alienating, and even "domesticating."

Between these extremes, much pastoral leadership is not the fruit of any deep reflection or serious inquiry. We might even state that it is the result of someone's personal dreams and passions, accepted by a group of followers, that later fail the test of time. Other examples grew out of dogmatism and rigidly applied conduct inherited or learned from other models, creating trauma, frustration, and severe limitations rather than contributing to the growth of the congregation.

However, we should be grateful to the many—and probably most—who, throughout the course of history, had a clear vision of the One who had called them, and developed an approach that is serious, profound, and responsible, and for whom the most important thing was service to others. We are thinking here of those who, through a sane hermeneutic taken in conjunction with the reality of their situation, sought a solid intellectual foundation on which to base their identity and develop their own life along with the life of their churches. These are people who have understood that the wholeness of the servant-leader and the interrelationships of leadership are of vital and transcendent importance for the health of a congregation.

In our Latin American context, we must not fail to recognize that the diversity of leadership models was nourished by patterns brought from abroad by missionaries during the nineteenth and twentieth centuries, models that were still evolving and only partially contextualized. In recent decades, imported "success" models have appeared, disseminated through television and other media, bringing great promises of rapid growth. Their influence has increased to the point of creating our own local versions adapted to the practices of the churches that introduced them, adopting styles of leadership that are not appreciated.

Different modalities within the ecclesiologies of the historically established denominations have also exploded. A moderately thorough reading of the New Testament makes it clear that in it there is no single ecclesiology and no single way of developing the life of the church. But so many new ideas and discussions have proliferated that not even the denominations themselves can keep up with the quantity of new methods. One consequence is that there is no one type of leadership. To the contrary, great diversity exists within churches, movements, and denominations, and that diversity will likely increase in the future.

In this study we will consider the question: What should be the role of the servant-leader in the context of this first decade of the twenty-first century? Even when we recognize that many servant-leaders try to harmonize their work with the Biblical pattern, in a definite spirit of service, we cannot avoid the fact that conflicts are inevitable. Those that cause most concern reflect the diversity of leadership roles that we could group in the following way:

1. The quest for power.
2. Denominational statements.
3. Response to popular pressure.
4. Coherence with ill-defined ecclesiastical ideas.
5. Ecclesiologies that accommodate or change in accordance with personal interest, even disregarding the history of their churches.
6. Events and social phenomena.
7. Emergence of a popular evangelical religiosity.

It is true that there are models that reveal that a major tension exists between what the New Testament presents as the basis for the role of servant-leadership—including the paradigm of Jesus—and the individualistic projections of certain leaders who develop an ecclesiology that best suits their personal aims. This stems from an ever-increasing desire to produce churches that are totally independent, even though they may be part of a denomination.

The emergence of a certain type of leadership has led to a counterproductive situation of frustration, a deterioration of "being evangelical," creating a superficial culture that has little to offer to society or cuts itself off from it completely. The assertion "I am an evangelical" becomes devoid of content. In Latin America, so much of the predominant leadership has distanced itself from New Testament models that it is no exaggeration to say that the pastoral function is that which has deteriorated most in recent decades.

At this stage there are two alternatives regarding church leadership: it either returns to the New Testament in its context as the clear basis for leadership and reflects seriously on it, or it allows the baneful ideas of leaders driven by "success" to take over permanently. Because, once the faulty ideas are assimilated, they are accepted as normal in the minds of the congregation. Once they have become fixed in the life of the church and adapted to a given culture, it is extremely difficult to turn things around.

For this reason, we must go beyond presently accepted models, or, at the very least, we are called not to stay within the framework that these models try to impose. If, however, we are able to leave these models and, through reflection and Biblical exegesis that rigorously respects the nuances of meaning, search out the model of servant-leaders—those who guide the congregation according to the New Testament—then and only then we will understand that there is much that can help us and discover facets that we have been neglecting.

By examining the current situation, constructing new ideas from a biblical position properly contextualized, and deconstructing other views, we can then begin the process of maturity and growth of servant-leaders and congregations.

1. Servant-leaders as Facilitators of Integral Mission

The theme of integral mission is increasingly significant in evangelical circles, regardless of denomination, but chiefly among those who are looking for an integrated gospel that sees every human being as a whole, in all dimensions of life.

Many people recognize that the gospel has clear social connotations and consequences that are inevitable when the gospel is presented in all its dimensions. But, for about a century and a half, for historical reasons that we cannot go into here,[2] we have been presenting an incomplete gospel, directed more or less exclusively to the individual. We learned ways of presenting the gospel emphasizing God's forgiveness (1Cor 15:3), the salvation of the soul, and eternal life, stressing that, one day, the saved would find themselves with the Lord. René Padilla points out that

---

[2] Cf. C. René Padilla, "Evangelización Integral" (Integral Evangelism), *Kairos,* No. 3, 2002. (www.kairos.org.ar)

this thinking leads us to accept the *benefits* of the gospel without the *commitments* that the gospel requires.[3]

What happens, then, to all the ethical challenges that flow from the gospels and the epistles? Where is love for our neighbor, with all that it means? And compassion? What about a cup of cold water? These demands are related to family, neighbors, work, and daily living.

Clearly, what was preached was a partial gospel which neglected social responsibility, or which pretended to meet that responsibility with the gift of a food parcel or some used clothing. How are we going to reverse this process of malformation in which we have been engaged for so long?

The change begins with leaders who understand the demands that Jesus himself makes. In large measure, our understanding of Jesus' words on leadership determines whether we become a community of servant-leaders or a community where people exploit leadership. Unless church leaders are willing to recover an integral gospel in order to present an integral evangelization, it is hard to expect change in our congregations.

Paradoxically, the situation of our times is forcing us to see with fresh eyes. The church can no longer exist as a bubble for members to be present at worship and absent from society. Harsh social realities are now affecting our churches themselves with greater severity as the days go by. These clearly are times that demand that we assume our responsibilities. In this context, the servant-leaders will be the ones who understand the magnitude of the whole gospel and begin teaching, training, and accompanying the congregation. It is a hard job that requires

---

[3] *Ibid.*

much patience. Many will prefer the status quo—to continue presenting the gospel in the way their grandparents did or as they were taught to do—but "more of the same" no longer satisfies what the Lord requires of the church.

The social impact of the gospel in the first century was very real. Even in the society of the twenty-first century, the values that caused that impact are present, whether they are lived out or not. Doesn't the fact that they are not recognized show that an incomplete gospel has been preached? Isn't this the world that God loves (Jn 3:16)?

God is calling men and women to an understanding of all the dimensions of the gospel, to live and teach that people can be redeemed.

a. The Role of Servant-leaders in the New Testament

It is impossible to present an analysis of all that the New Testament has to say on the subject, but we can look at one or two important pasages. One classic biblical text is Ephesians 4:1-16. It is the only occasion in the New Testament that the word *poimenas* ("pastors") appears referring to the pastoral role. The Lord distributes gifts among people and assigns them to specific functions, as verse 11 states. This assertion by the apostle may seem obvious, but for some reason he includes it, perhaps because of the same confusion seen today in people who attribute their calling to different subjective experiences. Why did Paul write this to the church in Ephesus? Probably because this congregation was best able to attest to the gift or calling of a servant-leader.

What gives definition, direction, and force to the term "pastors" is the discourse that follows (vv. 12-16). Paul immediately defines the role in terms of teaching, training people, and accompanying the whole congregation in both personal and corporate growth. Note how the apostle includes himself in the process: "we must grow" (v. 15). Observe also the number of plurals and the use of the first person plural. This is very important because the apostle is acknowledging before a congregation that he founded and taught, that he, too, is growing along with them. He reinforces this idea when he says ". . . until all of us come to the unity of the faith and of the knowledge of the Son of God, to maturity, to the measure of the full stature of Christ" (Eph 4:13).

When he says, "all of us," the apostle is offering us a very rich concept that includes balance, humility, dependence, mutual help, growth in unity and knowledge of the Lord. We should learn from the apostle, who confesses to the church with great pleasure that he "grows" thanks to them. This reinforces the idea that having a pastoral role does not mean that one has arrived, or that one is complete, or has the last word. Servant-leaders must acknowledge their weaknesses and strive to overcome them.

In this Ephesians text, the idea comes across with considerable force that servant-leaders are themselves growing as they help in the formation of others. This, far from being a sign of weakness in the eyes of the congregation, is a sign of strength. In this way, both they and the others accept their own weaknesses and make an effort to overcome them in order to continue to grow. When this happens, a person develops true authority in life. It follows then that giving what one has and letting one's growth be seen is the task of all. Growing is painful, because growth happens as we overcome weaknesses and walk alongside others sharing our own life story, so that they can share theirs with us.

This process makes it possible for people, regardless of how little or how much experience in the faith they have, to discover in the ministry of the servant-leaders that the relationship with Christ really works. He is the teacher.

Such an approach to the task of the servant-leader clears away hypocrisy. Who are the "real" pastors? Those who face up to their weaknesses and share their personal struggles. They are thus able to perceive other people's needs, help them in their experience with Christ, guide them with compassion, and travel "along with" them in the direction of God's plan to create a "perfect humanity." These are really servant-leaders.

The Pauline vision of the pastoral role is colored by his personal experience. When Paul is writing this letter to the Ephesians, his pastoral spirit spills over the pages because he lived the role with great fervor, every day, alongside the people. In this way Paul discovered that the servant-leader is not one who tries to control from afar, or pass down orders, or stand out or be recognized and admired, or have people under him, or demand to be heard without argument or contradiction.

Servant-leaders are those who remember with clarity how the Lord took hold of them, how he went on doing it during their lifetime, and how they were transformed by his loving kindness. And so, like their Master, servant-leaders find themselves moved to compassion for people and identify with them to the point where they understand them and live in solidarity with their struggles and their needs. This prevents them from feeling either superior or inferior to others.

All that has been said, far from diminishing the pastoral role and responsibility, enhances them. It implies that servant-leaders are placed by the Lord with the specific task of being instruments for the restoration of people, who belong to the Lord, not to them. Servant-leaders have to see their mission as growing out of that of their Master, whom they claim to follow. They have to help human beings, submerged in the inadequacy of their values and their limitations, to face life. They have to help human beings, oppressed by their life stories and unable to see a different world, to see other options, like those described by Jesus himself in his vision about poverty (Lk 4: 18-19).

This New Testament image of the pastorate is not limited to a date book, a desk, and a secretary—things that are not bad in themselves if they do not diminish the Biblical perspective. Our interpretation should continue to develop just as did that of the apostles in the development of the church in the first century. The Biblical writings show how their authors continually grew in their understanding of the mission of Christ and their own roles. We cannot overlook the fact that all this took place in the midst of various conflicts in the church. For example, although John does not use the word "church," his thoughts about it are reflected in the parable of the Good Shepherd (Jn 10). John speaks of identification, knowledge, dialogue, sympathy, care, seeking out, patience, and dedication. It is the sheep that are important for servant-leaders, because in them they find the Lord himself.

In this context, we understand Jesus' words in John 10:10: "I came that they may have life and have it abundantly." What does it mean to servant-leaders that they should be instruments of "abundance" in people's lives? It is interesting that the Taizé Community in its ecumenical New Testament in Spanish translates "abundance" as "exuberance."[4] This is a valid

---

[4] Comunidad Taizé, *Nuevo Testamento* (Barcelona: Editorial Herder, 1968), p. 132.

translation of the Greek comparative *perisson echein,* which does not suggest something above life, but life itself in its highest expression, the ordinary things of life in absolute fullness.

These concepts confront us with an inescapable reality: servant-leaders have the privilege of putting into effect the care, counsel, and guidance of people faced with the circumstances of life, in their internal journey to fullness of life. They carry it out as instruments of the Holy Spirit's working out of their redemption and growth.

In this first decade of the twenty-first century, the question is whether or not the servant-leaders are ready for this challenging task. Doubtless, the leaders will answer for themselves. However, the social circumstances of Latin America are presenting challenges that are utterly different from those of the past.

Foreign models of leadership have been of little use, especially because they are imposed and raise expectations almost exclusively of making money and material prosperity. In addition, they fail to understand our context, offering "more of the same" of what we have been hearing for decades. It also is obvious that many leaders, in their panic to achieve success, prefer to mimic these models rather than doing the work themselves. These foreign models have shown that in the pastoral ministry, however, one cannot ignore the need to work in context, to take cultural differences into account—ways of communicating, ideas of the family, the particular social situations aggravated by the economic systems that oppress the region—all part of the Latin American context put in place during the twentieth century.

It is time to strengthen our convictions and thoroughly criticize ourselves. Let us admit that the model of servant-leadership that Jesus offers us, and that was developed during the first stages of the church's formation, is lacking in the majority of the leadership we see today.

b. The Servant-leader's Role as Facilitator

It is not possible to find a definition that encompasses all of what is meant by servant-leader. Clearly we are talking about someone able to give of him or herself for the well-being of others.

The etymology of the word "facilitator" is linked to a phrase that I adopted some years ago: "Those who love teach." Teaching is inevitable for anyone who loves. It is stronger than the person, because love not only wants the best for someone; it strives to assure that that person succeeds, and to that end endeavors to *facilitate* the person's development as a human being. And if the person should stumble, love reaches out a hand to help start afresh.

It is easy to see this in fathers or mothers who really love their children. For them it is vital to see that their children grow up and develop abilities appropriate to their age, without getting behind or being precocious, with just the right timing. In the same way, being a facilitator can include accompanying, monitoring, overseeing, being silent, or perhaps saying something when the moment is right. It means doing things in such way that they have value for the people being accompanied, so that they can overcome difficulties and increase in stature. In this way, the *learning* becomes more important than the *teaching*. Leaders who are inclined to solve problems and make decisions for other people believe, without thinking, that their decisions are always best. Rather than facilitating learning, that sort of attitude atrophies and inhibits it.

Every believer daily confronts new situations that require reflection and problem-solving, and needs discernment in order to grow. In these situations the effectiveness of servant-leaders' ministry lies in fully understanding the diverse nature of situations and recognizing that their task is to be *facilitators of change* through *learning*. People only grow when they have learned how to learn, that is, when they have learned to reflect, to evaluate situations, and—in the light of the Word they have learned—to adjust and change, making wise decisions for living.

In the Scriptures, servant-leaders are called to clarify and deepen God's dialogue with his people. To that end the Lord calls servant-leaders to facilitate or make accessible the dialogue between Scripture and its readers. Perhaps a look at the opposite situation will help us to grasp the point. Some leaders use Hebrews 13:17 to enlist "total subjection" from their congregation. Clearly the author of the letter was trying to bring some clarity to a subject that, we might suppose, was causing some conflict in the community. However, it is essential to look carefully at Hebrews 13:7-8 to understand the concept fully. This text emphasizes that the primary quality of servant-leaders is that they should make the Word comprehensible, but the text goes on to say that what they are teaching has to be compared with the way they live. Then the author speaks of the faithfulness that servant-leaders owe to the unchanging Christ. In fact, in Hebrews 13:17, the author states that those servant-leaders who show consistency between what they teach and how they live are to be respected. So then, the task of servant-leaders is to teach, to clarify, to make the Word comprehensible, and to reinforce it with the way they live.

Every believer is called to please God, to obey him, and do his will (Rom 12: 2). The believer should also have the gift of both personal and communal discernment. So to "hunger for justice *(dikaiosune)* " (Mt 5:6) means to desire, in a most intimate and profound way, to live a life of obedience to the Word of God, so that this justice (doing what is right before God) comes into effect. And that is what, in the end, produces holiness. There can be no holiness without the profound desire to do what is right before God.

This is the tremendous ministry of servant-leaders! To guide their sisters and brothers—growing together with them—to live out this justice, so that one day we might be declared just.

If human experience is colored by the emotional, the rational, the volitional, and the sensual, a person's dialogue with the Word will be something very individual, so there is no easy pastoral response. Treading the way of holiness "without which no one will see the Lord" (Heb 12:14), servant-leaders are called to go through life together with all the members, learning and helping others to learn, enabling themselves and facilitating the dialogue between God and the believers, mediated by the Word. Under the supervision of the Holy Spirit, they comprehend and make comprehensible the Biblical challenge, especially that of the gospel.

It is necessary here to add a paragraph on people's responses. Up to now we have been looking at some biblical references and trying to contribute a few reflections about the pastoral role, but now we should be truthful: *treading the road of sanctification is not easy*. Let us recognize that, as human beings, it is extremely difficult for us to see our defects and limitations, and even more so when someone else brings them to our attention. We are often tempted to dissimulate and cover them up. Of course, our faults are an occasion of grief and shame to us, but it is here that the gospel has to do its work and it is here that the Spirit has to lead us in overcoming them.

It is notable that Scripture never hesitates to mention the faults of God's chosen servants, who carried out their ministry honorably. There they are; they appear just as they are, with all their limitations, half-truths and denials. They are portrayed as people wrestling with themselves and struggling about whether or not to obey the Lord. David is a remarkable example of someone who, on several occasions, opens his heart to show us his internal struggles, even recognizing his weakness to the point of saying, "Who can detect their errors? Clear me from hidden faults" (Ps 19: 12).

If leaders are seeking to be "salt and light," they must go through the difficult process of knowing themselves and accepting themselves in all their weakness, and from that point, gird themselves up to help themselves and help others so that the salt goes on flavoring and the light glows ever brighter. It would be a sad day should they appear before the Lord as salt that has lost its savor or light that has gone out, because of their ego.

2. Servant-leaders as Facilitators of Integral Development in the Church

According to Matthew's record, we see that Jesus twice used the word "church." The first time is in chapter 16, in the context of Jesus' asking his disciples questions to see if they understood who he was, and to establish what was to be the foundation of the church.

We find the second reference in a very special context. Matthew 18 begins with a power struggle among the disciples to establish who was "the greatest" among them. Jesus takes a child and continues his discourse with the child there on his lap. In verse 10, he warns about the ill treatment of children, and in verse 15 he admits the possibility that our sisters and brothers sin. In these circumstances, Jesus says, the disciples may not remain aloof. They must try to help the sister or brother. Something has not matured, and can be cured, restored. The task, then, is "regaining" them, seeing the need to accompany and support them through their process of transformation. In the same way servant-leaders can and should be accompanied.

We must not lose sight of the fact that Jesus used an internal dispute between the disciples to initiate the discussion. He used a child as the example of how they should treat one another; not as competitors, but as frail believers, who are vulnerable and may fall. And, in the case of a fall, there should be compassionate hands stretched out to help the fallen, not competitive hands stretched out to knock them further down. Human nature often behaves competitively, though, seeking success through the failure and frailty of others.

Jesus continues his teaching and exhorts his disciples: "if two of you agree on earth about anything you ask, it will be done for you by my Father in heaven" (Matt 18: 19). The Greek text helps us see something that Matthew surely heard from Jesus, which we need to recover if we are to understand the importance of harmony in the church. Matthew uses the verb "*sumphoneo,*" "be in accord," and "agree," the word from which we get "symphony."

To illustrate the text more fully, it might be helpful to ask, "What is a symphony orchestra?" Simply put, it is a collection of different instrumentalists who, under the baton of the conductor, bring their diversity together in harmony. To achieve this end, every one needs to recognize clearly that there is no one instrument more important than the others; all are necessary and each one has its particular sound. The finest sound is achieved when it is not possible to distinguish any one instrument in the ensemble, but all are in tune, playing at the right tempo, with each paying maximum attention to the others. The finest element of any orchestra is the quality of its harmony, which can delight the listener. Harmony is achieved, in part, by responsibility in performance, but even more by all the basic work that goes on before the performance. Listening to others more than to oneself in order to produce exactly the right tone, at the right moment, is unseen and often stressful work. The conductor knows just what she or he wants from the piece, and it is vital for the musicians to understand it, in order to bring it to fruition.

Once again, we see the wisdom of Jesus. The church preceded the symphony orchestra by one thousand six hundred years, showing us how each person's talents might be used in an integrated way with God as the master conductor to produce perfect harmony! The question is, are our leaders ready to turn their congregations into symphony orchestras? Who are willing to do such hard work? If servant-leaders manage to get the church to produce the right "music"—making music from the lives of its members—people will be captivated by the possibilities for growth and transformation, and want to be part of the community, making music which is pleasing to God. Of course, they must be willing to allow the "conductor"—the Lord, in this case—to direct the orchestra.

3. Servant-leaders as Facilitators of Pastoral Care

It has become popular to think that we can "counsel" others without knowing anything about their situation or about the topic on which we offer the advice. This idea is common in our culture and, as a result, is found in our churches, with all the risks that it entails. We generally assume that people are equipped to advise, based on their own experience, without taking into consideration the limits of that experience, and the lack of suitable training. Accompanying this idea is the dubious notion that "popular wisdom," which we "pick up" from sayings and odd experiences "here and there," is sufficient for counseling. Supposedly biblical texts appear in popular culture, such as, "Help yourself and I'll help you."

A healthy process is to help, assure, and counsel people toward an understanding of the nature of their difficulties, so that they find themselves in the midst of their problems, are able to make their own decisions and, where it is necessary, get whatever help is needed to arrive at a solution. In the process people grow and mature because problems are seen as occasions for personal development and growth, not as impediments impossible to overcome.

The first quality that servant-leaders must bring to their pastoral care is a deep respect for people. Servant-leaders are dealing with people, not inanimate objects. People feel and people suffer, and they often live with emotional stresses that paralyze them or stop them from thinking clearly. Jesus is the best example of the servant-leader. Looking closely at his encounters, we find that He always saw the person as a person, whether in a child, in a woman ostracized by society, or in a rich young man, whom he "loved" (Mr 10:21), although he had made the wrong decision.

Whatever the social or economic situation, Jesus saw people in need, and this evoked in him both compassion and profound respect. It is precisely in his conversations with people that we see Jesus seeking to understand people deep down, initiating a profound personal reflection as well as a critical analysis of their situation in order to fully transform them. It is the only way to provide fully integrated support.

Servant-leaders must understand the difficulties that exist in relating to people at such a deep level, at the level of their personal histories, their home experiences, their present situations, and their web of relationships. A counselor must resist giving simple, spontaneous answers to problems. Many recognize that they counsel people without having listened to them, or even worse, just praying about the problems as if they are going to be resolved by some kind of magic ("Pray for me, pastor"). The easy route is to introduce a bit of infantile mysticism—including just praying and leading people to believe that their problems are solved—rather than making the effort to truly understand the person or equipping oneself to help them with knowledge, wisdom, and personal commitment.

Reuel Howe suggests that *pastoral counseling is the essential means whereby a church can become a place of rescue and not a club, a hospital and a living spiritual garden, not a museum.*[5]

---

[5] Cf. Howard Clinebell, *Asesoramiento y cuidado pastoral* (*Basic Types of Pastoral Care and Counseling: Resources for the Ministry of Healing and Growth*) (Buenos Aires: Nueva Creación, 1995), p. 16. English original, only the Spanish translation available to the author.

Of the rich ideas in this quotation we would like to mention two. First, it contains the idea of *rescue*, which implies that the church exists to make integral salvation available to people who no longer have hope and expectation for their lives. Another is the idea of *hospital*, which suggests the idea of the church as a place of recuperation. "Rescued" people need a well-equipped trauma center in which to recuperate. We would not want people to arrive only to be badly treated or not cared for properly. How would we feel if we discovered that some illness of ours had been wrongly diagnosed? The first thing a sick person needs is to be treated with care and respect, like a person and not some animal. Even when we just go for an injection we want to be treated properly. To what extent is it the responsibility of the leaders to ensure that these two dimensions are present in the church?

When the church is both a place of rescue and recuperation, the Holy Spirit can work for people's restoration. The Lord's plan requires servant-leaders to be contributing to this end. And that can happen only when leaders have a clear understanding of their role, functions, objectives, and strategies.

On the other hand, it seems that some leaders prefer to seek success and fame based on the size of the membership list, public recognition, smart clothes, material prosperity, or being "too busy" for people or generally inaccessible. If, further, their ministries have to do with positions of authority, being in charge, being executives, entrepreneurs, and so on, the injured are not likely to find a place of rescue or recuperation there.

It is probable that many church members, in a time of crisis, go "from one hospital to another" until they find what they are looking for, or else become discouraged, give up the search, become accustomed to living with the crisis, and complain about their sad experience.

There still exists a vision in which servant-leaders give the best of themselves: to take on the pastoral care and counseling to bring about the restoration of people in their situations of crisis, illness and brokenness.

a. Servant-leaders and Their Co-workers

Church leaders, whatever their role, are being challenged to see themselves as people involved in a process of development and integration, open to transformation and enrichment.

However, in practice this is very difficult because competitiveness is ever present. Before describing the church as a body, Paul proposes the necessary starting point: "I say to everyone among you not to think of yourself more highly than you ought to think, but to think with sober judgement, each according to the measure of faith that God has assigned" (Rom 12:3). In spite of this, it is no rare thing in some leaders' meetings to see signs of a catharsis regarding conflictive relationships among them, and between them and their congregations. Some leaders seem overwhelmed by the tensions and pressures that other leaders impose on them.

For similar reasons, these leaders find refuge in the idea that "the Lord's anointed must never be questioned" because he is the one with "the vision." But, was Jesus never questioned? Were the apostles or the prophets never questioned? How are we to understand the loneliness of Paul's last days? Another defense that leaders often use is to assert that a kind of theocratic government is more Biblical, quoting from the Old Testament without acknowledging the need to seek answers in the New. In practice, this "government" works exclusively through the medium of some "anointed one" who has direct access to God's hotline, and so can discount every other opinion, including that of other leaders.

These extremes actually exist, despite the whole range of opportunities for integrated Bible study and training in biblical theology that are available. It should not surprise us, as there are similar situations found in the New Testament. Diotrephes (3 Jn 9) showed no respect for a senior apostle who had a wealth of valuable experiences worth listening to; instead he prattled and prohibited. It is no exaggeration to say that the church like any other community is vulnerable to competitiveness, to members acting out of place, and to manifestations of inferiority complexes, which are reflected in the desire of some to dominate the rest. There will always be those who use smooth talk in order to seduce.

A perennial question comes up: Who will pastor the pastors? Are some leaders so proud as to believe that they do not need it? Pride generates foolishness, the opposite of wisdom. Real wisdom recognizes our need for pastoral care, even though we are leaders. We all need to pastor each other. Pastors meet to pray and support each other spiritually, but they should also create opportunities for mutual confession, to restore and to be restored, to travel the road of humility and compassion. Often that means going against the stream.

Servant-leaders cannot avoid being open to observation. Churches are open systems in which anyone who joins can eventually settle in, exercise authority over others, manage groups, occupy pulpits, and preside over important activities. So it is not surprising that a person skilled in using words and manipulating people will exercise influence on a congregation. Furthermore, some people with many unresolved problems come to the church and settle into certain functions without having resolved their problems. They often transfer their work and family issues into the life of the church.

How do church leaders relate to each other in the face of this situation? Generally speaking, leaders rarely follow the route we have been suggesting, they do not generate a balanced image, and they encourage competition. Very powerful, self-centered, authoritarian pastors will tend to produce a style of leadership with very similar characteristics. On the other hand, more humble servant-leaders, with a love for people, and who do not seek advantage from them, who create space for discussion and biblical discernment, will, in time, produce other leaders with similar qualities.

Romans 12:1-8 is a brilliant text that can provide us with a great deal of understanding about the gifts of leadership. Paul points out the need for us to offer all our being to the Lord, in a spirit of worship (v. 1). He then highlights the continuous renewal that is produced in us when we are motivated by the desire to seek the will of God (v. 2). Next, as we have already mentioned, he notes that we should not keep on going without self examination, because there is a risk of thinking of ourselves more highly than we ought to think (v. 3).

Only after we have dealt with the question of relations between leaders and between leaders and the community, can we begin to consider the gifts that the Lord has bestowed on us to serve him in and through the church. We need to emphasize this need to sort out our relationships within the church before we can expect any gifts. It is only logical. How can I expect the Holy Spirit to provide gifts for use in the service of the Lord in the community, if the relationships among the sisters and brothers of that community have not been put in order? Using the symbolism of the cross, it is not possible to resolve the horizontal relationships—my relation with others—if I do not first resolve the vertical relationship—my relationship with God.

The New Testament message is actually quite straightforward on this point. We even have the necessary steps very simply detailed, but our unresolved conflicts often are more powerful. Instead of cultivating leadership models in line with this Pauline idea, whose source is the Lord of the gospels, we cling to models that impose power over others.

The gifts are God's tools. The most important thing about the mechanic's toolbox is not the box itself nor how fashionable it is, but whether it holds the precise tools that are necessary and in perfect condition to do the work that has to be done. Each tool has its own function. A hammer cannot be used to tighten a nut or to remove a nail. A saw cannot be used to hammer or to remove a nut. We could use many examples. Jesus would understand because of his experience as a carpenter. The problem is that we do not seem to understand that we have the privilege of being practical, useful tools in the Lord's hands, and we end up being useless, by insisting on rolling up all the functions into one person, and then trying to control the rest by insisting that our role is the most important.

Servant-leaders, in the first place, must recognize that nobody has all the gifts, all the tools. In the second place, they must also competently use the gift or gifts that the Lord has given them. This competence originates in the Lord, but it also improves and develops. Take for example somebody with a beautiful voice. Is it enough in itself? Surely we recognize that voice as a gift, but the voice gets better with use, its modulation improves through the help of professionals, and that way the gift is enhanced. And that is how it is with all gifts.

b. Servant-leaders and the Community

The Lord makes it clear that all the gifts or tools are necessary and that we have to make the effort to integrate them, even though that might not be easy. Only when servant-leaders put into practice this perspective of not monopolizing the gifts and using and refining those that they have received, we can expect the community to achieve it too. This seems almost obvious, but reality shows that it is a complex process.

We already noted that Pauline theology presents us with a very specific metaphor: the church is like a body. Paul made frequent use of this image because, for him, it offered a simple way of expressing the relationships among believers in terms of accompaniment and mutual support, not arguments and competition. In this figure, *no one* is indispensable, but we *all* need *everyone* and we help each other, and each person carries their own responsibility, so that the body—whose head is Christ—can function in every respect.

A healthy body grows harmoniously. It does not grow a leg first, and then a shoulder and finally an ear. Growth is simultaneous and proportionate. All parts of the whole change together. Paul speaks of the "joints" that connect the activity of the muscles, the blood that carries life, and the movements that adapt and complement each other naturally and spontaneously, growing in harmony. A sick or injured body, however, in which one leg is shorter than the other or an internal organ is not functioning properly can produce serious problems or deformities that end up affecting other body parts.

If people in the churches take the Pauline model seriously, they will find that within the body there is a mixture of sin and salvation, suffering and consolation, alienation and reconciliation, guilt and forgiveness, judgment and grace, disaster and triumph —a network of difficult problems and successful resolutions.

We must ask ourselves this question: What are leaders doing to help the church see itself as a body? To what extent do leaders grasp the truth of the concept and put it into practice? If people from the congregation are to care for each other pastorally, they need to see something similar taking place among their leaders. The primary task that the New Testament assigns to the pastorate is to accompany the church's harmonious growth—ironing out differences, stimulating growth, eliminating false doctrines, and excluding people who might seriously distort the nature of the church by only thinking of their own personal advantage. Pastoral care is not simply the commitment of a few leaders. It is an interaction involving the whole community. In a sense it is a cultural value of the whole church that it acquires with some effort.

For some twenty-five years the idea that pastoral care was the responsibility of the whole community has inspired a good deal of writing with various contributions under the general heading, "the church as therapeutic community." Several professionally qualified ministers have written on the subject (Daniel Schipani, Jorge León, Alberto Gandini, Hugo Santos, Daniel Tomasini, and others), but so far the idea has not been adopted by our Latin culture. The reason seems to be that our image of centralized "power"—whether priest or pastor or leader—leads people to reject pastoral care by someone who is not the pastor, and those who do pastoral work do not delegate it to others and have no desire to train others to do it. What goes through the mind and the heart of a person who sees an inaccessible pastor up on a platform, and after weeks of trying to get an appointment is finally conceded one? He or she will be inclined to accept whatever direction or advice the pastor gives however wrong it might be, or however remote from any comprehension of his or her situation.

John makes a very suggestive statement in his Gospel when he notes, "Although it was not Jesus himself but his disciples who baptized" (Jn 4.2). Why? He does this because there would always be those who would give a special category to having been baptized by Jesus himself, believing that this distinguished them from the rest. Remember the discussion in the church in Corinth, where the believers tried to identify themselves with the "hierarchy" of the leaders they followed. Some claimed to be followers of Peter, some of Paul, but some of the more self-promoting claimed to be followers of "Christ," and in that way put themselves on a higher spiritual level than the rest. Servant-leaders need to be aware of this tendency of people to establish castes among themselves.

To succeed in making the church into a therapeutic community, the servant-leaders need training. They in turn have to train, equip, inspire, and supervise those ministries dedicated to personal care, and this requires further education, more training, and consultation with other leaders and professionals as equal partners in the ministry. It is not easy! It takes a lot of humility, first of all, to accept one's own limitations in a situation where the people themselves are eagerly looking for "spiritual superstars."

The church, understood as community and as body, offers excellent possibilities for growth, development, and overall personal enhancement for every member including the servant-leaders. However, it requires an effort beyond the Sunday meeting or inspirational service. It has to do with the meeting together of people who recognize their need for help and who are willing to offer help to others.

The one really gratifying aspect of the pastoral ministry is seeing people grow. However, this growth, like faith, can develop only in community. This shows the importance of the church that grows harmoniously.

Final Reflections

How are we to reestablish the valuable role of servant-leaders as "salt and light" in a time of so much deviation, discouragement, and confusion? May we suggest that we follow the best examples that exist and that are worth emulating? We feel that this can occur only when we take two factors into account:

1. *The degree of impairment.* Until we say with the prophet, "My wound is severe" (Jer 10: 19), we cannot begin any process of change. It will take a lot of courage to produce a constructive critique of leadership as it is at present. We can say that a return to the Scriptures is essential. May the Word of God give us the right criterion and an honest word on what it means to be servant-leaders in our present circumstances. One suggestion is that we follow the Beatitudes of the Sermon on the Mount, contained in Matthew 5: 3-9.

   In personal life

   —Be aware of spiritual dryness (v. 3)

   —Mourn for any damage done (v. 4)

   —Be inclined to meekness (v. 5)

   —Yearn fervently for obedience to the Master (v. 6)

In relation to the lives of others

—Look on others with an eye to redemption (v. 7)

—Cultivate transparency of life (v. 8)

—Share comfort, solace, and peace (v. 9)

Ideas about the pastoral role in Latin America cannot be imported from abroad. We have our own rich cultural attributes which represent ways we communicate, use our space, relate with each other, live together, exercise solidarity, understand the concepts of pastoral care, and so on. In our search for a genuine response to biblical challenges, we need to take an in-depth look at these attributes again if we really want to work with those that are most conducive to a pastoral *praxis* that follows the servant-leader model.

2. *The need to turn to Jesus as model, paradigm, and ultimate reference.* If God wants to speak to us he will do it through his Word, in the context of prayer and profound compassion like that which the Master felt for people (Mk 6: 34). Turning to Jesus means looking at how his disciples interpreted the Master as they defined their own pastoral duties. After all, they had a wider perspective on the thinking of Jesus, beyond what we have in the Gospels. They saw him working and talking in many situations that have not been recorded. How did those disciples put into practice the perspectives they learned from the Master, in their own circumstances? How did they set about founding churches? What did they think about congregational life? Why was it so important to them to live in community, share needs, and even their own failures and struggles? What led Paul to say to brothers and sisters he did not know, "I can will what is right, but I cannot do it" (Rom 7: 18b)? Would there be any pastor today who would be moved

to confess from a pulpit what Paul revealed of his internal struggle?

There is no doubt that the Spirit inspired Peter to record what God had established in the gestation of his people and wished to reaffirm in the church: *the priesthood of all believers.* It is in this spirit that we should begin, if we really want to make radical changes, because that will force us to see ourselves without distinction of rank, under the very eye of God. From the Reformation until now, many congregations have tried to develop "the priesthood of all believers" in *praxis.* But these days, the idea is collecting dust in a corner, and a lot of people would prefer that it stay there. Is not this decade the moment when we should take this neglected objective from the debris in our churches and give it our serious attention? Could it serve the cellular church movement?

It is time to integrate all our efforts until every congregation, and every member within it, is performing a symphony under God's orchestration in perfect harmony!

9

Integral Mission in Worship

Josué Fonseca

To begin to write this chapter I did an exercise that I invite the reader to repeat in a spare moment: go through the hymnals and chorus books of different churches, observing what they reveal about their understanding of Christian worship. I was surprised by the results:

a. The evangelical hymnal of one historical church has only three hymns (out of more than five hundred) that make any reference to basic human needs, showing a lack of interest in social questions.
b. The hymnal of another historic church has no autochthonous hymns, but all translations, for the most part from English, showing a serious lack of concern for their people's own cultural values.
c. The hymnal of an independent church does not have a single hymn that refers to the cross of Christ, clearly pointing out some serious doctrinal limitations.
d. The songbook of a church related to the renewal movement did not include a single song or hymn in which the verbs were conjugated in the plural; songs were written exclusively with

the first person singular, a sign of excessive use of expressions of individualistic worship.

e. The songbook of a catholic parish has more than 350 hymns and songs, with a subject index and clearly defined sections entitled adoration, meditation, offertory, communion, thanksgiving, missionary vocations, and a section for the liturgical year. That is a range of music for worship that is a bit more balanced.

I reached other conclusions as well, but these provide a fair sample. Then I compared these with the hymnal of the local church of which I am a member, and took note of some of our virtues and faults. My questions are: How can we help our churches to be more faithful to the Bible in their worship? Are we going to be able to infuse our worship with the ethos of integral mission?

1. The Theology Reflected in the Worship Service

In 1912, J. Gresham Machen, the Reformed Church professor and theologian, distinguished three standard positions for understanding the link between Christian mission and the culture: the subordination of Christianity to the culture, the destruction of the culture by Christianity, or the transformation of the culture in order to put it at the service of God. Machen wrote:

> Rather than eliminating the distinction between the Kingdom of God and the world, or conversely retiring from the world in

> a kind of modernized intellectual monasticism, let us advance joyfully and enthusiastically to submit the world to God.[1]

For some decades, these three postures of Christian interpretation have defined both the theology of mission and the churches' development across the world, particularly in Latin America. The first way has been adopted, though very little, by some historical churches of a more liberal bent. For them the subjection of the Christian faith to the world's values has been so successful that to all intents and purposes they have ceased to exist. The second way is the one that seems to have been taken by the conservative churches, and perhaps by the Pentecostal churches too. They have strived to live the Christian life separated from, and in rejection of, the world, in the manner of the ancient monasteries, which produced religious sub-worlds which were supposed to eliminate all the cultural influences from Christianity. The third way is that of transforming and dedicating the culture to the service of God's Kingdom, which is clearly what we find in those churches who define themselves in terms of integral mission. It is this way that I would like to discuss in this work.

Following this line of thought, we can examine the kind of theology that is reflected in our public and private worship. In public worship services we can see these three theological postures in the contents of the liturgy. In churches that follow the first way, that of the subordination of faith to culture, worship forms and words follow the interests of the congregation, making much of human relationships in gatherings, like those of a social club, and relegating the Word and the relationship with God to

---

[1] J. Gresham Machen, *Cristianismo y cultura* (Christianity and Culture). (Netherlands: FELIRE, 1980), p. 10. Only the Spanish translation available to the author.

a secondary plane. Churches that take the second way, that of rejection of the culture, will have worship services that refer only to the relationship with God, heaven, and a community isolated from surrounding reality. They will use language that spiritualizes every idea in the world and seek to demonize every contact with all that is worldly. One can attend a Sunday service of one of these two models and immediately recognize the mission theology of the church.

So then, what kind of worship should churches with a thriving integral mission theology adopt as they seek to respect and transform culture to bring it into the service of the Lord? Integral mission, as we use the term here, means "the whole gospel, for the whole human being, by the whole church, in the whole world."

A short while ago, the leaders of a local church consulted their pastor about the definition of mission held by the church. The pastor replied, *"We believe in the theology of integral mission, but I confess that up to now I do not see it very well expressed in our church."*

It seems clear that the theology of integral mission, if we can describe it thus, has an unfinished task on the subject of worship and spirituality. This short work is an attempt to elucidate some clues that might help us in this undertaking.

2. Where Are We in our Worship Today?

In the past, we were told about the crisis of evangelism in Christian history. Furthermore, for centuries this sense of crisis in sound doctrine and theology has been maintained. Then, the second half of the twentieth century confronted us with the question of the nature of mission, and went so far as to create a discipline called "missiology." All of these subjects—evangelism, theology, and mission—have been critical issues for the Christian faith, especially at the end of the twentieth century.

These perennial tensions in the Christian faith appear to maintain their relevance in our current situation, but now we see clearly that a new crisis is emerging: a crisis of liturgy and worship. How could it be otherwise? New liturgical forms have appeared during the revivals and transformations of earlier centuries. For example, the sixteenth-century Reformation brought a new hymnody that came out in the vernacular. After the Methodist revival of the eighteenth century, Wesleyan hymns appeared. Perhaps another example might be the Pentecostal revival in Latin America at the beginning of the twentieth century that created an explosion of cultic expressions with a popular slant.

Now, at the beginning of the twenty-first century, Christian worship is again in a state of flux, not only in Latin America, but also across the continents. Christian churches are facing the challenge of new electronic liturgies. Pentecostal churches, which formerly rejected everything with a worldly sound, including musical instruments, are today putting on enormous productions with electronic bands that use great scenic effects and communication technology. Without warning church leaders, it seems that globalization and modernization arrived on the American continent, and neither evangelicals nor Catholics can escape its effects.

First we will look at these renewal liturgies[2] that are springing up in this atmosphere of modernization. Two factors seem to be

---

[2] I use the phrase "renewal liturgies" simply as a way of identifying them.

present in the novel liturgies of what is called the neo-Pentecostal revival, or of the mega-churches, which we have been experiencing for more than ten years now: marketing and individualism.

Marketing, as a form of expression derived from the world of consumerism, accentuates success, image, and advertizing in the life of the church. One key is to understand the religious marketing process in this way: show + crowds + money + show. Marketing has taken over the patterns of Christian worship in many places as follows: first, by imposing on the church the idea that public worship is the organization of an event that has to be well produced, with good—or apparently good—presentation, which becomes the content of the show-spectacle. It requires that the "show" be put on in the style of a TV program, including the use of make-up where necessary. Next, it expects the end result of providing a good show or a well-produced spectacle: the arrival of a large crowd of people. Of course, the crowds do not come overnight. The show must continue to be perfected until they come. When the people do come in large numbers, they need to be kept happy and entertained. They must never be given a badly rehearsed routine. And they must never be offended with doctrines or words that are not acceptable. The crowds become the measure of growth. They must be well cared for. Why? Because the crowd brings in the third element: money. The process of religious marketing is directed to this concrete, material, and specific end. Economic resources also become a measure of growth. When money is plentiful, the ministry grows, and we consider ourselves more spiritual, and the show becomes even more professional. The religious marketing process then continues on and on. Many evangelical sacred worship concerts follow this same pattern and help to confuse the audience, because they sometimes try to take the place of local church services and even criticize them.

Individualism is the other element strongly influencing this type of church. It acts as though it believed that the local church did not grow in the communion of the faithful, but in their isolation in the mass culture. Every individual in the crowd has their own agenda and pursues their own interests, without paying attention to the biblical teaching about the church as a body or community. A short while ago, a woman who had left her church several years previously, recounted, by way of testimony, her experience in a mega-church: *"I get what I want. I enjoy myself and feel good, without bothering about anybody or anything else. Nobody knows me there, so I am more comfortable."* If she is looking for emotions, she will find them in this kind of church. If she is looking for justification for her own private morality, she will find it in this kind of church. If she is looking for magical experiences, she will find them in this kind of church. If she is looking for an informal church, there she will be made to believe that the church has no institutional structure. If she is looking for pleasure, she will find it in this kind of church. If she wants rhythm, she will find it there. If she is looking for criticism of the traditional churches, she need not go elsewhere. It is like the supermarket, a place to find practically everything to eat and drink, but without any interaction between the consumers, save the occasional contact in line at the checkout. It is religious consumerism. Everything it offers is directed to the individual as an isolated being. In effect a powerful individualism is imposing itself on both the church and the worship service.

What is happening to the worship service in the more traditional or historical churches? Here too churches have their own difficulties. These congregations, rich in tradition and history, have existed for years, following models that little by little have become outdated. Their services are short and punctilious. They do not run overtime, because that would not please the worshipers. At the heart of the service is the sermon or exposition of the Word, which in many cases has very little to do with the actual life of the church. Often these churches will use every opportunity to denigrate charismatics and "renewal" churches. Clinging to the same rituals, this kind of worship is generally boring, and as a consequence turns off the young people. In a recent meeting of pastors, the minister of one of these churches asked if everybody had the same problem of communicating the faith to the children. He said, "*They don't want to believe.*" The truth may be that a local church that is characterized by its lack of commitment to mission and its improvised and repetitive services gives a good reason for people to reject the Christian faith as irrelevant. So they leave the church or look for alternative churches, including the esoteric ones. Yes, the traditional service also is in a state of crisis.

We see that there are similar phenomena in both the renewal liturgies and in the traditional churches. Both become ecclesiastical ghettos. Both give the people what they want. Both react strongly against each other. However, they also differ. While one allows itself to be deeply involved in the avalanche of modernity, the other rejects the modern. While one maintains its historical traditions, the other takes pride in its claim not to follow traditions.

Can integral mission offer some kind of hope for the local church in this critical situation?

3. Definition and Preparation of Christian Worship Services

Very little has been written about the impact of integral mission on the liturgical life of the church. Much more has been done to describe the community service aspect. We have already looked at what integral mission means. Now we must consider the issue of Christian worship.

William D. Maxwell has offered this excellent definition of worship:

> Worship is made up of our words and actions. It is the external expression of our homage and adoration, when we are assembled together in the presence of God. These words and actions are determined by two factors: our knowledge of the God whom we worship, and the human resources that we are able to bring to that worship. Christian worship is different from other forms of worship in that it is directed to the God and Father of our Lord Jesus Christ. Its development is different because the Spirit has been with and in the Church, counseling and guiding it since the day of Pentecost.[3]

What is Christian worship? It is to adore, to praise, to serve, and to dedicate oneself to God. And we express ourselves in worship according to our culture, with words, symbols, postures, and actions that have cultural significance. What is the cost of Christian worship? There is a price in terms of sacrifice, because the liturgy—which in Greek means *service*—implies a change of life, confession, commitment, and mission. To join in worship implies a readiness for the sacrificial offering of oneself to God.

Worship understood in the light of integral mission must include the whole content of the gospel, including its most complex challenges and teachings. The service of worship must include the whole human person, with all those potentialities and

---

[3] William D. Maxwell, *El culto cristiano* (Christian Worship) (Buenos Aires: Methopress, 1963), p. 15. Only the Spanish translation available to the author.

necessities that are experienced in our encounter with society and the world. It must include the whole Christian church, which carries with it the sense of *ecumenicity*[4] in worship. The totality of the gospel must find expression in our worship.

Our services also have to express an integral understanding of the growth of the church. Numerical growth is not the only kind of growth that is needed, if we are to be faithful to the Lord. One pastor, expounding his dreams for the future from the pulpit, said, "I dream that this church will vastly grow in number, and that many thousands will come to know the Savior." This aspiration seems to be common among evangelical leaders these days. Mission theologian Orlando Costas, however, distinguishes three dimensions in the true growth of the church:[5] extension, height, and depth. Growth in *extension* is actually numerical growth, and we are all agreed about that. Growth in *height* refers to the witness of the church's engagement in its community. We must surely all agree that there is no great advantage in having crowds in the congregation, while having a terrible reputation as a neighbor (though, truth be told, there are some churches that do not have a good reputation in their communities, because they are unaware of them). Growth in *depth* is about the development of discipleship and spirituality. Here worship and liturgy contribute to the integrated growth of the church, when they provide services of worship that are full of grace and blessing.

---

[4] The term *ecumenicity* is the term suggested by the biblical scholar Oscar Pereira with the aim of improving our understanding of the universality of the Church of Christ.

[5] Orlando Costas, *Compromiso y misión* (Commitment and Mission) (San José de Costa Rica: Caribe, 1979).

Christian worship, whether in private devotion or public expression, has its constitutive elements: songs and hymns, music, prayer, the Word, confession, the sacraments or offices, symbols, the offertory, and testimony. These elements need to be taken into account for the preparation, unity and celebration of the service, so that it reflects integral mission. How should we set about this in public worship services?

a. Service Preparation

The preparation of the service depends on the preparation of the coordinators or leaders of the service. This preparation is the responsibility of the church and its pastors. Some churches leave all to spontaneity; other churches, however, prepare their leaders. It is very important that the leaders of the service be trained and equipped as a worship team. That requires a commitment to this form of ministry, arranging regular meetings, teaching the basics of worship and the different aspects of the preparation and direction of services so that they are an invitation to praise God. We know churches that do not allow any layperson to lead a service without demonstrating genuine commitment to that ministry by taking part in coordinators' meetings.

b. The Unity of the Service

Public worship does not always have to include all the elements in a single service, but it does have to present the various elements that are included as a meaningful whole. The unity of the service is to be found in the thematic coherence of all the parts. Therefore it is vital that the Bible study or the theme of the sermon be known in advance, since this usually defines the theme of the service. Those pastors who improvise their message just a few hours before service do not make much of a contribution to the thematic unity of the worship in their church. We can find this kind of unity of motif in the Book of Psalms, in the liturgical festivals of the Old Testament, and in the Christian worship of the early church. Just as a Psalm begins and ends on the same note, so should our public acts of worship.

c. The Presentation of Worship

An act of public worship that has been prepared as a thematic whole is more fitted to give to God as an offering of praise. The offering of worship has its own cultural properties that are characteristic of the worshippers. Urban worship is different from rural worship, and a native service is different from a service in a Hispano-American culture. These cultural differences give to Christian worship a richness that we should value highly. The presentation of Christian worship also has an aesthetic dimension. We have to bring beauty into our services through our creativity and variety, our artistic expressions, our use of symbol and language that is worthy of the occasion. The use of crude language in worship does not help to make it beautiful for our God.

4. Christian Worship and Integral Mission

For an understanding of worship seen from an integral perspective, I would recommend the document *"Adoración y liturgia"* (Worship and Liturgy)[6] that was produced by the forty

[6] *Palabra, Espíritu, y Misión. El testimonio evangélico hacia el Tercer Milenio* (Word, Spirit, and Mission. Evangelical Witness Approaching the

participants of the Consultation which, under the same title, took place as part of the Fourth Latin American Congress on Evangelism (CLADE IV) celebrated in Quito, Ecuador, September 2 - 9, 2000. This document is interesting because it comes out of the work and reflection of a group of participants who put a great deal of effort into speaking and writing from the perspective of their own situation in more than twelve different countries, about their daily experience of the crisis in worship styles in our churches.

The document emphasizes that

> in liturgy we express what we are, what we believe and to whom we address our worship. We also communicate our mission in the world. Consequently there is a close link between worship and theology, worship and service, and worship and our self-understanding as a community that gives praise to God for salvation in Jesus Christ, in the fellowship of the Holy Spirit.[7]

For churches engaged in integral mission, we can distinguish five attributes that might be helpful for leaders of worship, pastors, and lay people.

a. Genuine Spirituality

The worship service in the Christian church is one of the disciplines of our devotion to God, which is the basis of our spirituality, of our worship. However, we practice other

---

Third Millennium), Documents of the Fourth Latin American Congress on Evangelism (CLADE IV) (Buenos Aires: Kairós, 2001), Chapter 18, pp. 203-209.

[7] *Ibid*., p. 203.

disciplines as well as public worship: retreats, devotions, fasting, meditation, holy days, and many others. Worship, or Christian devotion, goes far beyond services in church. It goes beyond rhythms and music. The search for a spirituality enriched by other Christian disciplines can be of great help in strengthening the public worship of the local church.

Apart from the devotional aspect, spirituality requires a coherent Christian ethic. In Isaiah 58, the prophet's denunciation speaks of people who say that they wish to know the ways of the Lord and draw near to him, but they fast to serve their own ends, they oppress their workers, they do not provide bread for the hungry nor hospitality to the homeless, they speak vanity, they wag a threatening finger, and hide themselves from their own kin. The prophet asks if this is the kind of fasting that the Lord chooses. The reply is negative. God desires worship and spiritual discipline coherent with an ethic that keeps the commandments. When spirituality and ethics come together, Christian worship, public or private, is enriched and edifying for all.

b. Multi-traditional Enrichment

Another aspect that worship rooted in integral mission should cultivate is respect for other liturgical traditions. In his book *Liturgia para el siglo XXI. Antología de la liturgia cristiana,* (Liturgy for the twenty-first Century. An Anthology of Christian Worship)[8] the Spanish author Sebastián Rodríguez examines worship in the Old Testament, the New Testament, and through the centuries. He presents examples of liturgical forms and materials, many different types of worship, and patterns of

---

[8] Sebastián Rodríguez, *Liturgia para el siglo XXI. Antología de la liturgia cristiana.* (Barcelona: CLIE, 1999).

worship typical of the various historical Christian traditions. Learning about the wholesome liturgical traditions will help us to enhance and enliven our services. Churches engaged in integral mission will want to strengthen their liturgical practice through this kind of study. The document quoted above from CLADE IV, "*Adoración y liturgia,*" notes, "Worship in Latin America should seek a balance between traditional and contemporary patterns and styles."[9]

Faced with the globalization of the forms of worship, which tends towards a uniformity in liturgy following a largely North American style, the suggestion of enriching our worship from other traditions could help us to nourish a liturgical experience which is more diverse, varied, and colorful.

We would like to suggest that churches learn from one another: the more traditional churches from the more renewed; and the more renewed, from the more traditional. Baptists could benefit from elements of the Anglican tradition, and Anglicans from the communal participation of Baptist worship. The same could happen between Pentecostals, independent churches, Methodists, Presbyterians and others. We only need to be open to the Spirit to learn from each other. We in the Protestant traditions also need to learn from Roman Catholic and Orthodox traditions, especially in those practices which we could easily adapt and use, as is happening these days in reverse, with evangelical practices and songs being used to help and enhance the worship of Catholic parishes, something that would have been inconceivable in former times.

---

[9] *Palabra, Espíritu y Misión* (Word, Spirit, and Mission), p. 206.

We do not need to do everything in the same way always. A variety from different traditions can bring a very special quality to our Christian worship.

c. Care for Personal and Social Needs

Christian worship engaged in integral mission also needs to concern itself with the specific social and personal needs of the surrounding community. The worship service is not some kind of space in which to separate ourselves from the reality of life around us. On the contrary, we should always be able to see reflected in our worship the human dramas of daily life. Sadly this is not always the case. Worship services in some churches never get anywhere near the needs of the people. Their spiritualized language is deliberately devoid of the hardships of unemployment, poverty, discrimination, sexual abuse, family violence, contempt for the elderly, abandonment of children, lack of opportunities for the young, alcoholism, drug addiction, sickness, urban decay, and many other human dramas. Not long ago, in one of the major cities of Latin America, there was a great public clamor about a person's disappearance. The story was covered in all the news media. The church leaders asked the pastor to pray about the case and invite the distraught family to an intercession service. The pastor's response was pathetic. He turned down the request without a word of explanation. The worship service was too preoccupied with the church's own affairs to bother about those of outsiders. A church engaged in integral mission does not neglect such an opportunity to testify in the community.

Christian worship committed to integral mission sees all social and personal crises as areas of service, as mission opportunities that need our help, and offers creative acts of ministry in response.

d. Folkloric Expressions

The document *"Adoración y liturgia"* of CLADE IV says:

> Over against the kind of Christianity that was imposed on our cultures in what was assumed to be some kind of "Christian culture" (the Catholic and Protestant evangelization of Latin America), we are today demanding a proper respect and appreciation of our culture as a means of liturgical expression.[10]

That means that in both language and music, symbol, style, and the aesthetics of worship we need to include the folk elements of each people. We can praise God in our native languages with our musical instruments and our own vocal styles, and do it without apologizing to anyone.

A negative example took place at a celebration of a new translation of the Bible in a particular ethnic community in Latin America. A music group was invited, a group very typical of the local culture, and sang in their own language songs translated from English accompanied on Spanish instruments. When they were asked to use their own instruments, and perform their native songs with their native musical style, they replied that they could not do that because they had been taught that such things were "worldly."

Folkloric expressions are very important for worship and for communicating the gospel, because they address not only the mind but also the heart of the people. One of the great advantages of many of the renewal churches in Latin America is that they include musical rhythms, melodies, instruments, and

---

[10] *Ibid.*, p. 205.

liturgical expressions that belong to the cultural traditions of our native peoples. *"Adoración y liturgia"* has this to say about the use of hymnody, music, and instruments from foreign cultures:

> Worship in Latin America, as well as being varied and heterogeneous, is distinguished by an interpenetration of cultures. It is true to say that we find ourselves in the presence of multi-cultural liturgies in which the foreign and the native flow into one another. We believe it to be right that we should continue to encourage these cultural exchanges that enrich the regional and denominational patterns of worship, and affirm the universality of Christian worship.[11]

e. Christian *Ecumenicity*

We have suggested above that the word *ecumenicity* is used to express more clearly the meaning of the universality of the church of Christ. The subject is not easy, but Christian worship really does furnish us with a valuable opportunity to learn to experience the catholicity of our faith. Believers today, from both Catholic and Protestant traditions, are learning to overcome their complexes and prejudices, and humbly experience these kinds of inter-church events.

Christian worship that is engaged in integral mission must also emphasize this ecumenical dimension. Current experience suggests that the damaging relationships that existed between the churches in the past are being left in the past. We have turned a corner from those days. Renewal groups are regularly noticing it in their lives, and so are the historical churches. Pentecostals and independents have fewer conflicts these days than in former

---

[11] *Ibid.*

times over this type of communion. Schools, universities, local councils, governments, and other public bodies are inviting pastors and priests to come together in particular religious acts. All this progress is essential to us, who believe in the integral mission of the church.

Conclusion

In accordance with the CLADE IV document *"Adoración y liturgia"* we need a theology of worship for Latin America that will enable us to reassess the relationship between culture and faith, that will lead us to a meaningful dialogue between our liturgical heritage and contemporary renewal, that will increase participation and promote opportunities to facilitate the sharing of liturgical ideas in the church, and that will produce well equipped liturgical leadership.

Every day there are more churches that recognize the importance of this work for the comprehensive dissemination of the gospel in today's world. These are churches that will try to redeem aspects of our culture and include them in our worship, and try to limit examples of religious consumerism that spring out of our rush to modernity. They are churches that pay more attention to the coherence and integrity of worship than to the volume of the amplifiers. They are churches that speak more in the plural of community than in the singular of individualism. Churches that want worship services to be alive and vigorous, but do not let themselves be trapped by a manipulated renewal. Churches that prepare the leaders of worship well, so that our services are shining examples of the spirit of devotion to God. Churches that speak not only about a spiritualized religious life, but that strive to ensure that their spiritual models take on all the riches of the different spiritual disciplines, with an ethical commitment to the true worship God requires. Churches that adopt the wealth of other Christian traditions in their liturgical activity. Churches that, like the Samaritan of the parable, do not pass by on the other side when they are confronted by personal and social needs. Churches that are using folkloric expressions as part of the language of worship. Churches that are seeking to live out an authentic Christian faith in communion with the rest of the Christian community.

Growing in worship with the insights from integral mission, in all the dimensions mentioned above, will bring with it the hope of a church in the future that is more alive, more biblical, and more faithful to the Lord's commandment in his Word. So be it!

II

Examples of Churches that Practice Integral Mission

10

"I'm Luis Pardo, folks"

Pedro Arana-Quiroz

This is the beginning of an old style Peruvian waltz, and it goes on ". . . the famous bandit." Luis Pardo was a rough Peruvian Robin Hood figure from the district of Ancash, to the North of Lima. He belonged to a well-to-do family, but his social conscience drove him to live among the marginalized and excluded. "That is why I love children, love and respect old people, and the Indians who are my sisters and brothers, and I give my heart to them." I have no idea why forty families gave this name to their "shanty town," though I tried to look into it. I do know, however, some of the more important aspects linking this marginal community to a local church, and how together they discovered a true kinship in the human community the God-Man came to save.

1. The Context

I was ordained a Presbyterian pastor on May 10, 1980, and was put in charge of a congregation called "Pueblo Libre," after the district of Lima where it was located. It was a middle and lower-middle class congregation, with a powerful vision and missionary passion. From its inception it was self-supporting, self-perpetuating, and convinced that Christian churches should, because of the nature of grace, be heterogeneous units or, to put it another way, "sociological miracles."

Since the seventies, I had been reflecting and writing about integral mission.[1] Now the time had come to put it into practice. I put my campaign plan together for the Consistory, our governing body, and received their approval. In a nutshell, the plan was as follows: that the liturgy, acknowledging its roots in reformed principles, would be indigenous in character; that the pastoral ministry would be maintained by the tithes and giving of the faithful; that the congregation would spread the gospel in order to grow, and would grow in the spreading of the gospel; that discipleship would be personal and integral; and that the congregation would create opportunities for the faithful to engage in the service of the people, especially the poor. All of this activity would take place in a specific area, time line, and community—"Pueblo Libre!"

I then reviewed a document about the situation, population, businesses, and services, that I had gotten from the Council of that district, which had a population of some seventy thousand. A few blocks from the city limits of Lima, there was a little *"Pueblo Joven"* (literally "Young Village"), the name that the military government had given to the shanty towns, marginalized groups, and ghettoes of poor people in the middle of different sectors of the city. Could this be the area for our missionary outreach? The prayers of our congregation, made up of fifty-eight people of some twelve families, had been, and still were, underpinning the project which was being initiated.

---

[1] See *Providencia y revolución* (Lima: El Estandarte de la Verdad, 1970).

2. The Meeting

One Monday morning at 9 o'clock—that was my time to go to the office in the church—I made for "Luis Pardo," the name that this community of forty-two families had chosen. Some children were playing on the ground in front of the community center. Everything seemed deserted. Gradually a few women appeared. I introduced myself as a pastor and I asked for their leaders. They found the chairperson of the Basic Education Program (PRONOEI).

We went inside the community center and I noticed a noise coming from the roof made of straw mats. Cats were chasing about and shaking down bits of dry dirt onto the thirty-odd people we were about to talk to.

The president, doña Susana, had the floor:

"You know that we're all Catholics here," she said.

"I suppose so," was my hurried response to such an unexpected beginning.

She asked, "But you still want to work with us?"

"Of course!" I said with no hesitation. And that is how our friendship started.

In the following days they asked me to take some babies to the Children's Hospital. And we met to discuss our initial projects, the first of which was a food program for children, supported by World Vision. Meetings multiplied and soon I was spending virtually half my time there, though I was pastor to a congregation. It gave me a great deal of satisfaction, but I kept a check on how much time the social ministry was taking up.

One thing was really annoying to me, though. People would make an appointment with me for nine o'clock in the morning, and come an hour or an hour and a half later. It was really annoying. I never said anything to them, but I would think, "Doesn't it ever cross your mind that I might have other things to do?" Or "How inconsiderate can they get, when we are trying to help them!" Then the World Vision promoter, Corina Villacorta, came to my aid and explained it to me. "Pastor," she said, "you need to realize that your timetable is different from that of this community. These mothers start work before four in the morning, when their husbands have their breakfast and go out to work. We start at nine. Later, they try to rest until seven, when they have to get the children's breakfast and get them off to school."

What a lesson! In Lima there are communities that have a different "space-time" culture. Integral mission has to take into consideration the situation in which we are ministering. I saw the importance of context again later, when we began helping the street children, the gangs, and the "heavy metal" addicts. Maybe Paul had this kind of situation in mind when he said, "I have become all things to all people, that I might by all means save some" (1Cor 9:22). But it is not an easy lesson to learn. I have known missionaries, both national and foreign, with and without studies in theology and missions, some with qualifications in anthropology or sociology, who still expected the communities they were helping to adapt to their hours, styles, and customs along with their program—a great recipe for failure.

3. Dialogue for Action

The roof of the community center had me worried. The flimsy rafters were giving way and the children, mothers, and teachers were in danger of a serious accident. In a meeting I asked the mothers:

"Why aren't we repairing the roof?"

"Because that would cost a lot, Pastor. Where are we going to find that kind of money?" they replied.

"Couldn't we organize some sort of activity?" I answered; "What do you think?"

"It sounds o.k.," I heard someone say. And other mothers joined in.

"A chicken supper, and we could sell beer."

I was saying inside, "What a mess I've gotten myself into, Lord!", when another voice joined in. . . .

"Kebabs with beer and a lottery?"

"We can make money selling beer!" another voice said.

I was thinking to myself, "What am I going to say to the Consistory?"

Then I saw a way out.

"How about a film?" I said. And practically in unison I heard,

"That's too much. How are we going to pay for it?"

Somewhat relieved, I told them that I had a friend who had a projector and films. So with the kind assistance of the Rev. Héctor Pina, the "Luis Pardo" community showed films from the Moody Institute of Science every Saturday for several weeks. The leaders and the mothers planned the project, and arranged and delegated the various jobs. And for several weeks, with some advance publicity, we saw, every Saturday, people paying to go in. The outcome was a new roof for the local hall. I saw then, and not for the last time, the tremendous capacity for organization and work of people we consider "the poor."

* * *

After several months of our presence and participation in the life of the settlement, one day a group of leaders, men and women, from "Luis Pardo" met with me and said, "We have been here in this place for seventeen years, and no institution or organization, either public or private, has shown any interest in us. But now, because of the films we have been showing, for the first time the parish priest from *Urbanización Palomino* has been to see us."

The parish priest had tried, without success, to dissuade them from showing these "evangelists'" films. The community persevered, however, because it was beginning to see that by taking certain actions, apparently quite small, they were able to improve the quality of their lives by their own efforts. They later managed to buy a sewing machine, which they made available for mothers in the community to use.

We were very much aware of the moral quality and the intelligence of the leaders of the community. A few of the mothers had completed high school. We helped them enroll in an open course in social work offered by the Pontificia Universidad Católica del Peru. They were the only ones in their classroom who were different. Their training enabled them later to provide the community with a day-care center for the children of working mothers, to have a source of income and opportunities for mutual support. I remember with gratitude the work and efforts of Elena Segura that brought all this to fruition.

* * *

December came, and with it came Christmas. Up to that point I had not even hinted at the possibility of preaching or teaching the gospel, even though I was longing to do so. The community arranged a Christmas supper and invited our church members. It was a gesture of gratitude and affection. They could now see us as friends, even very close friends. The priest, whom I knew, was also there, and I greeted him. The situation became a bit uncomfortable, because the people of the neighborhood directed all their attention to our church members. And then, the opportunity I had been hoping for came as a surprise. "Pastor," the president of the women's group said, "say something about Christmas." It was a short message. Afterwards several of the women asked if we could come and teach the Bible to the children.

The following Sunday, very enthusiastically, I told the congregation that the mothers of "Luis Pardo" *had asked us* whether, in addition to helping the children with their school work and providing a snack for them during the week, we could provide some Bible classes for the children on Sundays. They had taken the initiative! Our congregation had to respond to their need. I approached the young people and put the challenge to them. Several hands went up in response. Thank God for that!

Then, while I was shaking hands with members of the congregation, the mother of one of the young people in the team said to me, "Pastor, how can I let my daughter go with these people?" The question hit me like a bucketful of cold water. I shared it with my wife and we prayed about it and arrived at a solution.

One Saturday we invited the mothers of the young people on the team and the mothers from "Luis Pardo" to our home for lunch. That meeting was decisive for the future of the project. It was warm and friendly. We became friends and companions, as we broke bread together. We overcame many prejudices and the missionary vision went on finding channels of grace in evangelism, teaching, and social service.

4. Friends in Discipleship

A year went by. I was pastor of Pueblo Libre, but the greater part of my time was spent in "Luis Pardo." The congregation had started to grow and to get involved in community service. In our church building we opened our "St. Luke" medical center. The day-care center was functioning. We had an extension project in the *Urbanización Palomino*. We needed someone to help. We prayed about it and the answer came, with the provision of not only one person, but two. Roberto Van Treek, a young sociology graduate from Wheaton College in North America, came, with all his costs covered; and Bladimiro Chuquimbalqui, from our own country, from the Amazonas region, hoping to progress in life in Lima, approached our church and offered his services.

Our paths crossed again in Lima in August of 2001. Van Treek is a practicing clinical psychologist. He and his wife, Elena, whom he had met in our day care center and taken away, have two beautiful children. Elena is Director of the Peace and Justice organization in Chicago. Bladimiro is currently a sociologist and next year, God willing, he will graduate as a lawyer. He generously offers his services to a non-governmental organization that we started in 1987, called Integral Urban-Rural Mission (MISIUR). He helps in the preparation of new projects. They are still making an impact in people's lives. All this brings into relief the power that volunteers with vision and compassion for the poor can bring. They bond their professionalism with their faith, without any thought of gain, and give themselves in Christian service, following the steps of their Lord (Mk 10:45).

5. Some Obstacles

In sharp contrast to this voluntary effort is the municipal and state bureaucracy. When tuberculosis was diagnosed in some children in the project and in one of the high schools in the neighborhood, I approached the Health Center to see what they were able to do for the children and how we could coordinate our efforts. They had no medicines, nor were they willing to try to get any. I went to see the head of the epidemiology department in Lima Metropolitan Hospital, and the degree of indifference to the problem was as infuriating as it was astonishing. We were left having to limit our efforts to what a local church with a clinic could achieve with donated medicines and the generous work of a Christian doctor, David Posadas.

The strip of land which the people of "Luis Pardo" had taken over and built their homes was small in relation to the whole area. We encouraged them to set to work completing applications to the authorities for ownership rights. The first opposition to them came from their lower middle class neighbours. The second hurdle was the incompetence and disorder of the public administration and the corruption of the civil authorities and the lawyers they contracted. A third problem was the leadership's timidity in decision-making. At one time we found ourselves in a serious confrontation with the Belaunde government, which was proposing the destruction of all the shanty towns and slum neighborhoods in Lima. The leaders of the community came looking for me one night, faced with their imminent eviction by the police. We stayed together all night waiting for the violence, armed with the deeds that legalized their ownership, and flags that could be stretched in front of the doors so that the government forces would find themselves having to trample on them in order to get into the houses. In those days people still respected the national symbols.

There we came to realize that integral mission can mean social and even political leadership; that in Peru, as elsewhere in Latin America, the destructive forces that hinder our development are envy, indifference to human suffering, incompetence, and corruption. Then, in addition, there is a view of the Christian gospel that turns spiritual things into an abstraction and regards the exercise of civic responsibilities as something sinful, something which in our days is redeemed during the time of elections when some renowned other-worldly leaders become candidates to parliament because they have realized that they "were mistaken." And when they lose the world goes on just the same.

In August 2001 Van Treek and his family and my wife and I went back to visit our friends in "Luis Pardo." They all had houses built with sound materials, they all had their official documents, and several had come to know the Lord Jesus. We said, "It was well worth the effort of standing in solidarity with them!"

6. Mission is two-directional

One morning I arrived in the community and a robust dark-skinned lady came up to me and said: "Pastor, I want a word with you." Since I supposed it was something private we wisely moved away from the group. I heard, straight out, her confession: "Last night I nearly did something terrible." Her husband had come home drunk, he had attacked her and then gone to sleep. She had gone out looking for a large stone, and just as she was going back into her house to kill him, her Christian neighbor got up and persuaded her not to do it. She had confessed; she was truly repentant, and she needed the words of forgiveness and hope from the gospel. Several people came to believe in Jesus Christ as Lord and Saviour and are today members of another Presbyterian church, fruit of our missionary effort.

In the course of events, we made contact with the University of San Martín de Porres so that Social Service students could do their pre-professional internships in our church in "Luis Pardo." One of those students was Gina García, a cheerful young woman with lots of personality and beautiful brown eyes. She was not a Christian. But the contact with the children, the mothers, the believers, with the Word, and with the congregation were the means used by the Spirit of God to bring her to Christ. She married a young man in the church, Manuel Ortiz, and they had two children, Isaías and Cristina.

Two years ago they discovered that Gina had multiple sclerosis. The sisters and brothers would visit her, and we saw how, little by little, the degenerative disease was reducing her mobility, her touch, and her sight; but we also saw how her faith was growing, and how she was sustained by seeing "him who is invisible" (Heb 11:27).

I have often asked myself why we Christians separate evangelism and discipleship from social action. Why are we always tempted to think that we are the ones bringing help, when so often we are the ones helped at our point of deepest need by those whom we call "beneficiaries?" Gina has since passed into the presence of her Lord, but she helped us grow in our own faith and trust in the Lord.

11

Vignettes of a Servant Church

C. René Padilla

If I learned anything at the beginning of my work as a pastor in a small middle-class church in a residential district of Greater Buenos Aires in the middle of the sixties, it was that frequently the factors that most influence the life and mission of the church are not the result of human planning. They burst out on our journey and surprise us, like a refreshing rain shower on a hot sunny day.

This was an evangelical church like very many others, turned in on itself, with neither vision nor mission. Once a year a big "evangelistic campaign" was held, lasting two or three consecutive nights, and an evangelist from the denomination was invited for the occasion. As soon as this annual effort had finished, everything returned to its sad normality. The only certain result was the exhaustion of the members, compensated sometimes by the addition of two or three new "souls" in the congregation.

I was one of a group of three men called to form a new pastoral team in 1976, and we were agreed about one thing: this church required radical change. The big question was how to bring it about. The first thing we decided to do was to preach some sermons in a conversational style—with the possibility that the hearers make comments or raise questions—about the nature and mission of the church. At the same time we took some practical steps to ensure that the Bible teaching not remain on the level of abstractions, but that it be incarnated in that small faith community. One step, for example, was the publication of a weekly newsletter containing a summary of that week's sermon, for discussion by members of the congregation in mid-week house groups. Another step was setting up a monthly open forum to reflect in more detail on the themes of the sermons and the questions that had arisen from them.

Today, if I were a member of a pastoral team that found itself with the responsibility of helping a church escape from its self-absorption, I would still vote for starting with a teaching ministry with an emphasis on ecclesiology. *Every church, large or small, needs a clear vision of what it means to be the people of God in a secular society.* However, I am convinced that the decisive factor in the radical change of perspective that happened in our church in 1976 was not the teaching ministry, nor anything else we had planned. It was something totally unexpected. God intervened and surprised us. For us, this was like an unexpected shower on a hot day.

1. A Church for Sinners

One Sunday like many others, a young man named Rafael[1] suddenly appeared in church. After the service he told me his story. It was a tale of a former drug dealer, a born leader,

---

[1] The names of people mentioned here are pseudonymous.

experienced in the illegal business of prostitution, whose adventures had taken him to the United States. There, in the city of Boston, he had gone into a café one fine day following a young woman who had attracted his attention. The café was an outpost of evangelism of one of the churches, where every so often there was a presentation of the gospel. There, for the first time in his life, Rafael heard the good news of salvation in Christ. The message changed his life, and as a result the new believer decided to return to his own land with a double objective in mind: to share his faith with his old comrades in crime, and to buy a house for his parents. When he got back to Buenos Aires, with the idea of fulfilling his first intention, he was looking for an evangelical church, and that is how he came upon ours. When he ended his story he asked, "Would it be all right for me to bring my friends to this church?"

I could never have dreamed what my affirmative reply would mean to the church. The following Sunday we were literally "invaded" by a score of young drug addicts, male and female, invited by Rafael. What was our church to do with these dropouts—a church of "nice people" for whom social advancement had unequivocal priority over involvement in God's mission? And then again, even if the members of the congregation were really positive towards the drug addicts, how could they avoid their very presence in the church projecting a bad image in the neighborhood as a whole? And how were they to handle the question of the dangers of drug addiction spreading among the church families?

In the months that followed, the church suffered an identity crisis. Several threatened to leave unless we took strong measures to ensure that Rafael's friends not attend church under the influence of drugs, while others were experiencing a real *metanoia*, a complete change of attitude towards drug addicts, and as a result of their encounter with them, *a total reorientation of their understanding of the church and their part in it.*

It is possible that, during that time, some church members decided to seek fresh pastures where they did not have to graze alongside "odd" sheep like those whom Rafael led in. If so, it was not many. The great majority of members gradually learned to love with that same love with which God loves us in Christ. Consequently, several of the addicts got off drugs to embark on a new journey of faith.

A fine example of the transforming power of love in action among us in those days is Leonardo, called Leo. He was born in the simple home of a newsvendor, in the year that the famous Perón was toppled (1955), and he was 21 when he started coming to church. Of his twenty-one years, he had lived the previous seven in the world of narcotics. For a year he came to church without having the faintest idea what he was doing there. He went on taking drugs, but he attended church meetings, because he knew that there nobody was going to throw him out, that he was loved and accepted despite his lifestyle. One day, after getting into a street fight, he was put in prison. To his surprise several members of the church, especially the youth, went to visit him and take him clothes and food. In God's good time, Leo gave his life to Jesus Christ and quit the drugs. Today, he runs the "*Renacer*" (rebirth) home, a rehabilitation center for drug addicts, to which we will refer again.

If in 1976 someone had suggested "doing something" about spreading the seed of the gospel among drug addicts, it is quite certain that we would have refused even to consider the possibility. However, from that year on, in response to the challenge that God put in our way, *the ministry to drug addicts has been one of the main channels of the church's mission.* The thrust in the teaching, meeting schedules, budgetary priorities, and other aspects of church life spin off from that hub. The church was structured to serve people in those marginalized sectors of society.

To this end, Rafael was appointed to work with the church and was assigned the job of visiting the local bars seeking out victims of drug addiction. In this way the *Programa Andrés* ("Andrew Program") was started, and eventually became a major drug rehabilitation program.[2] The results, however, were not only for the benefit of the addicts; the whole church benefitted. The presence of young people like Leo was the means whereby God taught us one of the most important lessons that we needed to learn: *that the church of God is a church for sinners.* Of course that is not to deny that the church is the "communion of the saints" because it has been "sanctified" in Christ. For this reason the church does not withdraw from sinful humanity, but rather lives in solidarity with it and experiences the forgiveness of God by faith. Only the church that lives by the grace of God is in a condition to proclaim the good news of salvation in Christ.

2. "Let the Little Children Come to Me"

The ministry of rehabilitation of drug addicts became our church's entry point into the world of the poor. Alerted by the

---

[2] Sadly, in the 1980's the *Programa Andrés* severed its ties with the church, and became secularized to the extent of becoming a lucrative business. It was with the idea of recovering its original vision that two of its founding members left the program to start up "*Renacer,*" which up to now has kept its links with the congregation.

pressing needs that came into focus as a result of the *Programa Andrés*, a group of young people from the church started a weekly program of recreational activities and Bible studies in a primary school in San Fernando Oeste, a working class suburb of Buenos Aires. There a new community of faith was gradually taking shape. The church engaged the services of Mariana, a young teacher, to give some educational support to the children of the district, in a room rented especially for the purpose.

I can still remember some of the long pastoral conversations I had with that young woman, who at nineteen years of age felt herself continually challenged by the crisis of poverty and injustice facing the families of these young pupils. Mariana's remedial classes gave us eyes to see human needs that we had scarcely been aware of until that time.

One of the most severe crises that our church had to face arose from a disagreement among the members over our strategy for furthering the ministry in San Fernando Oeste. The conflict began in 1982 when the church had to decide whether or not to appoint a young social worker, named Viviana, as director of this ministry. She was anxious to move to the area with her family in order to get on with the work. But, as soon as the idea came up, people opposed to the project embarked on a campaign to prevent the appointment. One of the arguments was that Viviana had "communist tendencies," as evidenced, according to them, by certain poems she had written about street children in Buenos Aires. I shall never forget the "administrative assembly" in which the proposal was debated. *On that day the church defined itself theologically. It appointed a social science professional to manage a church ministry in a poor neighborhood.* We also lost five members who disagreed with the decision. Could it be a coincidence that they were all people who were financially well off?

Viviana was not just a social worker. She and her husband Mario shared a deep commitment to Jesus Christ, and it was that commitment that motivated them to move into San Fernando Oeste. A short time later another couple from the church joined them in their adventure of faith: Mariana, the teacher, and her husband Eduardo, recently married. John Perkins, the black prophet of Mendenhall, Mississippi, in his book *With Justice for All*, says that the first requirement, if a church is to serve the poor, is "relocation." Some members have to move to where the poor live, and put down roots among them. That is what these two middle-class professional couples did. During the major part of the eighties they laid the foundations of a new "Christian base community," which is still carrying out integral mission there today. Practically all the current leaders in that community were born and raised in the district, having been brought to faith while they were among the children whose lives were touched by the members of that group of young people from our church.

One of the ministries that developed in San Fernando Oeste to serve the community was a child care center and kindergarten, where every day from Monday to Friday some forty children of working mothers were cared for. Its originator was a young Swiss teacher who spent two years working with the outreach ministry of the church in San Fernando Oeste. The building where the kindergarten functioned was built with funds donated by the mother of this young woman when she asked people to give money for the kindergarten instead of buying flowers for her husband's funeral. For some years, until its closing, the kindergarten functioned with personnel from the district itself, both paid staff and volunteers.

3. "From Exclusion to Solidarity"

This is the title of a little book that Viviana, the social worker described above, published in 1995. Based on the thesis for her degree in social work, it draws together some of her real life experiences working with people infected by HIV/Aids. Once again, the experience took place in that same modest faith community in which God intervened and surprised us in 1976, and which almost inadvertently found itself committed to a ministry among drug addicts. Since those days, HIV/Aids has appeared on the drug scene giving the drama the character of real life tragedy. No longer is it possible to participate in that ministry without finding oneself involved in the need to offer pastoral care to both the carriers of the virus and their families and friends.

Under Leo's leadership, for a number of years the "*Renacer*" center, supported by our church and a church from another denomination, has taken under its care many drug addicts who were trying to sort themselves out. *The psychological treatment accompanied by a rich dose of faith, hope, and love, has had amazing results.* These days, that care has expanded to include accompanying some of those young people on their journey through the valley of the shadow of death, as victims of Aids. Several people have arrived at the church with this sentence of death in their bodies, have been received into membership of the church, and have experienced the love of God's family up to the day the sentence was carried out.

The main part of Viviana's thesis is based on the story of Gonzalo, a man who came to the "*Renacer*" center and the church with that illness which has been called "a place where the contradictions within our society are brought to light." When Gonzalo died he was forty years old, and in the last five he had had the experience of being part of the church. A few days before he died he said that those five years had given meaning to his whole life. The reason is clear: for him being part of the church took him from a dark world of discrimination to one filled with the light of solidarity and love.

4. Shaping a Christian Mind

In a society like that of Latin America, where institutional injustice is so apparent, one of the clearer signs of conversion to Jesus Christ is that move into social solidarity experienced by a local church of the middle class. That kind of *metanoia* can only happen through the action of the Holy Spirit who anointed the Messiah to bring good news to the poor, to proclaim release to the captives, and recovery of sight to the blind, to let the oppressed go free, and to proclaim the year of the Lord's favor.

It should come as no surprise that in a church that gives priority to following the crucified Messiah people should be called to the service of the outcast and the poor. I think for example of Walter and Alicia, two graduates from a university in the United States, whose "relocation" into a poor district on the edge of Greater Buenos Aires gave form and meaning to the presence of the good news of the Kingdom—good news to the poor. I think, too, of Marcos, a brilliant professional, who managed to combine research in the University of Buenos Aires with a remarkable apostolate among young drug addicts. He used to meet with them every week in an abandoned house in the city center to drink *mate* and study the Bible, and with them he spent a night in a police station, because the police had a "suspicion" that they were using drugs. That night, Marcos experienced for himself the abuses that are inflicted on marginalized people. In time, those experiences led him to leave his academic career and devote himself to the pastoral ministry.

At the end of the eighties, several of us members of the "servant church" of which we have been speaking organized the *Fundación Kairós* (Kairos Foundation). This little non-governmental organization (NGO) gave institutional shape to the vision of the Kairos Community, started in 1976: *to train disciples of Christ to live out their faith in every area of human existence, particularly in the professional field, and commit themselves to the integral mission of the church.* Today the *Fundación Kairós* enjoys the participation of some fifty professional people (volunteers, in many cases) who lend their services to the different ministries:

* Ministerios de Educación Teológica [Theological Education Ministries], including the *Centro de Estudios Teológicos Interdisciplinarios* [Center for Interdisciplinary Theological Studies, CETI], a program of theological education for Christian professionals who want to equip themselves for service to God and the church, and in their own fields. The *Fundación Kairós* also collaborates with the (Korean) Chung Ang Presbyterian Church in the *Instituto de Formación Biblico-teológica* [Biblical Theology Training Institute], whose program of theological education, directed at the popular level, is benefiting hundreds of students in different centers throughout the country.
* The *Centro Kairós*, a place for retreats, consultations, seminars, and workshops at local, national or international

levels on topics related to discipleship and the mission of the church.

* *Ministerios a la Familia* [Family Ministries] including programs of *EIRENE* (Peace), for people seeking training in ministry to the family.
* *Publicaciones Kairós* [Kairos Publishing] including the magazine *Iglesia y Misión* [Church and Mission] (by internet), the magazine *Kairós* and *Ediciones Kairós* [Kairos Books].
* *Ministerios communitarios* [Community ministries], specializing in the formation of a social conscience, particularly in evangelical churches, in terms of their solidarity with the most needy, the development of integral mission by evangelical churches, and the provision of loans for microenterprises among the poorest sectors of society.

The church that is committed to the poor becomes a sign of the new creation that burst into history in the person and work of Jesus Christ—a sign of hope in the midst of despair. So it is important that we should have a teaching ministry which combines theory with practice and is oriented towards creating, in the whole church and in each of its members, the Christian mind—a mind that conceives of the totality of human life as the locus of God's transforming work.

Conclusion

We can find many good reasons to criticize the church. Far too often it has been the primary cause of people's turning their back on God, because they believe that the Christian faith has nothing to offer them. Often that is true. But it also is true that whenever the church opens itself up to people who are marginalized and poor, God surprises it, making it a good Samaritan who responds to the needs of the neighbor with the resources of the Kingdom of God: faith, hope, and love.

12

"*Centro Cristiano de Alabanza*"

("Christian Center for Praise")

Mauricio Solís-Paz

While we were looking for churches engaged in integral mission we came across an example in Costa Rica, more specifically in San José, in the District of Alajuelita. Alajuelita is a community of some twenty thousand inhabitants, famous for its high incidence of criminality and drug trafficking. There the church "*Centro Cristiano de Alabanza*" ("Christian Center for Praise") is developing a ministry that is transforming the community, such as is rarely seen in Latin America.

The church originated in a home in 1994. With a congregation of about thirty people, including the children, people met to pray and study the Word of God. Their pastor, Alberto Castro, was a professional percussionist in the 1980's with several of the best tropical music groups in Costa Rica, such as "La Banda" and "Tren Latino." He realized that his true calling was to establish a community of people who would transform the whole life in their community through living out the gospel of Jesus Christ.

In eight years this congregation has become a miracle of holistic growth well worth observing. Despite the fact that the majority of members are people of meager economic resources, the church has managed, with divine assistance, to make an unprecedented impact on the surrounding community. By its example it has challenged churches with greater economic resources to share and redistribute God's blessings with the needy.

The church meets in a 650 square meter building on a 9,000 square meter piece of land that was purchased as a huge leap of faith, that is, without the necessary financial resources, believing that God would honor his promise to provide for all their needs. Worth noting is that, at their inception, none of the ministries of the church had the necessary funds to start their work. The leaders simply stepped out in faith, and God rewarded their actions.

Today the congregation has grown to about one thousand five hundred people. The majority are residents of Alajuelita with very limited means. The church has three services a week and a youth gathering. People have been attracted by the impact made on the community by the testimony of the church or through the social services it offers. The church has ministries for children, young people, women, and men.

1. The Tasks of Integral Mission

Evangelism

Its evangelistic passion to spread the Word is one of the distinguishing marks of the church. The leaders have initiated creative strategies for communicating the gospel. One ministry made up of some fifty people uses various methods including mime, clowns, theater, a hip-hop/rap dance group, open air preaching, personal evangelism, and concerts to minister in the parks and squares of San José.

Another ministry, called "The hundredth sheep," goes around the streets, the shanty communities, and the parks in the high risk areas of the city, at midnight on weekends, offering coffee, bread, and warm soup to the desperate people they meet in the street. They serve the alcoholics and the drug addicts, homosexuals, prostitutes, and homeless people, bring them the gospel and pray for their lives.

At various times throughout the year the church also does mass evangelism, with up to three hundred people visiting in the poorest quarters of Alajuelita, visiting house to house with food and clothing, sharing the gospel, and praying with each family. On Fridays there is a service for the purpose of presenting the good news to people who have not made a commitment to Jesus. Every activity of the church has—and should have—an evangelistic motive.

Discipleship

Aware of the need for an integral transformation and formation of its members, the church has a discipleship program that aims at educating people biblically and theologically as well as encouraging a passion for evangelism and the exercise of leadership. House groups meet weekly to study the Word of God. The service on Tuesdays emphasizes teaching and generally follows a series of biblical expositions.

Worship

Worship is encouraged as a lifestyle that transcends musical or artistic expressions. The congregation aspires to worship in all that they are and do. Consistent praise and worship are encouraged, dynamic and participatory. and with a Latin flavor. The church has a music group called "Restoration" that has produced a CD. There also is the ministry of dance that combines modern, traditional, and messianic dance and has rediscovered many Costa Rican cultural values. A children's dance group also performs.

Community action

The church is committed to cultural, political, economic, social, and spiritual transformation in the community. Various projects respond to the many needs of Alajuelita. The following are among these projects:

The Oasis Foundation: Since one of the major problems in Alajuelita is drug abuse, especially "crack" and alcohol, the church opened a rehabilitation center for men. The center provides food and shelter, holistic health care, counseling and pastoral care, and occupational skills training so that after recovery the men can return to their families, enter the work force, and live a normal life. The center has cared for an average of forty people a month for the last two years.

"For you, Ma'am": This is a refuge for women who have been victims of physical violence or who are addicted to drugs. The women can live there for a period of up to ten months. They learn skills for dressmaking, crafts, beauty care, and baking.

Home for the elderly: The church set up a temporary home for old people that provides food, laundry, hairdressing, and supplementary health care. It has a capacity for eight people.

Children's lunch program "Oasis": Situated in the most deprived area, it is funded by a secular company (a computer software manufacturer), and operated by the church. It provides for an average of one hundred twenty children a day, and some mothers. The program is a door into the community, which has a very high level of unemployment.

Education Center "Oasis": As a way of making some impact at the social level, the church opened a nursery school, which then became a bilingual primary school. It began three years ago and now educates one hundred children up to grade 4. The teachers are members of the congregation.

Financing: To finance the community service projects described above, the church developed a series of production programs over the last two years including the following:

Service enterprises: The rehabilitation centers are maintained by offerings and the income from the work of internees who undertake such activities as painting and repair of vehicles, automobile mechanics, welding, carpentry, painting, craft sales, construction, etc.

Bakery: Some people from the rehabilitation centers have learned how to make bread and cakes, pastries, and biscuits of all kinds, which are sold by home delivery and in shops, mini-markets, and supermarkets. The also sell directly from the bakeries.

Coffee shop: A coffee shop has been opened on the church property to attract people from the neighborhood into the church. The shop produces some income through the provision of snack meals.

Copy center: Since the church is close to centers of education, two photocopiers were installed to serve the students and local residents.

Internet café: At the end of 2001 an Internet café opened with ten computers, where people, especially young people, can access the Internet.

Gym: The church opened a gym that offers separate classes for men and women. It is a way of catering for physical health and attracting people from the community to hear the gospel. There are *aerobics* classes with Christian music, weights, machines, and other equipment.

Bus: The church has a second-hand bus to serve the school children. The bus also provides transport for church members, and is for hire to generate income for the church projects.

Communion

The church called "*Centro Cristiano de Alabanza*" is a therapeutic community accepting and welcoming all who come there. Study groups, various ministries, and marriage enrichment meetings all foster a strong sense of community. A ministry for deaf people signs the worship services and arranges meetings for them, their families, and friends. The church also arranges frequent meetings, retreats, vigils, and fraternal get-togethers.

Pastoral leadership

Alberto Castro sees himself not only as pastor of the church, but also as pastor of the community, which means that his ministry extends beyond the boundaries of the congregation. He keeps in touch with other Christian ministers, state institutions, and churches abroad.

Pastors' network: Recognizing that it is impossible to undertake the mission in Alajuelita alone, the church seeks to promote the unity of churches in the area as a first priority. For the last three years, every Friday pastors of the twenty local congregations meet for fellowship, Bible study, prayer, and planning to address the needs of the different churches. This has helped churches with less economic resources by mean of offerings within the network.

Tithing: The church decided to give a tithe of its tithes for distribution among the poorest congregations of the district. Similarly, at the end of each year, they give a "Christmas present" to the poorest pastors to help provide for their families.

The church engages in the struggle for freedom for those who are oppressed by the forces of darkness and by economic, emotional, and spiritual powers. There is a service of pastoral counseling, and the church encourages the development of the gifts of the Spirit among its members.

2. Principles We Can Learn

The following list of principles learned from the "*Centro Cristiano de Alabanza,*" though not exhaustive, may encourage other churches interested in integral mission:

—Develop a holistic perspective that seeks to bring the power of the gospel to bear on all aspects of life in the neighboring community.

—Involve yourself in the community with the intention of transforming it.

—Set out passionately to reach those who do not know Jesus, with charisma and drive and a lot of faith.

—Do not wait until you have all the resources to embark on a ministry, but at the same time set up productive initiatives, in order to avoid being dependent on other sources of income.

—Try to grow in every way, in number, spiritual depth, understanding of the Word, the transformation of character, response to people's need, influence on the community, and the sharing of resources.

—Do not be satisfied by doing social action alongside evangelism, but in a comprehensive way seek to transform the whole situation with the gospel of Christ.

13

Proclaiming Jesus Seven Days a Week in a Corner of Buenos Aires

Dafne Sabanes Plou

It is a corner in the district of Colegiales, tree-lined and traversed by many vehicles. The avenue that passes in front connects two prominent areas of Buenos Aires: Belgrano, with its vigorous commerce and elegant buildings and parks; and Chacarita, which is home to one of the main rail terminals and the city's huge public cemetery. The church building on this avenue does not attract much attention. Built in the classical style typical of churches constructed in the first decades of the twentieth century, it is solid and austere. At the main door of the church, the recently restored and well-polished wooden floor reflects the sun's rays piercing through the simple stained-glass windows. The age-old wooden pews are arranged in a circle –a sign, a clue that in this church people like to meet their sisters and brothers face to face, when they worship together, as a token of their communion.

In the center of the church is a bare altar. Laughter, conversation, and a multiplicity of color fill the church. A group of children from the Sunday School, helped by their teacher, are preparing their contribution to the next worship service. They are showing off the attractive large-headed puppets that they made with their own hands and painted in the brightest of colors. They will use them to present their message to the congregation.

In the hall, the hubbub gets louder. There, the teenagers are starting their weekly meeting. Greetings, jokes, the arpeggio of a guitar, and attempts at a new song create an atmosphere of welcome, which embraces and affirms. In the kitchen young people of both genders are starting to make pizzas which they will share with the teenagers later, and on the rear patio a group of teenagers kick a ball around while they wait for the rest of their friends to arrive for the meeting.

It is a Friday evening in winter, and it is getting dark. Already some fifty people are in the church, involved in various activities. But nothing is unusual about that. This church never tires of the task of proclaiming the message, which goes hand in hand with service or showing acts of kindness to each other. With 40% of its confirmed members under the age of thirty, this congregation has an impetus for integral mission in which every member, regardless of age, is regarded as an agent of the gospel. As a consequence the different gifts are encouraged and the church considers the neighborhood its parish.

1. Two Church Traditions, One Congregation

Established at the end of the 1970's and beginning of the 1980's, The Church of the Good Shepherd in Colegiales is the product of ecumenical and interdenominational work, of several evangelical and mainstream protestant churches in the northern part of Buenos Aires. Facing a situation that was causing a great deal of anxiety among the people who lived in this part of the city, several church forces favored the growth of a spirit of unity, and opened the way to deeper and more specific dialogue among the members through united services, interchanging pulpits, engaging in fraternal meetings, and exchanging visits by women's groups, children, and young people.

As a result of that work, with the favorable and sympathetic consideration of the requests by the churches at the national level, the Church of the Disciples of Christ in Colegiales and the Evangelical Methodist Church of Belgrano decided to come together in a single church building to develop their mission jointly. The members themselves came to this conclusion and with great evangelistic vision set about merging their traditions and doctrinal emphases to clear the way for new experiences. In their discussions both congregations did their best to make sure that their members always felt accepted and respected. By doing this, they managed to create a strong sense of fellowship, which in time leavened the development of a missionary effort that spread powerfully across the local neighborhood.

The congregations decided to meet in the church in Colegiales, because it was the older one. The Disciples of Christ had begun work in the district ninety years before, while the Methodists had set up a few blocks away in Belgrano in 1940. On June 30th, 1986, the two congregations confirmed their union. They saw this act as responding to Jesus' call, "that they may all be one...so that the world may believe that you have sent me" (Jn 17:21). They took the name "Good Shepherd" because they saw their neighborhood as a flock that needed to be tended with great care, affection, and commitment, as well as with the challenge to follow Jesus Christ and to be light and salt in this environment.

2. A New Impetus to Evangelism

The union gave the congregation renewed strength. They began to design their mission to the district with a fresh vision. Committees responsible for this or that aspect of church life that had been quite compartmentalized began to plan in a more integrated way. They decided that their activities should no longer be segmented, but that all should be seen as components of a single undeviating evangelistic and missionary task. All this was coordinated by leaders committed to working as a team, including the pastor, with a vision that tried vigorously to put into practice the universal priesthood of all believers.

How were they to respond to this new vocation? How were they to communicate their enthusiasm for evangelism to the neighbors? What should be the main emphases of their programs? What priorities required immediate attention? To answer the many questions meant that the faithful began to see a whole new way of being the church.

The great Latin American cities, like Buenos Aires, can dazzle us with their well-preserved historical relics, huge commercial centers, busy avenues, and modern glass buildings. But behind this overt splendor are people who bear the burdens of devastating structural change. The vast international debt eats up most of our economic resources, and the neo-liberal policies imposed to make these payments give priority to the creditors, while stripping away the social and economic rights of the people.

In districts like Colegiales, mainly middle class, the economic change has impoverished the inhabitants and attracted new squatter families who live illegally in abandoned houses or crowded rented apartments in the big old houses, with several families sharing the same sanitary facilities. Though a number of people still own their own houses, the chance of being able to move to a bigger place as their family grows is extremely limited. Small two-room apartments are living quarters for parents with children living amid great difficulties with no hope of improvement for the future.

Several of the "Good Shepherd" families live in these circumstances. But when the congregation decided to organize themselves in teams of visitors, with the intention of making real contact with the neighborhood, the members were shocked to discover that the problem was even worse than they had thought. The idea behind the project was to bring together evangelism, community work, and Christian education. The problems in the area deteriorated with the repeated salary cuts for office and manual workers that left people unprotected and without job security and the increased informal economy that developed without any respect for the rules that safeguard workers' rights.

The economic situation began to affect family life, relationships in the neighborhood, and people's values. Squatting created a situation of illegal occupation. Overcrowding began to drive people away. The majority of the children and young people spent the better part of their days in the street. That meant that an important portion of their secondary socialization took place there, on the street, with its own rules and dangers, including the notion that the only moral sanction was that exercised by the state, in the guise of the police.

This problem of the children and teenagers demonstrated the need for, and possibility of, an integral mission that, centered on them, would affect the whole family and involve members of the congregation in many different ways, according to their particular gifts and abilities.

3. Opening New Spaces

The congregation decided not to have an evangelism committee, nor to leave evangelism to any one group. They also decided that if they wanted to really reach people they had to open their doors, not only to invite people in, but also to see to it that their worship and other activities were appropriate for the people to whom they wanted to bring the Word. So the church dismantled some of the traditional structures and patterns often found in evangelical congregations. As the children and young people become central to the life of the congregation, demands increase, commitment grows, the old patterns of meetings change, and all the vacant spaces in the church are adapted to their needs.

So where do adults fit in this scheme of things? In many cases, their role is leadership; in others, in leadership training; for the majority, in the down-to-earth task of being there and accompanying the young folks in their activities. If children and young people who have received the gospel begin to share the Word in their homes, their parents often respond by coming along to the church, even if only out of curiosity. The question is, are the adults ready to welcome them, and, if so, how will they do it? What kind of witness to Jesus is going to be suitable for people often weighed down by enormous problems? Can there be some sharing of hope in a crisis that offers no respite?

As they started to cover the district and make contact with their neighbors in the streets around the church, the teams of visitors began to ask all kind of questions. They assessed the multiplicity of needs and decided that they should begin by offering concrete help to families. During numerous visits they found that the children and young people had nowhere to do their homework or to study. The overcrowding meant that the children had to do their homework on the floor. It is impossible to concentrate when the whole family is in the same room. One of the leaders remembers a child trying, carefully, to trace the outlines of a picture with his worksheets on the bed. Obviously, it was impossible, but there was nowhere else to do the work except the floor, which was rough and unpolished.

The problem required an urgent response. So, in addition to the normal work with children and young people, the church members introduced a program of support for school children, every afternoon, for all who needed it. How to do it without any resources apart from the tithes and offerings that were already designated in the church? The church decided to spread the project among a wider group of volunteers, to include people of all ages, and they organized it in such a way that none of the volunteers would feel over-burdened. They worked in shifts that enabled more people to be involved. It was a lot easier for some people to commit themselves for a few hours once a week, than for a few to do it every day.

They soon uncovered a lot of talent in the congregation. Retired teachers of different subjects flocked to help, offering weekly sessions to reinforce what the young people were learning. Housewives and young people sat with the youngsters while they did their work. After a while they started serving snacks and organizing recreation and games. After each work session they also included a simple devotional meditation. Then, once they had things going, the participants were invited to join in the traditional children's and young people's activities in the church.

Soon, it was simply not possible to limit the work to after-school assistance because the volunteers became aware of other more serious needs. They had to think about a more integral form of support, because these children were so burdened with socio-cultural problems that they had neither the will nor the reason to take any initiative. Education was not as yet seen as a means of social advancement. Included in the group were victims of mental and physical violence. So it was essential, with some of the new participants, to work with their emotional problems too.

The pastor and adult leaders had to give a lot of attention to providing pastoral help for volunteers, who often found themselves in difficult situations that were not easily resolved. Consultations, personal conversations, and informal group discussions enabled the work to mature, with a determination to overcome the obstacles and face the challenges that emerged in the day-to-day encounters, with a message of hope. Today there are thirty-five people engaged in this work from Monday to Saturday. Most of them are young people less than twenty years of age.

An open church program complements the witness of the educational support work. Twice a week, the local people and passers-by know they will find just the right welcoming atmosphere in the church to spend a few moments in meditation or personal prayer. The pastor is there to discuss any personal problems and to lead communal prayers.

4. Young People as Evangelists

Some forty percent of the Good Shepherd congregation are young people under the age of thirty. The community service programs reach about three hundred people, of whom a hundred and eighty are children and young people. About fifty families get material help from the church in various ways.

The driving force of all this work, which goes hand in hand with evangelization, is the lively body of young people and teenagers. As we have already seen, they are very much involved in the educational support work. They also arrange their own weekly meetings and camps for fellowship and evangelism, which have a very special dynamic because of their ability to integrate people.

The working arrangements seemed to appear naturally, almost without thinking about it. The young people and teens are involved as helpers for the little ones, and the older youth work with the older children. The interchange and joint participation between groups is constant, and leads to activities developing their own culture and language. Once a month the teenagers and young people arrange a youth service on a Saturday night, which usually goes on until after midnight. In a "midnight oil" city like Buenos Aires it is important that Christian youth take advantage of that time of night to share the Word of God with their friends. At that hour a lot of young people wander the streets in search of entertainment, and this is a good opportunity to offer open doors and enthusiasm to enjoy a few moments a bit different than normal, and to make some new relationships. The "over eighteens" also have a spiritual celebration once a month in a family home. It provides an opportunity for one of the families in the congregation to make their home available for the occasion, which always includes a few new people.

Holy Week celebrations provide another chance to put on special events for the youth. Every year a Resurrection vigil starts on Saturday night and continues until breakfast on Easter

Sunday, culminating in the Easter service. Dozens of young people join the vigil. They invite their friends along to sing and read and pray for over twelve hours. Events like these strengthen this kind of group and encourage personal growth. The exchange of experiences enriches everyone and enhances the life of the congregation.

The young people also take the responsibility for the camps, whose primary purpose is to evangelize and bring new believers into the community of faith. Living together in these camps helps smooth some of the rough edges and promotes a better understanding of each other. The young people do not all come from the same social background. Some of them come from middle class families that manage quite comfortably. Others have suffered severe deprivations from childhood and have had to work from a young age. Members of the group remember one little girl asking why it was that they ate so frequently at camp. Living together helps people understand social and family situations, which would not normally be experienced or appreciated from a casual contact, but they are there and, if not attended adequately, could create conflicts in the future. Although the life histories may be very different in socio-cultural and economic terms, the group has found that the differences disappear when they dedicate themselves to the task of evangelism, especially when they are working with children.

During the camps the young people and teenagers are actually equipping themselves for the church's work. Generally speaking, the congregation has avoided holding training courses, because the leaders believe that learning by doing is preferable. The adult leadership of the church puts this into practice at the camps and other activities by accompanying and providing the necessary guidance to produce new leaders.

The young people communicate hope to their friends without any deliberate effort. Inspired by the positive spirit of the group, some of the members have returned to studies they had abandoned. And everybody, in one way or another, has begun to join in the activities that are set up. That has given the group its own dynamic and ways of working.

An important step in the process of evangelism was that the new believers among the youth started, bit by bit, to invite their families to attend the weekly services. Today, several of those families are in process of being integrated into the church. The young people not only share the gospel with their peers and those younger than themselves, but also with their own families. Two services are arranged each year for parents, with the involvement of the whole congregation, but those young people who have recently come to know the gospel have a special part. They have also held the first camp for parents. Sixteen married couples came and joined with a great deal of enthusiasm in what was, for them, a totally new experience.

The opportunity provided by the educational program has inspired several of the neighbors to offer their services in teaching and helping, including several of the parents of the children involved. When the parents come to get their children they often stay around to chat in the church hall. Sometimes they talk about their own affairs, other times they seek advice from the pastor or the volunteers. The important thing is that they discover that the church is a place to meet with people, a place which has willingly welcomed their children and is willing to welcome them, with the same commitment to the gospel. Several of the neighborhood volunteers have become a part of the church as well.

While visiting the families in the district, the young people have encountered situations of desperate social need. Because of that they have arranged with the congregation to prepare food parcels for the neediest of the people. Now the young people have taken on the responsibility for this work. They make up the parcels from the contributions of the congregation, visit the families, and share their problems, knowing that in so doing they are communicating the love of God who cares for every person.

All this youth activity is sustained by a spirituality centered on the study of the Bible, with group reflection and prayer. Prayer has its own special place in the regular meetings of the young people, and that nourishes and strengthens the countless tasks they undertake with such dedication. This spiritual dimension always plays an important part in the camps. They encourage both the spiritual impetus to work in solidarity in community service programs, and the strengthening of the personal life, which sustains their Christian commitment.

5. Evangelism that Welcomes and Cares

The Church of the Good Shepherd has always recognized that an element of its evangelistic task must be a willingness to offer a warm welcome to new people with a disposition to care for them in love and solidarity. Powerful preaching and calls to conversion are worthless unless all who make up the community of faith realize that their mission is to draw in new believers knowing that, as they evangelize, they themselves are being evangelized.

"In serving I am served; in offering the gospel I receive the gospel; in welcoming I am welcomed" is one of the mottos of the church. We have a dynamic of interrelationships through which the members of the congregation, new and old, take on the responsibility of sharing the Good News, of walking together in fellowship, of taking care of each other, and showing love and concern.

This is how the young people received the message and were able to pass it on. They are all, in one way or another, conscious of their responsibility for the mission of the church. They see themselves as agents of evangelism, not only in word, but also in action, conduct, and disposition. The same thing is true of the adults in the congregation. All of them in different ways, without consideration of age or gender, know that they share in the responsibility of proclaiming, receiving, accompanying, and giving; and they know, too, that they will receive the same treatment from their sisters and brothers, including whatever material and spiritual support they need, should the situation arise.

An intense revolving ministry, to which new people of all ages are added each week, sustains the work of the congregation. Team work, with the participation of the pastor and lay people, young and old, means that the work is always carried out with great dynamism and at the same time ensures that the people willing to dedicate themselves to it do not exhaust their energies. This joint leadership process has meant that far more people are leaders, and the leadership has its own support network. It means they always know their co-workers are caring them for. Then an informal network of support, based on personal friendship, springs up naturally from shared objectives and convictions. The personal well-being of the leaders and their families is also a continuing preoccupation of the pastor.

Looking at the daily life of a congregation, it is hard to speak of "models." Congregations are made up of people, with all their virtues and vices, trying to respond to the call of Jesus Christ with faithfulness, in every aspect of life, trusting in the grace of his love and mercy. Nevertheless, there are certain characteristics of this kind of ministry. We mentioned earlier that at The Good Shepherd the seats are arranged in a circle so that the congregation can see each other face-to-face in every activity as an attempt to be in personal contact as they share their faith. This is no minor detail for this concept of evangelism that welcomes and cares, but rather it sustains and nourishes the dynamic of evangelism, and gives it passion.

The message of Jesus Christ changes the lives of individuals and of congregations. When a congregation takes on the mantle of agent of the gospel, its life changes. The church becomes more real and more fundamental, because the proclamation of new life in Christ carries with it the scope for new ways of relating to each other, of seeing each other as sons and daughters of the same Father, in love, respect, and solidarity.

Printed by
Roberto Grancharoff e hijos
Tapalqué 5868, Buenos Aires, Argentina
Te. 54-11-4683-1405

Another title by *Ediciones Kairos*

TERRORISM AND THE WAR IN IRAK
A Christian Word from Latin America

By

C. René Padilla and Lindy Scott

The attack on September 11, 2001, was a dramatic blow on the long-held assumption that the United States had a defensive system which could guarantee safety to its citizens and protect the world. It marked the beginning of a "war on terrorism" which raises very serious questions with regards to the possibility of world peace in the future.

Is the war in Irak a "just war" or an expression of zealous nationalism?

To what extent can Christians support the war in Irak without seriously compromising their Christian stand?

Does the "war on terrorism" guarantee generations of peace without a radical revolution of values?

These and other relevant questions are addressed from the perspective of Latin American Christians. This is *must* for thinking Christians in the United Sates!

Another title by *Ediciones Kairos*

TERRORISM AND THE WAR IN IRAK
A Christian Word from Latin America

By

C. René Padilla and Lindy Scott

The attack on September 11, 2001, was a dramatic blow on the long-held assumption that the United States had a defensive system which could guarantee safety to its citizens and protect the world. It marked the beginning of a "war on terrorism" which raises very serious questions with regards to the possibility of world peace in the future.

Is the war in Irak a "just war" or an expression of zealous nationalism?

To what extent can Christians support the war in Irak without seriously compromising their Christian stand?

Does the "war on terrorism" guarantee generations of peace without a radical revolution of values?

These and other relevant questions are addressed from the perspective of Latin American Christians. This is *must* for thinking Christians in the United Sates!